Making College Better

AC SS

Adolescent Cultures, School & Society

Joseph L. DeVitis & Linda Irwin-DeVitis
GENERAL EDITORS

Vol. 68

The Adolescent Cultures, School & Society series
is part of the Peter Lang Education list.
Every volume is peer reviewed and meets
the highest quality standards for content and production.

PETER LANG
New York • Bern • Berlin
Brussels • Vienna • Oxford • Warsaw

Making College Better

Views from the Top

Edited by Joseph L. DeVitis

PETER LANG
New York • Bern • Berlin
Brussels • Vienna • Oxford • Warsaw

Library of Congress Cataloging-in-Publication Data

Names: DeVitis, Joseph L., editor.
Title: Making College Better: Views from the Top / edited by Joseph L. DeVitis.
Description: New York: Peter Lang, 2018.
Series: Adolescent cultures, school and society; vol. 68 | ISSN 1091-1464
Includes bibliographical references.
Identifiers: LCCN 2017018113 | ISBN 978-1-4331-3479-1 (pbk.: alk. paper)
ISBN 978-1-4331-3480-7 (hardcover: alk. paper)
ISBN 978-1-4331-4498-1 (ebook pdf)
ISBN 978-1-4331-4499-8 (epub) | ISBN 978-1-4331-4500-1 (mobi)
Subjects: LCSH: Education, Higher.
School improvement programs.
Educational leadership.
Classification: LCC LB2325 .D46 2018 | DDC 378—dc23
LC record available at https://lccn.loc.gov/2017018113
DOI: 10.3726/b11306

Bibliographic information published by **Die Deutsche Nationalbibliothek.**
Die Deutsche Nationalbibliothek lists this publication in the "Deutsche Nationalbibliografie"; detailed bibliographic data are available on the Internet at http://dnb.d-nb.de/.

To William T. Greer, Jr., a college president
who never lost his humanity

Contents

Introduction

JOSEPH L. DeVITIS

These are not the best of times for colleges and college presidents. Often prized as national, state, or local treasures, colleges and universities, in these troubled times, are under continual siege from a wide variety of internal and external interests groups and stakeholders: faculty, parents, students, alumni, the media, board members, legislators, and other politicians (elected and would-be), among others. Yet postsecondary leaders are still expected to deliver all the goods—no matter what the times:

> Colleges and universities are told to do more with less while, on the other hand, demands for innovation persist. The call for access and universal education remains. The desire grows for the development and delivery of new intellectual properties and products. While all these demands have increased, resources have shrunk. (Rowley, Lujan & Dolence, 2001, p. 8)

Simply put, this book joins the efforts to make college better. The different paths to improvement have already proven to be difficult. Amid all the contestation and controversies, our undertaking proffers insightful counsel from a host of presidents and chancellors who represent a wide array of higher education institutions: liberal arts colleges, large public and private universities, comprehensive regional universities, religiously affiliated colleges, historically black colleges and universities, women's colleges, and community colleges. These academic leaders typically face daily multifaceted, complicated tasks that might drive many mortals to give up the ghost:

> In the course of making a decision, an administrator must perform a complex act of taking into account any number of goals (short and long range), constituents, interests, opportunities, costs dangers, and at every point … keep constantly in mind the forces and resources that must be marshaled. (Fish, 2008, p. 64)

To make matters worse, administrators often do so in a semi-domesticated environment in which they feel as if they are herding cats. Faculty can routinely ignore them and their relations with administrators can be downright frosty and adversarial. College leaders also face student and parent demands for more compliant and convenient customer service, outside audiences who seek more active campus involvement, and athletic boosters who desire wins above all else. Some commentators on university administration paint an even gloomier portrait than does Fish:

> The hard fact is that on the modern campus, no one really wants to be led. Every current and former college president we've met has related how every proposal he or she made was greeted by a chorus of no's or simply stone-faced resistance. … Indeed, when presidents call for something new, they usually find they have no real allies. (Hacker & Dreifus, 2010, p. 43)

While realizing the above concerns, our contributors are attuned to these important needs: trust among all constituencies, effective strategic planning, building viable campus relationships, fostering town and gown interaction, and ameliorating political squabbles on and off the quadrangle. Like many successful leaders, they have a firm grasp of their campus culture, work on nurturing strong communication networks, hone in on mission and core values, and are not afraid to recommend "out-of-the-box" solutions. (Leslie & Fretwell, Jr., 1996) They walk a high wire to balance all manner of competing interests in the hope of creating a better college.

In this volume, they are pleased to share their knowledge as they seek the light at the end of the tunnel. They understand the promise and rewards of the modern academy—an institution that still warrants their constant care and vigilance. Above all, they are realists who continue to believe in a real future for all those students who enter the walls of ivy, stone, bricks, and mortar.

PART ONE: VIEWS FROM THE PRIVATE SECTOR

In Chapter One, "Foundational Truths about Higher Education," Jonathan Brand, president of Cornell College (Mount Vernon, Iowa), addresses the large demographic shifts, considerable financial pressures, and sharp external criticisms that imperil today's American campuses. He explicitly examines several important disjunctions that the academy must effectively deal with: disconnects between higher education and families; competition among academic institutions; disagreements in discussions of breadth and depth of knowledge; and divisions between postsecondary education and the world of work. Ultimately, President Brand contends that colleges and universities must develop deeper foundational learning goals to prepare students for their futures.

In Chapter Two, "Liberal Arts Colleges: Building Capacity to Thrive," Steven C. Bahls, president of Augustana College (Rock Island, Illinois), defends liberal arts schools within the context of changing social and economic demands. He claims that they will need to focus more on postgraduation goals and outcomes, showing how liberal education has instrumental value; reallocating resources and costs; and revamping shared governance to make it more effective. President Bahls warns against dependence on academic and campus life silos. He seeks a more integrated collegiate structure. He also advocates for more strategic "lean management" while encouraging faculty entrepreneurship to better serve students.

In Chapter Three, "The Future of the Liberal Arts College, or How to Keep Smiling on the Edge of the Crevasse," Brian Rosenberg, president of Macalester College (Saint Paul, Minnesota), explores where liberal education is trending and how to allow it to sustain its viability. He predicts that few private liberal arts colleges are likely to die in the near future unless they are quite small and already struggling. But liberal arts institutions in general, he argues, will require more adaptability and less redundancy. President Rosenberg forecasts that many will welcome a more diverse student body as they fight to attain adequate revenue. Furthermore, he contends that they will tend to discard the fiscally unmanageable teacher-scholar model of pedagogy and move toward more cross-disciplinary structures.

In Chapter Four, "Making College Better—For Whom?" Timothy L. Hall, president of Mercy College (Dobbs Ferry, New York), argues for improving colleges and universities by making them better for *all* students—many of whom come from low-income homes and are underrepresented in elite, wealthy, and more "exclusionary" institutions. He focuses on student success and "inclusionary excellence" rather than serving only the "best" clientele who might boost institutional reputation. President Hall shows how innovative strategies, programs, and practices can yield higher college completion rates, help close the achievement gap, and tear down demographic hurdles.

In Chapter Five, "Rethinking Fit, Choosing to Include, and Educating World Changers," Elizabeth (Beth) J. Stroble, president of Webster University (Webster Grove, Missouri), elaborates how university faculty, staff, and students can contribute to global awareness in ways that benefit all concerned. Emphasizing the power of diversity and inclusion in their myriad forms, she depicts a private university's integrated strategy and systemic design for student success locally and abroad. President Stroble describes a network of campus locations and partnerships worldwide that affords Webster's constituents expansive opportunities for international understanding, collaboration, and transformation.

In Chapter Six, "The Soul of a Christian University," J. Randall O'Brien, president of Carson-Newman University (Jefferson City, Tennessee), analyzes how faith, or soul, can be integrated into the heart of the university. After tracing how Colonial colleges were founded by church organizations, he argues that the secularization of higher education corroded the fundamental functions of faith. Citing a host of esteemed clerical and nonclerical thinkers, President O'Brien contends that religious colleges and universities should extoll both academic freedom and a commitment to their theological heritages. He closes with numerous examples of how soulful living and learning can flourish on today's campuses.

In Chapter Seven, "From Either/Or to Both/And: The Journey of a Lutheran College to Interfaith Living," Paul C. Pribbenow, president of Augsburg University (Minneapolis, Minnesota), provides a stark example of how his institution's traditions, values, and identity have made it a force for interfaith progress. He shows how his university has highlighted diversity beyond ethnic and racial boundaries through the agency of vocation, "critical and humble" inquiry, communitarian engagement, social justice, and the readiness to be open to reform. These goals have been implemented in curriculum, campus life, and service learning. President Pribbenow's presentation underlines the significance of preparing students for a world of diverse beliefs, today and tomorrow.

In Chapter Eight, "A Case Study: Transforming a Catholic Women's College," Patricia McGuire, president of Trinity University Washington (District of Columbia), enumerates the challenges and achievements in saving an institution from near closing and then seeing it become a vital, special place. The renovation entailed creating a far more diverse student body by enlarging access to African-American women in particular. In addition, Trinity focused on a working-class clientele in general and modified its curricula, majors, and programs to keep pace with the times (e.g., establishing a much needed nursing program). President McGuire also guided Trinity in building bridges to organizations in the District of Columbia, especially in areas relevant to the College's revamped academic structure.

PART TWO: VIEWS FROM THE PUBLIC SECTOR

In Chapter Nine, "Learning to Thrive: A Perspective from Texas Woman's—A Large Public University," Carine M. Feyten, chancellor and president of Texas Woman's University (Denton, Dallas, and Houston), shows how her University strives to fulfill wide dimensions of student development and deeper purposes for higher education in general. Her chapter considers the creation of personal meaning and growth in whole personhood. Given her institution's mission as primarily a woman's college, she reaffirms commitments to female leadership, education in health, and "learning by doing," especially service learning. Finally, she utilizes a health care model as a practical metaphor for exploring ways to well-being at her University.

In Chapter Ten, "Making College Better through a Reimagined Undergraduate Research Focus," Beverly Warren, president of Kent State University (Kent, Ohio), stresses the need for increased attention to inquiry-based learning at the undergraduate level and how public research universities are especially equipped to develop strong models of undergraduate research engagement. She offers several examples of successful programs and shares her own institution's journey to a more robust undergraduate vision. President Warren argues that this reimagined focus affords undergraduates distinctive and critical opportunities for both academic and leadership development.

In Chapter Eleven, "Public Comprehensive Universities: The People's University at a Crossroads," Sandra J. Jordan, chancellor of the University of South Carolina Aiken, first provides a historical and philosophical account of the role and scope of regional state campuses. She characterizes them as "important social investments" that afford accessibility and practical and professional education to a vast plurality of the college population. Chancellor Jordan also understands the many challenges facing these campuses: changing student demographics, decreased state funding, increasing regulation, shifts in faculty roles, adapting to new technologies, the impact of the recent recession, and competition for students. She concludes with specific possible solutions surrounding the benefits of diversity, student advocacy, and local and regional collaboration.

In Chapter Twelve, "The Role of Public Regional Universities in the 21st Century," Elsa M. Nuńez, president of Eastern Connecticut State University (Willimantic, Connecticut) begins by describing how those schools, particularly in Connecticut, were born and eventually grew to be key players in American higher education. She discusses a plethora of obstacles now confronting them. President Nuńez offers several remedies to revivify those universities: reaffirmation of institutional identity in terms of mission; core values; campus/system alignment; strategic planning guided by responsiveness, relevance, and more access for diverse students; engagement; accountability; and advocacy. She shows how each component can be nestled within campus units and offices in order to assure applied learning opportunities as well as wider economic and social benefits.

In Chapter Thirteen, "How Transformational Change Can Prepare Historically Black Colleges and Universities (HBCUs) and Minority-Serving Institutions (MSIs) to Be Competitive in the 21st Century," James A. Anderson, chancellor of Fayetteville State University (North Carolina), analyzes the unique status of the latter campuses—ones that are often caught in a web of confounding issues in today's higher education landscape. In the face of new demographic changes and fiscal constraints, he recommends more intentional, coherent, and evidence-based educational designs; closer monitoring of goal achievement; more effective pedagogical methods; and ensuring more academic quality and market accountability through better assessment of learning outcomes. Ultimately, Chancellor Anderson calls for more transformational leadership to attain those difficult aims.

In Chapter Fourteen, "Energizing Higher Education in Tough Times: A Historically Black College President's Perspective," Kevin D. Rome, president of Lincoln University (Jefferson City, Missouri) presents a coherent set of recommendations for improving postsecondary education, especially HBCUs, during an era of limited resources. Pointing to the need to educate students as "holistic contributors" to society, he deals not only with current campus issues, but also with crucial concerns beyond college graduation. President Rome seeks a kind of synergistic bond between internal and external contingencies. His ultimate goal is student success in college and in the world of work.

In Chapter Fifteen, "Making Community Colleges Better," Edward E. Raspiller, president of John Tyler Community College (Chester and Midlothian, Virginia), focuses on salient features of why two-year colleges are vital to higher education and society. Along with a discussion of their values, purposes, and programs, he uses a microscopic lens for an in-depth exploration of how community colleges can share services in a scarce economy and tough political climate while connecting workforce development and globalization in more concrete ways. Finally, President Raspiller emphasizes the need for agile, proactive leadership in a world of ever-changing conditions and environments.

* * *

In closing, let us work to insure that our colleges and universities can continue to improve the lives of individuals and society as a whole. Let us strive to make college better.

REFERENCES

Fish, S. (2008). *Save the world on your own time.* New York: Oxford University Press.

Hacker, A., & Dreifus, C. (2010). *Higher education? How colleges are wasting our money and failing our kids—and what we can do about it.* New York: Times Books/Henry Holt.

Leslie, D. W., & Fretwell, E. K., Jr. (1996). *Wise moves in hard times: Managing resilient colleges and universities.* San Francisco: Jossey-Bass.

Rowley, D. J., Lujan, H. D., & Dolence, M. G. (2001). *Strategic change in colleges and universities: Planning to survive and thrive.* San Francisco: Jossey-Bass.

PART ONE

Views FROM THE Private Sector

CHAPTER ONE

Foundational Truths ABOUT Higher Education

JONATHAN M. BRAND
President, Cornell College

INTRODUCTION

An education should prepare graduates for a democratic society. It should teach them how to lead enriching lives. And, of course, a college education should help students to achieve career success, especially obvious following the 2008 recession. Yet, there is no widespread agreement on what that preparation should include or how colleges and universities will know when their students "get there."

At the same time that they face external criticism, many colleges and universities confront nearly insurmountable financial pressures. For multiple years now, demographic patterns in the United States have presented a challenge not only to small residential liberal arts colleges but to all of higher education. There are fewer traditional students available to attend college, and, as a result, there is fierce competition for them. Colleges continue to close each year, and many others fear for their future.

The current political push for workforce development and a proposed oversimplified collegiate rating system[1] that focuses on degree completion, job acquisition, and starting salary have also put these institutions in a defensive and awkward position. The last decade has been marked by dramatic scrutiny of higher education institutions, not only by government officials[2] but also by the media that seem to exacerbate the issues. As one example, an increasing number of print and online articles in national and international *fora*, and several articles in leading news venues have placed student loan debt within the context of the long-term value of a college education.[3] Put another way, people are strongly questioning the worth of college, especially in relation to its perceived cost.

In response, colleges and universities are spending significantly more time and energy trying to measure and communicate the quality of their students' experiences. But, significant tensions have hindered the progress. For example, students and their parents may seek one outcome from a college education while colleges and universities may believe that students need something else. Higher education institutions have different histories and missions. They are thus fragmented in their responses to families. Many colleges and universities struggle to find a balance between a broad liberal arts education and a more narrowly focused professional one. Finally, employers, for their part, have expectations in terms of preparedness for their new hires, and they presume that colleges and universities will automatically meet them.

In the aggregate, the environmental factors and these points of contact create the perfect storm for colleges and universities within this highly charged climate. Wealthier institutions can withstand the criticism better; under-resourced ones struggle and even fail. Such obstacles also provide an opportunity for improvement, no doubt, neither obvious nor easy, but helpful all the same.

There is, thus, a particular urgency for colleges and universities to present a cogent case for the education they offer—to measure student learning, student success, and the career benefits of a liberal education.[4] And, it's a good story. After all, even if unemployment persists and wages stagnate, employment remains highest among college graduates. What better reason to attend and graduate?

In this essay, I argue that colleges and universities must dig deeper into learning goals in order to: (1) bridge the perceived gap between a liberal education and professional preparation, (2) graduate students with the skills employers covet, (3) ease the temporal disconnect between a dynamic external environment and the pace of institutional change, and (4) make clearer the value of higher education for students, their parents, and employers. The aim of this essay, thus, is to suggest a set of global, foundational learning goals that would prepare future generations of students. Further, a college education would be uniformly recognized as invaluable.

THE DISCONNECT BETWEEN HIGHER EDUCATION AND FAMILIES

Imagine Alex and Angelica, two "average" public high school seniors preparing for college. They communicate differently than their predecessors. They have always known cellphones and the Internet. They spend, on average, two to three hours per day in their various media/communications activities such as texting and social media.[5] They are comfortable communicating their ideas in 140 characters or fewer.

There has been more and more pressure on new generations of students to do everything. Alex and Angelica both run cross country and participate in band and choir. They are members of the debate team. Alex works at the local supermarket and Angelica at the pizza parlor. Together, they do community service two Saturdays each month through a local organization. And, of course, they have their homework. In addition, in their high schools, they have been tested and tested more than previous generations. Alex and Angelica prefer to do their research online, finding the specific information that they need to support their ideas. On average, they have about 1 hour of homework each day, including weekends.[6] That must be all that they need to do because Alex and Angelica are both near the top of their class. Their parents dismiss the issue of grade inflation; Alex's and Angelica's good grades are all that matter. When asked, Alex and Angelica state that business is the major that most interests them, consistent with the national trend.[7]

Alex and Angelica have also been raised with significant financial pressures surrounding their college choices, especially in light of the Great Recession in 2008. The recession was hard on their parents who have already endured decades of wage stagnation. Alex and Angelica's parents know that tuition, until recently, has risen at a rate that eclipses a number of other sectors, and feel strongly that college for their children has to be affordable. The fact of the matter is that, even though college graduates, on average, have higher rates of employment than noncollege graduates and out-earn them over a lifetime, they also believe that college students nationwide struggle to find gainful employment. Alex and Angelica's parents also believe that many graduate with significant debt that limits their post-graduate options. As a result, debt is out of the question for Alex and Angelica because it only limits what they can do after college, and they must graduate in four years.

Alex and Angelica's parents are interested, above all else, in ensuring that their children are gainfully employed after college and have the ability to live independently.[8] For them, employment is the primary measure of a successful college education and, in turn, of a successful college. College is about job preparation and the most direct path to it. Like many parents, Alex and Angelica's want a guarantee that Alex and Angelica will be employable the moment they graduate from college, but they can't articulate specifically what those skills are that lead to employment. That is why, in their eyes, engineering or business is the perfect major because they know that many employers seek graduates with those degrees.[9] Particularly in a tougher economy, Alex and Angelica's parents are looking for the value-added aspect of a college education. They rightly ask, "Can my child get a job straight out of college, especially when I believe that I will have to pay so much for my child to get that education?" It goes without saying that Alex and Angelica need to go to the college with the best reputation at the best price and whose graduates get the best jobs; the reputation of a school is important insofar as a college's reputation increases its perceived value.

THE DIVIDE WITHIN HIGHER EDUCATION

Though there is widespread belief that higher education needs to take measuring itself more seriously, the variation in assessment approaches fosters great disagreement about the utility of each.[10]

There remains a growing gulf between the wealthiest, most prestigious institutions and every other college nationally. The former schools have the financial luxury of not worrying about their existence and continue to secure a larger portion of the student pie. And, these same schools are significantly less interested in measuring student learning: "For almost every category of assessment activity, the more selective an institution's admission standards, the less likely it is to employ various assessment approaches or use the results."[11] After all, these same schools have nothing to gain from these assessments. The value is either hard to establish or the value is self-evident based primarily on reputation. Further down the financial continuum, schools with more limited resources struggle to stay afloat.

In addition, some institutions consider what they do as self-evident *ex post* justifications of what they already think that they do well. Rather, they should honestly reexamine their academic offerings within the context of what is foundational for students and adjust them based on what they actually learn from those measurements.

There is also a profound disconnect between the rate of change in society and that accommodated by institutions of higher learning. No doubt, all schools endeavor to meet the changing expectations of students. However, colleges and universities implement change slowly. They struggle in the face of acute competition and financial pressures to continually make themselves relevant to their "customers" and the world into which they will go after college. This inability to move quickly hinders the capacity of schools to respond to their cultural realities.

If you ask Alex and Angelica's parents about colleges and universities, especially the elite liberal arts colleges, they repeat the cultivated media stance that they should be wary: they believe that higher education institutions provide little value to students, and do so at an excessively **high price**, and allow students to graduate with limited skills, few employment opportunities, and staggeringly high debt (on which many students default). Further, colleges and universities **resist accountability** and do not measure student learning in ways that are useful to students, their families, and the larger world. They raise tuition annually at **rates faster and exponentially greater than do other services or sectors**. They **clandestinely operate welfare states**, in which they subsidize poorer students by providing aid to them that is funded by wealthier students who pay the full, advertised sticker price for college. Their decision-making processes—rooted in notions of sharing governance with faculty (and students)—are both **inefficient and medieval**, and allow faculty to resist needed changes. **They build palaces for their students**

simply because they can—such as luxury residence halls, new comprehensive athletic facilities (with climbing walls), lazy rivers to float down, and well-appointed student centers.

While this hyped stance may sell newspapers and magazines, it's generally pulled out of context, highly anecdotal, and certainly not the full picture. And, these perceptions surely do not speak to the vast majority of colleges and universities in the United States.

THE DIVIDE BETWEEN THE BROAD AND FOCUSED

A further problem, debated for years, is between a broad-based liberal education in which one studies across many academic disciplines versus a more professional or practical focus in which one studies for one kind of job.[12] Increasingly, over the last few years, colleges and universities have focused more and more on how individuals can apply their abilities to any content and in any context—as compared to the strict transmission of substantive knowledge. It would be folly, however, to think that an education should be all about the instruction of process. Ultimately, employers assume either broad or specific knowledge as the basis for any undertaking. Critical thinking requires a base of **substantive knowledge.** It is hard to imagine being a productive scholar in, say, French literature, without having direct knowledge of French texts. It is hard to imagine assessing the existence of gravitational waves without an understanding of physics.

Alex and Angelica's parents want them to get a practical education—geared toward getting a job. And, it is unpersuasive to them that studying, for example, Russian literature might prepare students in ways that employers want. But, Accounting 101 does. On the other side of the ledger, proponents of the liberal arts claim that Alex and Angelica are likely to have multiple careers over their lives and, thus, need preparation not for one job but for many. They need to evolve with the world, being ready to assume jobs that don't yet exist.

No doubt, if there is any good to emerge from the Great Recession, it is that it has more quickly healed the split between the arts and sciences and professional fields on college campuses. More colleges and universities are adding professional programs within their liberal arts curricula. But under the current scheme of learning outcomes, the divide will never fully disappear. One camp sees the importance of an education that prepares students to be leaders in a democratic society. The other believes that the primary outcome of college is job acquisition. These two schools of thought rely on different learning outcomes.

But even the term "learning outcomes" misses the point. It suggests that there is an endpoint to learning—that learning is about checking a box or crossing a finish line. Done and moving on. And it supports the misguided impression that college provides a finished product with degree conferral, which implies that learning is for all intents and purposes over. However, life is never about a finite endpoint. One is always moving past something or on to something else, or addressing something unforeseen. There is no finish line. The orientation toward learning outcomes suggests the mastery of skills that allow people comfortably to arrive somewhere. In reality, though, it is the beginning of their professional lives. It is not an arrival anywhere; it is another start.

Educators question whether they can effectively reconcile the dichotomy that a college education is either a broad exposure to the academic disciplines OR a laser focus on career preparation. Leaders in higher education increasingly recognize that the distinction between the liberal arts and professional fields is an illusion generated by history and the media. I share the belief that the liberal arts as an educational philosophy is preparation for **any** profession. It has always been and still is. The nondiscipline-specific skills advanced by the liberal arts are sought devoutly by employers in **all** fields.[13] Now we can ask the question: how, then, can one argue that a liberal arts education is anything but professional preparation?

THE DISCONNECT BETWEEN HIGHER EDUCATION AND EMPLOYERS

On the face of it, numerous published surveys elucidate the abilities as well as the gaps that employers expect from college graduates. Survey results regularly indicate that employers wish to hire good communicators and find, in fact, the opposite. College graduates simply cannot write at the level expected. They also don't adequately focus on details, as another example indicates.[14]

A 2013 study by Eduventures found a split between what prospective students seek in a college education, and what employers look for in employees. Students identified three *sine qua non* goals of college: (1) in-depth knowledge and expertise in a major; (2) pursuit of personally fulfilling career prospects; and (3) skills to help enter into a specific career path. Career preparation is clearly on their minds. Meanwhile, the top three skills that employers seek are: (1) the ability to work in a team structure; (2) the ability to communicate verbally with people in and out of an organization; and (3) the ability to make decisions and solve problems. In fact, the study indicated that, "only two of the traits employers look for are in the top ten goals students want to achieve." And colleges are in the middle of these disjunctions as they try to meet the needs of their students as well as of those whose responsibility it is to hire them.

Reports, including one undertaken by PayScale/Future Workplace, tell a relatively similar story. Gaps exist in student preparedness in relation to the well-established learning outcomes affirmed, for example, by the Association of

American Colleges & Universities (AAC&U).[15] Colleges and universities teach critical thinking; hiring managers still emphatically state that that skill eludes college graduates. In their opinion, it is actually the largest gap in student abilities. Attention to detail matters in every endeavor, including college. But students aren't gaining that skill either according to employers. Communication is central to a college education but is a shortcoming routinely noted.

From the perspective of colleges and universities, it would be easy to become defensive in the face of these claims. However, they contain a measure of truth regarding higher education as a sector that requires serious attention. For example, one study stated that college students don't make significant progress in developing their critical thinking skills over four years of college.[16] At some institutions, they do not make adequate progress in their writing. And, what about problem solving and decision-making skills? Though more schools are trying to provide opportunities for students to hone these skills, they still remain highly theoretical.

Nonetheless, college and universities, for their part, provide data and anecdotal reports on all the ways they ready students for their futures. These data are subsequently used at both ends of the college pipeline as evidence to employers and prospective students alike that higher education institutions are indispensable. A dizzying array of third-party rankings, ratings, and scorecards insert another layer of information that either supports or refutes them.[17]

From the practitioners' perspective, it's always about the employer's needs because college is just a passage into the more permanent period called real life, including employment. But, as we know only too well, college is not an end after all. It is both a beginning and a means to an end. The purpose of higher education is to educate future leaders and community citizens in a pluralistic democracy. Students should learn how to lead enriched lives, grounded in themselves such that they can develop meaningful relationships and give full expression to their personal interests. They must be open to discover new experiences. And, such learning is near impossible to measure.

THE CORNER OFFICE

Hard as it is to do, responsive and courageous are the terms I would use to characterize how colleges and universities should approach measuring learning. Assessing learning has value, and students, families, regulators, accreditors, alumni, and governmental officials either require it or, at a minimum, expect it.

One answer to the debate about appropriate student learning goals lies with The Corner Office, a weekly New York Times column that provides an opportunity to listen directly to employers across multiple sectors. These employers discuss their leadership philosophies, lessons they have learned in their professional

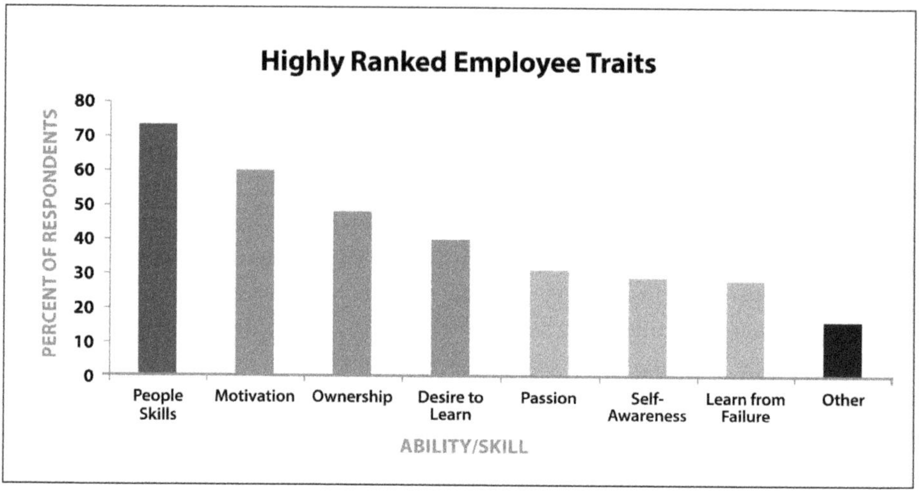

Figure 1. Results of survey of 100 "Corner Office" interviews. The most common responses may be assigned to three general "trait classes." The category labeled "other" includes a variety of skills that were mentioned by 3% to 26% of respondents; the average value is 16%. Additional information is presented in Appendix B.

careers, as well as the skills and attributes that they value in employees and what they look for when interviewing candidates. A total of 100 columns between August 21, 2014, and July 8, 2016, was analyzed in order to determine whether a consensus existed. Not surprisingly, CEOs interviewed over the last two years were aligned; these CEOs consistently mentioned eighteen separate skills and abilities they consider significant, seven of which emerged in particular (Figure 1).[18]

Those attributes identified through The Corner Office are not precisely what students, on average, value today, what schools are necessarily teaching, or what anyone is necessarily measuring as goals. Employers interviewed in The Corner Office believe that college graduates/employees must know themselves well and know how to apply themselves to larger efforts through a team. Specifically, the information gathered from these CEO interviews would suggest that employers assume a basic intelligence and a wish to learn that manifest themselves in three "trait classes"—teamwork/collaboration represented by people skills (the first bar in Figure 1), high motivation (the second, third and fourth bars), and considerable self-awareness (the fifth, sixth, and seventh bars).

Like many American high school students, our hypothetical prospective college students Alex and Angelica "recognize that it is most important for recent graduates to be proficient in skills and knowledge that cut across majors, including critical thinking skills, the ability to apply knowledge in real-world settings, written and oral communication skills, teamwork skills, and ethical decision-making."[19] Notice, though, that the term, critical thinking, *per se*, appears **nowhere** among the most central traits in The Corner Office interviews.[20] It is not that these employers don't value critical thinking. Rather, it is that they are identifying capabilities that, together, **undergird** it. They offer skills that are embedded in critical thinking.

Thus, the answer may lie in the question: what are the skills or appreciations that are even anterior to capabilities like critical thinking, analysis, or teamwork? For example, would it be important for students to learn, above all else and in *all* instances, that they may not know all that they think they know on a topic or that what they know is incomplete? Can students then be convinced otherwise or be receptive to learning what they don't know? There is value in learning how to give and take—to disabuse others and to be capable, in turn, of being convinced otherwise with new evidence and facts. Might these skills be essential to a lifetime of personal and professional success in any undertaking?

I do it. You do it. At some point, we all do it. We are guilty of enforcing our own ideas by selectively curating our own information. In ways that merely conform to our beliefs, we miss the opportunity to take a broader view or learn from others. Further, students who are not receptive to the possibility that they may not know everything, or that what they know may either be wrong or incomplete, will not impress their future employers with critical thinking skills or the ability to work on a team. It is vital that students "come to appreciate context, trade-offs and data … master how to recognize complexity, to argue effectively for their positions and to reconsider and challenge their own beliefs … [or learn that] actions inevitably have multiple implications and that many decisions involve not simply choosing between "good" or "bad" but evaluating a set of consequences and uncertainties, both desired and undesired."[21]

FOUNDATIONAL SKILLS

The answer rests in *going deeper* in terms of essential learning goals. That is, there exists an even more fundamental set of learning goals, including capabilities, that could provide the bedrock of learning, an optimal focus for a college. Without attaining certain basic skills, these larger learning goals as delineated, for example, by the AAC&U, are simply not possible to master. Thus, what I would like to suggest is a structure for foundational goals that could bridge the divide between the liberal arts and preprofessional education and prepare students to thrive in any number of settings.

1. **Recognition of One's Inability to Know Everything.** The AAC&U defines critical thinking as "a habit of mind characterized by the comprehensive exploration of issues, ideas, artifacts, and events before accepting or formulating an opinion or conclusion."[22] There appears to be widespread support

among colleges/universities, accrediting bodies, the U.S. Department of Education, and employers for the notion that critical thinking is a vital learning goal. In fact, there are increasingly claims that people today confuse opinions with facts or reach opinions that are not rooted in established evidence.[23] Professors today increasingly report that more students cherry-pick their information from the Internet to support the outcomes or conclusions that they seek. The sheer accessibility of information leads many to think that they know more than they do. In cherry-picking information, students might ignore existing evidence that invalidates the conclusions that they have reached. Yet, students can't experience a critical thinking process without first knowing that they don't know everything. Students must question observations, assumptions, values, and opinions. Failing to grapple with contrary evidence entirely negates critical thinking.

By nature, individuals, not just students, embrace their ideas. That can make it difficult to accommodate the ideas of **others**. Thus, colleges and universities cannot hope to eliminate this practice in one class or two or even through an academic major. It is far too engrained for simple retraining. It takes **multiple** years and **multiple** experiences in **multiple** settings in order for individuals to appreciate and act on the reality that one's understanding is limited to what one knows and may not be as complete as one might think. It takes an act of breathtaking humility to undergo this process.

At bottom, colleges and universities would do well to focus on helping students learn that **they may not know everything** or that **what they know may be incomplete or inaccurate.**[24] The trend away from facts exacerbated by the Internet's cheap access to information both valuable and unreliable presents a major threat to the academic enterprise and the work that graduates will undertake after college. Maintaining an open mind is essential as a preface to critical thinking. In so doing, students should realize that they need others who can offer additional and/or more accurate perspectives.

2. **Grit.** The significance of grit has been in the public eye under several names: resilience, perseverance, resolve, follow-through, and stick-to-itiveness. At one level, it might seem obvious that persisting through challenges is critical to success, particularly because things rarely go as one expects. Such claims square nicely with past experiences that many of us have had in overcoming obstacles.[25] One countervailing body of evidence suggests that grit is overrated relative to intelligence;[26] however, it must have value if a student is to make the most of his or her intelligence.[27] The response falls to higher education to encourage situations in which students are required to persevere—and to learn how to persevere wisely.

3. **Ethical decision-making.** Ethics is consistently listed as a *sine qua non* goal of student learning and thus noted by the AAC&U. The value of learning how to make principled decisions is the moral center of the world of higher education. It is the very germ of our existence, and cannot be overestimated in its ubiquity as the substrate for one's life. Students need guidance in learning how to make "good" decisions—appreciating how decisions might impact others or the larger social good. Simply, right and wise choices assume a black-and-white world with clear correct and wrong answers. However, education forces us to see the gray and to make hard decisions that are neither right nor wrong in some immutable way. What we really want students to gain over time is wisdom. Ethical choices spread democratically through higher education in every discipline, bar none.
4. **Communication.** This is a widely accepted learning goal, whether it be in written, oral, or some other form. However, communication presumes several essential skills that make it effective. For example, communication requires a committed and honest **ability to listen.** It requires individuals **to ask effective questions,** which indicates an ability to identify assumptions, biases, misinformation, and omissions.[28]

   Further, it is often the case in the work setting that members are not expected to think only of their ideas but also are actually expected to develop the ideas of others then and explain, refine, and/or defend them. Therefore, there is value in teaching students **how to develop, modify, and refute other people's ideas.** Finally, effective communication is compromised if students have not learned **how to interact with each other in civil and respectful ways.**

   Open and respectful conversation is particularly central to high-functioning teams. Without it, a group cannot expect to arrive at their best results. The current generation of students believes strongly in an environment that is conducive to everyone.[29] They are redefining courtesy and diplomacy. In so doing, they are struggling to find a civil way to discuss incredibly difficult topics. Students need to be capable of hearing someone else's position, which may differ from their own, and wrestling diplomatically with it. They need to challenge and be challenged, all with respect and maturity. Thus, learning how to hear someone out and even advance her ideas is a particularly essential learning goal at this time.
5. **Teamwork.** Colleges and universities often identify Teamwork as a vital learning goal. But, many schools hope that one way or another students will get the importance of teamwork by simply offering them opportunities to work with others. That is not adequate. Students need guidance in learning **how to choose a team, how to contribute to a team, and/or how**

not to contribute to a team. High-functioning teams have members who serve different purposes (as a function of their different strengths), which is why the highest functioning teams are also diverse.[30] Students need to learn those intricacies. They also need to understand how **others** can contribute to a team, not only themselves. Further, high-functioning teams require **effective** communication. They also require strong **interpersonal skills**, which involves **empathy** and **respect**.

6. **Motivation/Drive**. Individuals who are motivated to excel find greater success. They have the ability to resist distractions and to be mindful of the subject undertaken. In brief, motivation is based on, but not limited to, our biology—our predispositions. Motivation is changeable. It can be cultivated, based on the context. Psychologists to corporate executives maintain that motivation is that from which grit springs as well as the will to do or think about most anything. The recognition that individuals are **accountable for their work** also powers motivation.

Colleges now gravitate to several forms of experiential learning, including internships in organizations or businesses, service learning/community service, off-campus study, and academic research, as effective complements to in-class work. In fact, studies establish that "working on a project that took a semester or more to complete, having a job or internships where they applied what they were learning, and being extremely involved in extra-curricular activities" sharpen students' strengths.[31] Thus, students need out-of-class opportunities to apply what they have learned.

Intelligence and Substantive Knowledge

1. Broad intelligence
2. Core knowledge in a discipline and broad knowledge

Foundational Skills (Some of Which Make Critical Thinking/Cognition Possible)

1. Recognition of one's inability to know everything
2. Grit
3. Ethical decision-making
4. Communication
   a. Listening effectively
   b. Asking constructive questions
   c. Learning how to modify, refute, or develop the ideas of others
   d. Acting with respect and civility
5. Teamwork
   a. Choosing a team
   b. Identifying one's productive role on a team

    c. Supporting others on a team
    d. Having strong interpersonal skills
        i. Demonstrating empathy and respect
6. Motivation
    a. Resisting distractions and remaining focused
    b. Willingness to think about or try new things
    c. Recognizing one's accountability
7. Application through experiential learning
    a. Undertaking internships
    b. Participating in service learning/community service
    c. Traveling for off-campus study
    d. Engaging in academic research

CHALLENGES

Of course, if these are the learning priorities, there are many obstacles that could sabotage them. For example, what if students and their families are unable to overcome the financial obstacles? What if they are not interested in these goals—because they either believe that they are trivial or are unwilling to invest the time and effort to achieve them? After all, parents say that their children need to know how to make widgets so that they are employable. Employers, though, say that they need employees who know how to make *better* widgets. In this instance, it won't matter what colleges and universities try to do to improve the educational experience. They are left in the middle of warring goals. And, the learning taxonomy is rendered useless.

Which of these goals can a college realistically teach or students realistically learn? For example, if a professor hopes to teach U.S. history in a manner that will also teach listening skills, can that professor develop class exercises or activities that will accomplish those goals? How would such a class function? Can it be done? What if faculty members are cynical or skeptical about measuring student learning, believing that it either cannot be measured or it just happens serendipitously? Academic freedom generally means that professors have the liberty to teach in the manner that they see fit or that best accommodates their strengths. Further, would shared governance and faculty autonomy impede these goals? Academic departments within colleges and universities tend to operate in decentralized and autonomous ways, which can compromise efforts to unify learning across an institution. These present additional challenges in harmonizing teaching to specific goals.

Would the lack of uniformity across higher education also undermine such work? After all, the United States has over 4000 colleges and universities. Each is different. Each has its own location, geographically and historically, and its own mission and values. It is unrealistic to think that each institution should embrace a universal set of learning goals. Each institution needs to interpret such a taxonomy within its unique context. At the same time, colleges and universities confer degrees and prepare students to excel after college. Employers still expect students to graduate with a foundational set of skills. Thus, schools need to be earnest not only about those areas where students succeed, but also about those where students do not. This honesty means a willingness to make changes in light of ongoing results.

There is also a risk that such learning cannot be accomplished in only four years. For example, data show that students nationwide don't make progress in critical thinking while in college.[32] This result may not be a function of poor teaching in higher education. Many factors contribute to it. It may reflect that learning takes years, or that high schools are not geared to these goals. It would, thus, be necessary to achieve curricular alignment with secondary schools and even graduate schools, and is that even possible? Likewise, at the other end, the question arises as to articulating these skills with those in the professional world and beyond. Over a lifetime, foundational skills are a work in progress.

APPENDIX A

AAC&U Current Learning Measurements

The Association of American Colleges and Universities (AAC&U) released a commissioned study in 2007 delineating what employers seek from college graduates-employees.[33]

1. The ability to work well in teams—especially with people different from yourself
2. An understanding of science and technology and how these subjects are used in real-world settings
3. The ability to write and speak well
4. The ability to think clearly about complex problems
5. The ability to analyze a problem to develop workable solutions
6. An understanding of global context in which work is now done
7. The ability to be creative and innovative in solving problems
8. The ability to apply knowledge and skills in new settings
9. The ability to understand numbers and statistics
10. A strong sense of ethics and integrity

These skills square nicely with the essential learning goals that the AAC&U articulated through its LEAP Campaign, which groups its goals into the following areas:

1. Knowledge of human cultures and the physical and natural world
2. Intellectual and practical skills, including
   a. Inquiry and analysis
   b. Critical and creative thinking
   c. Written and oral communication
   d. Quantitative literacy
   e. Information literacy
   f. Teamwork and problem solving
3. Personal and social responsibility, including
   a. Civic knowledge and engagement—local and global
   b. Intercultural knowledge and competence
   c. Ethical reasoning and action
   d. Foundations and skills for lifelong learning
4. Integrative and applied learning, including
   a. Synthesis and advanced accomplishment across general and specialized studies

These abilities then need to be honed and "demonstrated through the application of knowledge, skills, and responsibilities to new settings and complex problems."[34] This is what colleges and universities refer to as "experiential learning."

Eight years later, a similar AAC&U study revealed that "[w]hen it comes to the types of skills and knowledge that employers feel are most important to workplace success, large majorities of employers do NOT feel that recent college graduates are well prepared. This is particularly the case for applying knowledge and skills in real-world settings, critical thinking skills, and written and oral communication skills—areas in which fewer than three in ten employers think that recent college graduates are well prepared. Even in the areas of ethical decision-making and working with others in teams, many employers do not give graduates high marks. …"[35]

APPENDIX B

Most Commonly Cited Corner Office Learning Goals (Number of Citations by CEOs, $n = 100$)

Teamwork/Communication

People skills/collaboration/community/teamwork (73)—This factor was the most sought after attribute: how do people fit into the existing structure, how do they treat others, how do they build the culture of the company? At its most basic level, how likeable is a particular person? If a person cannot work well with others or does not collaborate well, their contribution will be compromised.

Motivation/Detail-Focused

Motivation (60)—This is a significant trait that employers look for. Why do these candidates want this particular job? What do they intend to achieve in this job? What are their aspirations? Motivating factors, within and without the workplace, allow employers to get a feel for an individual's commitment and determine if they will be an asset to the company.

Ownership (48)—Employers want employees to be invested in the company, to have ownership. If an employee feels a sense of ownership, he or she will care about the company's success and outcomes and tend to work harder.

Growth mindset (40)—Employers want employees who have a growth mindset. They are curious and are not only willing to learn but also wish to learn.

Passion (31)—In the workplace or out of the workplace, passion is a positive trait in an employee. "If they're passionate about something, I know they're going to bring that passion to the workplace" (Sally Smith, 12/13/2014).

Self-Awareness

Self-discernment (29)—Do candidates for employees know themselves? Are they aware of the areas in which they struggle? Are they willing to ask for help? If they are aware of the areas where they have room to grow, they can work to improve them.

Learn from failure (28)—This relates to the idea of a growth mindset. Failure is a learning opportunity. It is common for employers to ask: "what is a mistake you have made and what would you have done differently." A person who recognizes or acknowledges their mistakes and takes ownership will learn from them, not making the same mistake again.

Many of the same findings were confirmed in another recent study, "How Hiring Managers Rate the Skills Gap," conducted by PayScale/Future Workplace.[36] These hiring managers noted that new employees have shortcomings in such areas as:

1. Critical thinking/problem-solving
2. Attention to detail
3. Communication
4. Writing proficiency

Public speaking and interpersonal skills/teamwork also show up in the top eight major gaps.

NOTES

I would like to thank my mother, Alice Glarden Brand, the best writer I know, for working through this chapter, sentence by sentence, with me. I would also like to thank Mimi Vukelich, Cornell College Class of 2017, and Ben Greenstein, former Associate Dean of the College and Professor of Geology, for their great work related to The Corner Office.

1. In the fall of 2015, the Department of Education abandoned an actual college ranking system in favor of the "College Scorecard"—a "customizable consumer-oriented website" that potentially allows students and their families to compare colleges according to many different metrics. Retrieved from https://collegescorecard.ed.gov/
2. See Sophie Quinton, More States Start Funding Colleges Based on Outcomes, August 15, 2016, in Stateline, Pew Charitable Trusts. Retrieved from http://www.pewtrusts.org/en/research-and-analysis/blogs/stateline/2016/08/15/more-states-start-funding-colleges-based-on-outcomes?utm_source=Sailthru&utm_medium=email&utm_campaign=Issue%3A%202016-08-16%20Higher%20Ed%20Education%20Dive%20Newsletter%20%5Bissue%3A6914%5D&utm_term=Education%20Dive%3A%20Higher%20Ed
3. See *U.S. News and World Report* 6/26/15 and *Real Clear Policy* 7/3/15, for examples.
4. These outlets include *The Washington Post* (6/19 and 8/30, 2015), *The Financial Times* (8/25/15), *Forbes* (5/18 and 8/17, 2015), and, from Jonathan Brand in the *Huffington Post* (6/30/15).
5. https://www.hhs.gov/ash/oah/adolescent-health-topics/americas-adolescents/day.html
6. https://www.hhs.gov/ash/oah/adolescent-health-topics/americas-adolescents/day.html
7. See Aina Katsikas, "Same Grades, Better Performance," *The Atlantic*, January 13, 2015. Retrieved from https://www.theatlantic.com/education/archive/2015/01/same-performance-better-grades/384447/
8. See https://www.washingtonpost.com/posteverything/wp/2016/09/02/meet-the-parents-who-wont-let-their-children-study-literature/?utm_term=.c9c8f4d6f12c&wpisrc=nl_most-draw7&wpmm=1
9. See Susan Adams, "The College Degrees Employers Most Want," *Fortune*, March 29, 2012 at: https://www.forbes.com/sites/susanadams/2012/03/29/college-degrees-employers-most-want/#6e06e1b8661e
10. See Malcom Gladwell, "The Order of Things," in *The New Yorker*, February 14 and 21, 2011.
11. See page 11, George D. Kuh et al., "Knowing What Students Know and Can Do: The Current State of Student Learning Outcomes Assessment in U.S. Colleges and Universities," National Institute for Learning Outcomes Assessment, Urbana: University of Illinois and Indiana University, 2014.
12. See "Re-Educating Rita," *The Economist*, June 23, 2016. Retrieved from http://www.economist.com/news/special-report/21700760-artificial-intelligence-will-have-implications-policymakers-education-welfare-and
13. See *Fortune Magazine*, "What Future Leaders Need to Learn in College," June 2, 2016. Retrieved from http://fortune.com/2016/06/02/what-future-leaders-need-to-learn-in-college/
14. See Scott Jaschik, "Well-Prepared in Their Own Eyes," *Inside Higher Ed*, January 20, 2015, at: https://www.insidehighered.com/news/2015/01/20/study-finds-big-gaps-between-student-and-employer-perceptions
15. See Appendix A for a fuller delineation of the AAC&U learning outcomes, including from its LEAP initiative.

16. See the results related to Critical Thinking from the Fall 2015 ACT College Assessment of Academic Proficiency survey. There, the national average for **first-year students** at all levels of institutions was 59.7 out of a possible score of 80. The national average for **seniors** at all levels of institutions remained unchanged at 59.7.
17. See *U.S. News and World Report, The Princeton Review, The Wall Street Journal,* and *Forbes*.com as examples of different rankings, and the U.S. Department of Education's Scorecard.
18. See Appendix B for more information on the learning goals culled from the interviews in The Corner Office.
19. See page 9, Hart Research Associates, *Optimistic About the Future, But How Well Prepared? College Students' Views on College Learning and Career Success*, commissioned by The Association of American Colleges & Universities, April 29, 2015.
20. Of the 100 CEOs, only 10% of them identified critical thinking as a general construct.
21. Robert, J. Zimmer, "Free Speech Is the Basis of a True Education," *Wall Street Journal,* Eastern edition (New York, N.Y.) August 26, 2016: A.11.
22. See *Assessing Outcomes and Improving Achievement: Tips and Tools for Using Rubrics*, edited by Terrel L. Rhodes. Copyright 2010 by The Association of American Colleges and Universities.
23. The most prominent matters that have involved claims of cherry-picking have been in the scientific arena. See, for example, Ryan Buxton, "Neil deGrasse Tyson's Warning for Politicians Who 'Cherry-Pick' Science," *The Huffington Post,* August 28, 2015.
24. See the Socratic Paradox: "I know that I know nothing."
25. See Angela Duckworth, "*Grit: The Power of Passion and Perseverance*," New York: Scribner, 2016.
26. See Jerry Useem, "Is Grit Overrated," *The Atlantic*, June, 2016.
27. And, the additional work that occurs as a result of someone being persistent also has to be work that is done in the right ways (see Claude Steele, *Whistling Vivaldi*: *How Stereotypes Affect Us and What We Can Do*, New York: W. W. Norton & Company, 2010). Working hard in the "wrong" or counter-productive ways does not achieve anything.
28. See Yoni Appelbaum, "Why America's Business Majors Are in Desperate Need of a Liberal-Arts Education," *The Atlantic*, June 28, 2016.
29. http://www.latimes.com/opinion/op-ed/la-oe-chemerinsky-gillman-free-speech-on-campus-20160331-story.html
30. L. Hong and S. E. Page, Working paper, *Diversity and Optimality* [Loyola University (Chicago) and University of Michigan (Ann Arbor): 2002].
31. See "Real Data Revolution," *Trusteeship*, The Association of Governing Boards of Universities and Colleges, July/August, 2016, p. 15.
32. See again the results related to Critical Thinking from the Fall, 2015 ACT College Assessment of Academic Proficiency survey. There, the national average for **first-year students** at all levels of institutions was 59.7 out of a possible score of 80. The national average for **seniors** at all levels of institutions remained unchanged at 59.7.
33. Peter D. Hart Research Associates, Inc., *How Should Colleges Prepare Students to Succeed in Today's Global Economy?*, commissioned by the Association of American Colleges & Universities, released on January 10, 2007. Retrieved from https://www.aacu.org/sites/default/files/files/LEAP/2007_full_report_leap.pdf
34. From "Essential Learning Outcomes," which is a part of the Association of American Colleges and Universities' LEAP campaign. See https://www.aacu.org/leap/essential-learning-outcomes for more on the LEAP campaign.

35. See page 12, Hart Research Associates, *Falling Short? College Learning and Career Success*, commissioned by the Association of American Colleges and Universities, released on January 20, 2015. Retrieved from https://www.aacu.org/sites/default/files/files/LEAP/2015employerstudentsurvey.pdf. See also Scott Jaschik, "Well-Prepared in Their Own Eyes," *Inside Higher Ed*, January 20, 2015. Retrieved from https://www.insidehighered.com/news/2015/01/20/study-finds-big-gaps-between-student-and-employer-perceptions
36. https://www.payscale.com/data-packages/job-skills

CHAPTER TWO

Liberal Arts Colleges

Building Capacity to Thrive

STEVEN C. BAHLS
President, Augustana College (Illinois)

> "The report of my death was an exaggeration."
> —Mark Twain in a letter to Frank Marshall White (May 31, 1897)

Many have predicted the slow demise of traditional liberal arts colleges. President emeritus of Beloit College, Victor E. Ferrall, Jr., writes in his book, *Liberal Arts at the Brink* that "the handful of voices supporting the liberal arts ... are being drowned out by the economic forces driving colleges to vocations and by the rising chorus of advocates for the abandonment of liberal arts education."[1] Robert Zemsky in *Checklist for Change* argues that colleges and "faculty are encamped just north of Armageddon [looking] over the edge and see the destruction that would await them."[2] Harvard business professor Clayton Christensen contends that change will disrupt traditional colleges, arguing that "private universities without national recognition and large endowments are at great financial risk."[3] Jon McGee, of College of Saint Benedict and Saint John's University, offers the direst prediction when he concludes that due to "changing demographics, changing economics, and changing cultural expectations ... most colleges and universities will need to find a new point of sustainable mission, market and management balance."[4]

Presidents and boards wrestle with the response to these dire predictions for their institutions. Is McGee correct that they should lead their institutions to new missions and new markets? I don't think so. Instead of jettisoning mission, liberal arts colleges should respond to disruptive change by building the capacity to thrive within mission. Doing so requires a more deliberate focus on outcomes in order to enhance the value of the humanities. Building that focus requires more effective shared governance and employee engagement to align faculty, staff, and board members for a joint agenda to build capacity for change.

This chapter argues that the model of a residential liberal arts college is not deeply flawed, and it is not relevant only to the past. Instead, liberal arts colleges need to be intentional in continuing to evolve within their traditional mission, just as they have been evolving over hundreds of years. Liberal arts colleges will remain an important part of higher education for decades to come within traditional models, but only if leaders build the capacity for their colleges to meet the social and economic changes in this country and this world.

The most effective college and university leaders are able to accelerate the pace of change, within the traditional models of liberal arts colleges, by understanding that investment is required in four areas:

- Deliberate action to focus on outstanding outcomes, particularly those after graduation.
- Aggressive steps to enhance the value of humanities and other traditional liberal arts majors.
- Aggressive actions to reallocate resources and bend the cost curve.
- Effective shared governance to build a joint agenda for change.

DELIBERATE FOCUS ON INTEGRATING THE CAMPUS EXPERIENCE AND ENHANCING OUTCOMES

Those who predict the demise of liberal arts colleges ignore the reality that these colleges do more than simply prepare students for jobs. Most traditional liberal arts colleges enroll primarily 18–22-year-olds, whose families expect much more than a job upon graduation. They expect a "coming-of-age" experience where students grow in mind, body, and spirit. In fact, with its small, residential, nurturing campus, a traditional liberal arts college has many natural advantages in providing a coming-of-age experience that no other sector in higher education has. Liberal arts colleges that are able to "tune-up" their curricular and cocurricular offerings to assuage families' concerns about outcomes upon graduation are positioned to thrive when compared to their counterparts in other sectors.

Liberal arts colleges cannot take this advantage for granted if these coming-of-age offerings aren't deliberately coordinated and aligned. Liberal arts college administrators too often assume that impressive residential campuses, strong athletic programs, and an impressive array of co- and extracurricular activities will ensure student growth into the future. Small college administrators should not rest on their laurels, since these functions can often be disaggregated at a lower cost.

In fact, one could argue that each part of what makes liberal arts colleges special could be done as well by others. Many studies show that online courses, for example, when done properly with motivated students, can be as effective in conveying information (and even critical thinking skills) as traditional face-to-face classes. And these classes can often be delivered at a lower price than the typical liberal arts college charges its students.

But it is not only classes that might be offered with greater value elsewhere. Students enrolling in online courses can usually find more attractive housing in the community than traditional residence halls (often with amenities like swimming pools and exercise facilities) at a lower cost than for residential students. And most communities have competitive club sports teams for young adults that provide many of the same advantages as college-sponsored sports, without all the rules imposed by colleges and athletic conferences. It is not far-fetched to predict that future students might take a combination of online courses and live courses, living in housing developments catering to students and engaging with the community through club sports, local music ensembles, and other student-oriented community activities at a fraction of the price of attending the local liberal arts college.

Would this disaggregation of the components of a residential liberal arts education jeopardize the success of residential colleges? It depends. A college that successfully aligns these functions will make the whole more valuable than the sum of the parts. That requires integrating the primary functions of the college, moving away from the trend of decentralization and silos. Residential life programs and athletics must integrate better with the academic program. The college should develop a cohesive set of student learning outcomes, and each activity should be expected to integrate those learning outcomes into their programs. With that integration, liberal arts colleges can continue to achieve better outcomes than the disaggregated and uncoordinated alternative.

As part of providing value in the integration of the components of a liberal arts college, colleges must show extraordinary value in post-graduation outcomes. Too many students and their families assume that the majors and programs offered by liberal arts colleges, particularly humanities majors, are not in demand by employers. In fact, many employers value the critical thinking and analytic skills that liberal arts colleges' graduates have mastered due to the more in-depth general education requirements that most liberal arts colleges excel in.[5] Likewise, lifetime earnings are often higher for those with humanities majors than more technical majors such as computer science and engineering.[6] Savvy parents and students recognize that college should prepare students for their first and last jobs—and that the integrative, critical and creative thinking emphasized by liberal arts colleges is a more durable education for a lifetime of changing jobs and careers.

I've come to conclude that successfully conveying a liberal arts college's long-term value for students is much more than marketing—either at the college level or the national level. Too often, our intended audiences regard marketing the value of the liberal arts with skepticism. They don't want to see the sizzle—they want to see the beef. Well-intentioned campaigns like the one by the Council of Independent Colleges to market the advantages of the liberal arts can't compete with the drumbeat of many of our politicians (including President Obama, though he later apologized) joking about art history majors or devaluing the practical application of the liberal arts.[7]

More impressive than slick marketing campaigns touting the success of featured graduates of the college are solid efforts by the college to ensure strong employment and graduate school outcomes for all graduates.

One important strategy is to supercharge the institution's efforts to focus on outcomes, starting with a student's first year. At Augustana College, we have invested heavily in rethinking our career services office to meet the needs of today's students. The college has transformed its career services operations from four to fifteen professionals over two years by the establishment of a centrally located campus hub called CORE (Careers, Opportunities, Research, and Exploration). The office promotes a four-year program to integrate all of the services that enable students to obtain the important first job (or graduate school acceptance) while at the same time helping students to achieve other outcomes—a commitment to find one's calling in life, a durable work trajectory, and a commitment to lead a life of service.

Too often, an institution's major student advising services are siloed and not coordinated. Academic advising is often done in isolation from career planning. By the same token, career planning is often not deeply connected to experiential learning or even vocational exploration.

Augustana's CORE center seeks to create an integrative experience for students from the first day of their arrival at the college. This integrative experience provides more value than the sum of the traditionally disaggregated parts.

Augustana's CORE center is a four-year program, made easy for the students by creating a simple pathway for them to navigate toward their first job or graduate school program. To chart the path, we devised a tool called the Viking Scorecard that asks students to track their professional preparation for life after graduation.[8]

The process that most students go through to pick a major is too haphazard at many institutions. Too many students never seriously confront decisions they made in high school about their majors. How well do most 16-year-olds really know what they want to do with their lives? Too often, their preliminary choices of majors are heavily influenced by parents or friends, without much of a critical examination. Students are best served by a deeper reflection upon their vocational calling. This reflection is best seen as a process in which students are able to discern where their skills, passions, and talents meet a deep societal need. Such reflection, however, doesn't take place in a one-time counseling session with a career services officer. Instead, vocational reflection is a series of experiences in the classroom, in co- and extra-curricular activities, in internships and in conversation with family and friends, all linked together by intention. For most it is akin to a spiritual experience—what am I called to do? It is important for students, as part of this process, to ask who they are before they ask what they want to do.

At Augustana, an institution affiliated with the Evangelical Lutheran Church in America, an important part of our campus ministries program is to assist students with vocational reflection by helping them draw together the many experiences they have that touch on their calling in life. As the percentage of Lutheran students at ELCA colleges declines as well as general interest in denominationally based spirituality, Augustana has relocated a chaplain to the CORE center to aid career services professionals in facilitating meaningful vocational reflection.

As students are wrestling with finding their calling, colleges must be more deliberate in giving them the tools necessary to be successful. Employers increasingly believe that quality internships and leadership in co- and extracurricular activities are as important as grades, majors, and quality of the institution. For liberal arts colleges to ensure students have the post-graduation outcomes they (and their families) desire, it is important that students have the high-impact experiences in college that employers are looking for.

Quality internship experiences require a team effort. Delegating full responsibility for internships to an internship office is not enough. It must be an integrated effort. Faculty members, with their connections in the field, can often best match students to the most appropriate internship experience. Faculty members are usually in the best position to urge students to pursue internships and can often match students to high-impact opportunities. Coaches and other student life professionals can do the same. But matching students with quality internships is not enough. Faculty, coaches, and other student life professionals should help students reflect on what they've gained and learned from the internships. Students need to be challenged by faculty to use internship opportunities to inventory their passions, skills, and talents as well as asking whether the experience helps them be passionate about a deep societal need.

Colleges should look for more ways to integrate the classroom with hands-on opportunities in the field. Faculty should not view what happens in the classroom as separate from what students learn outside of the classroom. At Augustana College, for example, our Upper Mississippi River Center offers hands-on opportunities for two hundred students each year to engage in real life projects that assist aging Mississippi River communities become more sustainable. These projects involve students working with various city officials to design actionable plans to address pressing community issues like water quality, lead abatement, and mass transit ridership. Students pursuing such projects are encouraged not only to learn about the communities' problems, but also to propose and implement actionable solutions to them. Communities have recognized the value of students developing new solutions to old problems and have agreed to defray the costs of involving students through generous contracts with the center or grants to the College.

To further encourage students to engage in internships and service learning, Augustana College provides a $2000 grant to each student to pursue such high-impact experiences. These can also include study-away programs and intensive research projects with faculty. Nearly all students at the College use this grant. Students frequently engage in guided reflection with their faculty members, coaches, and other student-life professionals about how these experiences help them discern their vocational calling. Augie Choice grants also have the beneficial impact of ensuring that students from less wealthy families have the same access to and participation in high-impact experiences as more wealthy students.

Free-standing career services offices do not provide the integrated experience necessary to achieve the very high placement rates in jobs requiring a college degree, or acceptance into top graduate schools that families are demanding. Augustana's CORE Center, located at the heart of campus, engages students, faculty, coaches, and others in an integrated program that helps ensure students will engage in meaningful career reflection and benefit from the high-impact experiences offered to maximize the probability of post-college success in both the short run and the long run.

ENHANCING THE VALUE OF HUMANITIES AND OTHER TRADITIONAL LIBERAL ARTS COLLEGE MAJORS

Most philosophy majors do not become public philosophers. A relatively small percentage of English majors end up as English professors. Most successful careers are benefited by these majors, but do not require them. Too often, as students are preparing for the job world, they perceive that their humanities majors do not open as many doors as hoped for. I find that the humanities majors who have the greatest challenges are those who have hunkered down in their major, not taking advantage of other activities that enhance their skills in a way that will allow them to market their major to employers. Once again, this is often due to the siloing of functions at our colleges: faculty members are concerned with academics, and student life professionals are concerned with co- and extracurricular activities.

One approach to enhancing employability by those who do not have preprofessional majors is to double major. Most liberal arts colleges make it easy for students to double major. Often students report that one of their majors follows their passion and the other major is designed to get a job. Often the second (job-oriented) major is strongly encouraged by parents and relatives. While double majors have their advantages, few institutions do much to ensure that the double majors are an integrative experience that helps students answer their callings in life. Liberal arts colleges, with their attractive full-time faculty/student ratios, are in a better position than other sectors to address this issue. Many colleges have established interdisciplinary "contract" majors where one or more professors guide students in an integrated course of studies outside of traditional majors.

Because employers are looking at experiences (e.g., internships and other activities outside of the classroom) as much as majors, faculty teaching traditional majors at liberal arts colleges should be alert to linking their majors with experiences outside the traditional boundaries of the major. There are four categories of these experiences colleges should consider:

Certificates or other programs short of a major or minor. The best of these programs, usually available to all majors, combine several classes with internship experience. At Augustana College, for example, the College offers a nonprofit administration program. The program requires three or four courses with an internship. This combination provides students with not only the knowledge but a base experience from which to demonstrate a set of skills in demand by certain employers. Many students in humanities majors have a special passion to think deeply about making their communities and the world a better place. Nonprofit organizations are often a wonderful way for students to pursue their passions. Similar programs are in development in filmmaking, fundraising, and gerontology.

Opportunities for humanities majors to gain quantitative/computer skills. The United States Department of Labor projects many of the faster growing job classifications in the future will be those requiring some level of quantitative skills.[9] Students in the humanities are not routinely required to master the level of quantitative skills to which students in pre-professional (business, accounting, and psychology) majors are exposed.

Colleges with the most robust humanities programs in the future will devise ways to connect students in the humanities with quantitative skills. But how do we help our students overcome their fear of not being successful in quantitative areas? One answer is to look for ways for the humanities to put the "A" in changing STEM to STEAM.

One example of how we are linking Arts to the Science, Technology, Engineering and Math emphasis is through a data analytics program at Augustana that provides a minor designed for non-mathematics and non-computer science majors. Jobs in data analytics (including business analytics, analytics in public policy, healthcare analytics, and cyber-security) are among the fastest-growing job categories and the most in demand by employers. While construction of databases is best left to computer scientists, humanists with a meaningful, but not extensive, knowledge of statistics can bring much to these job categories. The most important task of a data analyst is to form the right questions, an aptitude rooted in strong critical thinking skills. Data analysts need to ask the difficult questions—is the database reliable, what should be in the database, how can the data base be best parsed and how can it most ethically be used? One could argue that humanists might be best positioned to ask these questions.

The evolving economy offers a dizzying array of opportunities for humanists. Businesses that are socially oriented are growing rapidly. Those combining graphic design and creative skills are in high demand. Students with new media skills can combine the best of the major they are committed to with a marketable skill to advance what they learned in their major.

Skills credentialing can enhance humanities majors. Increasingly, employers are demanding skills certifications or other evidence of demonstrated practical competencies for first jobs. Often that certification is more important than the major. Humanities faculty should look for ways to help their students gain these certifications and other competencies. Often liberal arts colleges shy away from programs that provide their students with these competencies due to the cost of the programs or the belief that they do not have the technical capability or expertise to deliver these competencies. During these times of constrained resources, which are likely to continue, the best way to develop these resources is with mutually beneficial partnerships with those outside the institution.

Such partnerships do not come naturally to many liberal arts colleges. Faculties are sometimes concerned with loss of control over programs or partners driving an agenda that might be too commercial or otherwise inconsistent with the institution's values. Academic departments are often siloed, meaning that determining who drives partnerships that provide certifications and other competencies sometimes devolves into political wrangling.

Our best partners are those who share the institution's mission and ideals. Partnerships with commercial enterprises that have all the answers should be approached with skepticism.

Two partnerships at Augustana help illustrate these points. Recently a graduate of the College approached me with a novel idea. He was a Classics major who went on to get a graduate degree in film and media. He observed that many jobs available in film and media do not require a film or media major—rather most require creative people who have technical skills. More important than major are skills behind the camera, editing skills (made easier by relatively inexpensive, user-friendly editing software), script-writing skills, and business and marketing skills. The common thread among all of these skills is critical thinking.

After conversation, we determined to relocate his small but successful film-making company to the campus. In exchange for no rent and a modest stipend, FreshFilms will provide fellowships and internships to dozens of students, with majors from across the campus. Faculty members have fully engaged with this company in part because of its connection to an Augustana graduate passionate about producing quality films by engaging the creativity of our students.

Another example is the Sustainable Working Landscapes Initiative[10] at Augustana. Partnering with cities and counties within easy driving distances, students from all majors develop project-management and problem-solving skills through multidisciplinary work that serves community needs. As an example, the college contracted with an adjacent county to develop strategies to remediate lead paint in the older homes of the community. Students from various majors developed a communications plan to encourage difficult-to-engage residents to participate in the project. Other students used data analytics to determine homes most at risk, in order to apply the first dollars where needed most. Other students worked with county officials to develop innovative ways to obtain public and private dollars for remediation. Still other students connected with local hospitals and other non-profit organizations to leverage their resources and expertise.

Liberal arts graduates, particularly humanities majors, have the integrative, critical, and creative skills to make a difference. Combine this with the passion of most humanities majors to make their communities better and the transforming power of these disciplines is as strong as ever. With creativity and relatively little investment, liberal arts colleges can help students put the A in STEAM as well as enhancing all professions with greater creativity.

AGGRESSIVELY REALLOCATE RESOURCES AND BEND THE COST CURVE

Liberal arts colleges are simply too expensive for many families. This is particularly true for those schools that do not have the endowment or other resources to fund the gap between what families can pay and the price of the institution. Most liberal arts colleges, including my own, have partially addressed this issue with aggressive tuition-discounting policies. These schools have increased tuition and fees at double the recent low rates of inflation, while increasing the tuition discount by about one percentage point each year.

This high-cost/high-discount approach to pricing is a natural and reasonable response to the widening disparity between lower-income Americans and upper-income Americans and the concomitant shrinkage of the middle class in the United States. Tuition discounting transfers resources from wealthier families to less wealthy families, allowing colleges to maintain (or increase) enrollment and inject a measure of equity into college admissions.

Of course, the high-tuition, high-discount model is not sustainable. At Augustana College, for example, our tuition, room and board is about $50,000 with an overall discount rate of about 50%. If we continue to increase tuition at 4% each year, which is double the low rate of inflation, but increase our overall discount rate by 1% per year, our tuition will be in excess of $340,000 annually in fifty years. But the good news for students is that the discount rate will be 100%! While this model has enabled liberal arts colleges to maintain strong enrollment, it cannot continue indefinitely. High "sticker prices" will discourage many families from even considering our colleges.

What should the pricing model of the future be? College leaders who have engaged in tuition resets (substantial reduction of price with an associated substantial deduction of discount) have regretted it. Not only do they lose the Chivas Regal effect (isn't the college worth less than higher-priced colleges?), they also lose the ability to shape their classes. Rarely do tuition resets materially reduce costs, given that the targeted net revenue per student is usually the same before and after the strategy is employed.

The solution to the pricing dilemma within the liberal arts sector must be more than a simplistic price reset or other gimmick. Liberal arts colleges are too expensive, and even if a family can afford to pay the full price or most of the price of a college, they are increasingly unwilling to do so. More and more families view liberal arts colleges (above a minimum level of quality) as a commodity, using their purchasing power to bargain with financial aid offices.

The resistance to the cost of liberal arts colleges is, of course, likely to increase. Many state grants to support residents attending private colleges are eroding. Likewise at the federal level, there will be considerable debate about free or debt-free public education for the majority of American families. While these proposals may or may not come to fruition, the debate will keep the spotlight on the high cost of college education and the perceived desirability of finding a "bargain" when selecting a college.

To break this cycle, liberal arts colleges need to take two approaches. One is to bend the cost curve to become affordable to more families. The other is to have a steadfast focus on outcomes—particularly employment outcomes and graduate-school-acceptance outcomes. When these approaches are pursued in tandem, the institution will increase its value proposition. Increasing the value proposition will help the institution become more than a commodity, and instead become a sought-after investment for families.

But creating great outcomes for our students can only work if they can afford access to them. Yes, many liberal arts colleges have bent the cost curve, but most need to do much more. In the wake of the recession, most liberal arts colleges have picked the low-hanging fruit in cost savings, making finding future savings more difficult. For the independent college sector as a whole, the cost-cutting to date has been accompanied by tuition and fees increases at roughly double the rate of inflation, meaning net price (tuition and fees minus financial aid), adjusted for inflation, has not increased since the Great Recession.[11]

Most liberal arts colleges have a difficult time reducing costs. Reduction of costs often means the reduction in the number of employees, but laying off employees is an anathema at liberal arts colleges, where the concept of community is cherished.

Colleges have controlled their costs since the recession by reducing student/faculty and student/administrator ratios modestly, moderating salary and benefit increases, limiting travel, and other expenses and, in relatively rare occasions, closed programs. Trustees frequently urge leaders to be more aggressive in cost reductions, and administrators and faculty push back. Providing a quality education, particularly with the liberal arts model, is inherently costly because it involves small classes and one-on-one interaction. Trustees urge that small majors should be dropped, but those small majors are often in the core of the humanities. How can liberal arts colleges maintain their identity, faculty members correctly ask, without classics, philosophy, art history, and religion majors?

Other cost savings initiatives are more difficult at liberal arts colleges than larger colleges, particularly in the public sector. Most faculty members and presidents are loathe to provide much online education, given their belief that face-to-face interaction is the best way for students to grow in mind, body and spirit. Though many liberal arts college have seen growth in adjunct and other contingent faculty over the past two decades, the growth has not been as dramatic as higher education institutions in other sectors. Liberal arts colleges value the community and commitment to students created by full-time faculty teaching the bulk of the classes. While most liberal arts colleges have offered new academic programs, additional athletic programs and a host of new co- and extracurricular programs, smaller undergraduate institutions are more limited in new program addition than their larger public counterparts. Many at traditional liberal arts colleges correctly surmise that the addition of numerous graduate programs threatens the focus on the undergraduate arts and sciences core. But, at the same time, most senior administrators of liberal arts colleges worry that the reliance on a single product—residential, undergraduate liberal arts—does not provide the necessary flexibility to diversify offerings that might enhance the institution's sustainability.

Most of the expense reductions since the recession have not been strategic. Hiring freezes for administrators, staff, and faculty do not create a strategic direction. Freezing the growth of each department's non-personnel expenses will damage some departments more than others while doing nothing to advance the institution's mission. While many institutions have maintained the quality of their programs notwithstanding these cuts, deeper cuts will damage quality, risking a spiral of more cuts. Many presidents and boards hope for better days, but then remind each other that hope is not a strategy.

Other nonprofit sectors of our economy share the same post-recession stress that liberal arts colleges face. I have the privilege of serving as vice-chair of the board of a regional healthcare system. Hospitals have longed faced similar economic pressures that liberal arts colleges face. Reimbursements for services, like tuition and fees, have not kept up with the rate of inflation. Doctors, like faculty members, tend to place a high value on autonomy and are sometimes resistant to administrators advocating a quicker pace of change. Not-for-profit hospitals face increasing competition from the for-profit sector, as well as clinics placed in drug stores and even grocery stores. Smaller health systems outside of major cities often face the same challenges as smaller colleges in the same communities, particularly attracting and retaining the number and quality of professionals (e.g., doctors and faculty members) in high-demand specialties.

Health care has been more aggressive than higher education in addressing these issues, perhaps because the crisis in health care is more acute. Those leading higher education would do well to examine how health care has addressed its issues. This examination could provide a road map for higher education, and I would suggest two responses by health care systems merit particular examination by higher education.

Application of the principles of lean management. Many health systems have employed principles of lean management to bend cost curves and develop better outcomes for the dollars invested. Principles of lean management assume that the best way to control costs and gain better outcomes is to examine processes from top to bottom, engaging those involved or impacted by the process with a trained facilitator. Often those involved in the process are promised no job loss (though there may be job reassignment or retraining) in order to encourage their full participation. The result is an interactive process where solutions are proposed, examined, and revised.

Lean management processes are particularly well-suited for liberal arts colleges.[12] Because liberal arts colleges tend to be decentralized communities with many members suspicious of top-down decision-making practices, the cooperative, grassroots aspects of lean management are particularly attractive. Further, many small colleges have thinly staffed business offices without the time, resources, and sometimes expertise to examine each and every process at the college.

The lean management process at Augustana yielded both better outcomes and cost savings. An employee at the Augustana mailroom asked why we needed to staff a U.S. Postal Service substation at Augustana, when the local post office would provide many of the same services at no cost. Another employee, in receiving, asked why we maintained so many paper records of the parcels received. Could we use bar-scanning technology and free up resources for other uses? Other projects included optimizing the use of faculty time in advising through a combination of technological solutions and lower paid administrators handling the less complex advising questions students posed. The lean process also assisted with optimizing use of our IT professionals and our communications and marketing resources. These are just a few of the many examples of how empowering employees to address inefficiencies can yield meaningful savings. Perhaps the biggest advantage of the lean management philosophy at Augustana has been to create a culture where all internal constituencies continually examine key processes to improve outcomes for students, while minimizing unnecessary expenses. In doing so, employees accept change more readily and adopt lean as a way of thinking.

To identify the areas to most productively apply lean management, Augustana hired a national consulting firm to take a top-to-bottom review of our efficiency. The firm specializes in working with venture capitalists in reducing the operating costs of the businesses they acquire. These consultants concluded that with proper planning we could reduce 7% of our expenditures. Though the college rejected some of the advice as being inconsistent with its mission and values, the suggestions were used to seed the lean management process. We expect in the next three years to realize two-thirds of the savings suggested by the consulting firm.

Benefitting from economies of scale. Many smaller health systems do not have the capacity to provide all of the medical specialties needed in their communities. In health care, the response has been a wave of health-system mergers and larger hospitals acquiring smaller critical care hospitals, applying their experience to the smaller hospitals and allowing them to serve the needs of smaller communities.

It is unlikely that higher education will witness the mergers and acquisitions seen in health care. To date college mergers have been relatively rare, largely because colleges and universities, unlike hospitals, usually have a strong and loyal alumni base that would eschew mergers and likely stop their considerable charitable contributions in response to perceived loss of institutional identity and independence.

But institutions of higher education can realize some of the same economies of scale, through affiliations that are far short of merger. An example is the Five Colleges of Ohio consortium that develops ways to share backroom resources as well as academic programs. Associations of colleges are relatively rare, outside of a few (e.g., Associated Colleges of the Midwest, Great Lakes College Association). Even loosely affiliated colleges give up a bit of autonomy in the areas of affiliation, anathema to faculty and presidents.

Though many assume that the best opportunities for liberal arts colleges to affiliate is through shared backroom expenses, my experience is that there are not, in fact, massive savings here. Most of these expenses are place-based, so the opportunity cost of negotiating joint purchase and similar agreements is often not justified by the savings. The best opportunities for meaningful collaboration are in academic programs with low enrollment and in programs requiring a high degree of expertise. I agree with the classicists that argue that a college cannot have a top-shelf classics program without four or five positions. But I also agree with the chief financial officers who say staffing in small departments needs to have a relationship to the number of students taking courses from those departments.

The ability to link classrooms real-time via video conferencing holds tremendous potential to both control costs and advance better outcomes. Consider a religion department that has experienced declining enrollment over the years. One college may have a strong but undersubscribed Islamic studies program, while another college has a strong but undersubscribed Judaic studies program. Linking these schools electronically for the same live classes nearly preserves the valued face-to-face instruction small colleges offer, while at the same time allowing them to attract faculty and ensure those faculty that they will have the chance to teach their coveted specialized courses, because the combined enrollment of consortium students will justify it.

Another way that smaller regional health care systems have remained prosperous is through affiliations with larger and perhaps more prestigious health care systems. Doing so provides access to specialties beyond those available in smaller communities, and offers a wealth of healthcare analytics to provide better outcomes at lower prices to patients, all resulting in improved margins for the partners in the collaboration. Liberal arts colleges should consider the same.

Most small colleges have long collaborated with larger universities, often flagship state institutions, in offering 3:2 programs (three years at the liberal arts college and two years at the flagship university) in programs such as engineering and architecture. Liberal arts colleges should consider more affiliations to gain the expertise needed for advanced courses, without having the expense of hiring a full-time faculty member. Options holding promise include regular visitorships or exchanges with R1 institutions, retaining R1 faculty as lecturers, and cross-enrollment arrangements. R1 institutions often welcome such arrangements in order to create a pipeline to graduate programs and provide new types of opportunities for their faculty members.

BUILDING CAPACITY FOR CHANGE

Many of the actions suggested in this chapter require that institutions undertake a more rapid pace of change than they are accustomed to. Some may threaten faculty and departmental autonomy, while others will take considerable additional effort from an already overburdened faculty and staff. Knowing what to do for sustainability is easier than effectively implementing the needed steps to achieve it. Change comes more naturally if a college has built up its ability to work together toward common goals. To build the capacity for change, colleges need to develop a stronger approach to both shared governance and employee engagement. They also should take intentional steps to foster entrepreneurial faculty and administrators.

Shared governance. Effective change within liberal arts colleges is seldom top-down. Given faculty traditions of self-governance and autonomy, there is no better way for a college president to defeat an initiative with academic implications than to mandate it.

In my 2014 book, *Shared Governance in Times of Change: A Practical Guide for Universities and Colleges,*[13] I made the case that institutions investing in shared governance have greater capacity to harness solutions to the problems facing liberal arts colleges. For shared governance to be effective, I argue, colleges and universities must move from the traditional definitions of shared governance to one that creates greater alignment of faculty, administrations, and boards. The three traditional approaches to shared governance described below all fail to sufficiently align the board, the faculty, and the administration to address the increasingly complex problems they face.

- Shared governance as equal rights to governance. Sometimes faculty members believe shared governance means that all important decisions at a college or university are jointly made—including decisions involving facilities, budgets, and administrative personnel. Those holding this view would usually make exceptions for academic decisions, where they would argue that faculties have the sole responsibility.

  This view is a sure cause for deadlock and indecision. For some faculty members, deadlock is the preferred state of affairs as it preserves the decentralization and independence they value. This, of course, is unacceptable for institutions needing to move forward. In the Association of Governing Board's *Strategic Imperatives. New Priorities for Higher Education*, the AGB appropriately noted that "despite higher education's traditions of thorough, broadly inclusive, and perhaps unhurried deliberations, boards may also need to push institutions to become more nimble and more deadline-driven in their decision making."[14]
- Shared governance as consultation. Many board members see shared governance as an obligation to consult with the faculty before making major decisions.

  While consultation with the faculty is important in matters of the direction of the institution, it's only effective when the consultation is careful and thoughtful—not when it is little more than window dressing.

  Consultation with faculty is a necessary component of shared governance, but consultation alone is not sufficient for effective shared governance. Even when they've been consulted, many faculty members are prone to feel they have not been listened to if decisions don't go their way. Further, for matters at the heart of the academic program, faculty members do not want to simply be consulted. They believe that they own the academic program.

  Viewing shared governance as seeking faculty input is an incomplete view. It addresses neither what role faculties have in actually shaping policy nor how decisions are made when the board and the faculty disagree.
- Shared governance as a rigid set of rules of engagement. This view is most commonly espoused by the American Association of University Professors *Statement on Government of Colleges and Universities*.[15] The AAUP rules were designed to prevent colleges and universities from diminishing the role of faculty. The rules seek to affect a system of checks and balances in an attempt to increase communication between boards, administrators, and

> faculty members. In reality, many have viewed the AAUP *Statement* as rules of engagement, since it defines the domains of governing boards, the president, the faculty, and the students.
>
> The AAUP's *Statement on Government of Colleges and Universities* is a helpful reflection on how to share governance, but implementation of true shared governance should not be viewed as a set of legalistic, one-size-fits-all rules. If the AAUP *Statement* is viewed as little more than rules of engagement, it is unlikely that shared governance will be truly effective.

Moving beyond these traditional definitions, I would suggest a fourth way of viewing shared governance; namely:

> A system of open communication to align priorities, to create a culture of shared responsibility for the welfare of the institution, and to design a system of checks and balances that ensures the institution stays mission centered.

Shared governance, then, is not an elaborate set of rules of engagement nor is it a friendly partnership. Rather, it suggests a strategic alignment guided by four principles:

- Strategic goals are to be jointly developed, but tactical decisions are best left to the constituency best positioned to make and implement them. To achieve this, presidents must be committed to giving the faculty the information and support they need to see the "big picture" issues.
- Open communication is necessary to align priorities and discuss generative issues. Chait, Ryan and Taylor in *Governance as Leadership: Reframing the Work of the Nonprofit Board,* identify the core of generative thinking by boards as acting creatively in discerning problems and engaging in "sense making" prior to decision making.[16] Faculty members, by training and disposition, are particularly adept at engaging in discussion at this level.
- Appropriate checks and balances are essential to ensure that the institution remains mission focused (i.e., faculty govern the detail of the academic program, while the board and the administration provide the budget).
- A common set of metrics must be adopted in order to measure the success of the college and its academic program.

Developing a system of shared governance around aligned priorities requires a president with a skillful and steady hand. Presidents must be overt in lauding shared governance and must urge board and faculty leaders to do the same. The president must foster a strong commitment by the board, administration, and faculty, alike, to share key decisions such as strategic planning not just at the end of the process, but in the generative phases. At Augustana, for example, we invite 40 faculty members to join our 40 board members every other year at the board retreat to discuss major issues facing the college. At nearly every board meeting, we are intentional in creating space and time for faculty members and board members to interact outside the formal structure of the board meeting. Shared governance can't be effective without trust, and trust is hard to build without personal relationships.

Effective shared governance requires a strong commitment to transparency with the faculty. Boards are often committed to transparency, but think of it in external terms only, not necessarily being transparent inside the institution. Faculty can't be expected to share governance if they aren't fully informed about the challenges facing the college. Shared governance can be most effective when the board and faculty understand and agree on the key strengths, weaknesses, opportunities, and threats. Faculty must also commit to being transparent with the board, particularly with respect to student learning outcomes.

The president must work to ensure that shared governance advances accountability to mission and to student learning outcomes. A common focus on outcomes helps protect against shared governance amounting to nothing more than a consensus on how to protect the provincial interests of the participants.

The greatest obstacle to shared governance at most institutions is ineffective faculty governance of the academic program. If faculty members cannot effectively organize themselves with the requisite degree of centralized decision making to ensure timely, high-quality academic decisions, it's difficult for the board and the administration to share college governance with them. A faculty that is dysfunctional usually does not have leaders or governance processes that can coherently speak for the faculty, making effective deliberation almost impossible. A president can be supportive by articulating the importance of faculty governance to a strong academic program, and by helping faculty understand the difference between faculty governance of academics and shared governance of the institution. Faculty leaders should be given support by appropriate stipends or release time as well as adequate professional leadership development opportunities. Finally, the president should take care not to circumvent faculty leadership by developing a "kitchen cabinet" or other informal network for building consensus with the faculty outside its governance structures.

When a college uses shared governance effectively to align priorities, it can shift from ad hoc decision making to building the capacity to cope with higher education's many challenges. I have seen shared governance most effective during the development of a strategic plan to prepare for the future. That's when a college can effectively address such difficult questions as program expansions, program retrenchment, affordability, and campus diversity and inclusion.

Employee engagement. Within the employee base of a college or university, shared governance focuses primarily on engaging faculty and senior-level administrators.

But for institutions to be effective, all employees must be engaged. This is particularly important for liberal arts colleges where the sense of community is often greater than at universities organized around multiple quasi-independent colleges or schools.

Experienced presidents know that mid-level administrators, when not engaged, can quietly sideline many important initiatives. Conversely, when engaged, mid-level administrators have tremendous capacity to identify problem areas before they become insurmountable, and to develop creative solutions to those problems. Staff members who feel engaged also have tremendous capacity to help the institution advance, both within their job descriptions and outside of them. A friendly hello from a groundskeeper or a housekeeper can go a long way to helping students feel welcome. A report by a food service worker that a particular student seems to be suffering from depression can be a valuable early alert. And an encouraging word from a campus security guard can make a huge difference in how students conduct themselves.

Employee engagement, like effective faculty governance, requires substantial efforts by senior administrators. Administrators and hourly employees, like faculty, expect respect and transparency. Like faculty, all employees need to understand the importance of their role at the college. They need to understand that their efforts are acknowledged and valued by senior administration. Engaging employees also means giving employees the tools they need to be successful.

The first step to improving employee engagement is to measure it. Instruments like the Gallup Employee Engagement Survey, a simple twelve-question survey, provide comparative information on engagement within higher education as well as other sectors. Administering one of these surveys every year or every other year lets presidents examine the progress made at their institutions and the areas needing improvement.

FOSTERING THE ENTREPRENEURIAL SPIRIT OF FACULTY AND STAFF

Many would contend that liberal arts colleges and their employees are not known for entrepreneurism. Observers unfamiliar with the traditions of the academy might even suggest that change at a liberal arts college proceeds at the speed of a glacier. The conventional wisdom holds that faculty, with all the protections of tenure (real and imagined) are more interested in preserving the comfort of the status quo than confronting the discomfort of embracing the changes necessary to best educate a changing generation of students.

Some of these stereotypes are accurate for some of our faculty. But most are patently false. The greatest problem is not active resistance to change, but a lack of engagement and a sense of powerlessness in the crafting of a change agenda. At several institutions I've observed, faculty have felt disenfranchised because of headstrong administrators or a board not deeply connected to the institution's mission.

Most faculty members, at heart, can be entrepreneurs. They are intellectually curious. They value critical thinking. They are personally committed to their students and most will do all in their power to provide their students with the best outcomes. Like entrepreneurs, they value the independence they need for creativity; but given the increasing demands on the majority of faculty members, even the most entrepreneurial lack the time or resources to pursue fresh thinking, let alone risk taking. Effective presidents need to help unlock the entrepreneurial potential in these faculty members. They can do so by creating a culture that values and rewards innovation while providing the resources and time faculty need.

In order to facilitate faculty entrepreneurship, the president needs to:

- make a cogent case for taking risks to advance mission,
- provide faculty with the tools for risk-taking and entrepreneurship,
- remove the barriers of traditional bureaucracy, and
- provide pathways for moving plans into action.

When shared governance is effective, meaning that faculty, administration, and board are aligned with a common understanding of problems and a common approach to strategies to address those problems, faculty are likely to understand how their individual entrepreneurism can provide better learning outcomes for students, while adding to the financial strength and reputation of the college

It doesn't take a huge amount of money to stimulate creative thinking at a liberal arts college. Often it requires no more than a summer stipend, a modest amount of release time, or an allowance for travel to explore new ideas. At Augustana, just after the 2008 recession, several donors came forward to create a fund of $500,000 to support innovative program development. We've sustained that fund by allocating the same amount of funding from the college's reserve for depreciation. This dedicated reserve is meant to provide for capital expenses related to repairing, renovating, or replacing buildings. New program development, like an investment in buildings, is a one-time investment that provides benefits for many years to come. For the sustainability of our institutions, it's as important to invest in new programs as in new buildings.

At Augustana, funding for startup expenses has allowed us to grow enrollment during times others are having difficulty shoring up the student body. And given the nature of innovation, ideas should be expected from unlikely sources. Two examples at Augustana are a hockey club proposed by the head of our opera program, and a gerontology program now under development by a music professor.

Finally, it's important to help busy faculty members cut through bureaucracy. Too often new ideas—particularly from younger faculty and staff members—are derailed before they can be fully developed. It's the familiar refrain: we've done that before, it will never be accepted by the faculty, it will never be funded by the administration. This chills the creation of new ideas.

At Augustana, the provost appointed an Augustana Future Initiatives Think Tank (A-FITT). Faculty and staff members invited to join must be in the first half of their careers and must not be part of faculty governance or the senior administrative ranks. They must have shown willingness to apply creative solutions to problems. A-FITT has provided its recommendations to the faculty, the administration, and the board of trustees. Several suggestions that would have been dismissed under normal governance structures (such as recruiting for an active e-sports program) are now under active consideration.

CONCLUSION

Liberal arts colleges have endured for centuries, gradually changing with the times, as have our students. Today's schools have survived not because they are mired in the status quo, but because dedicated boards, administrations and faculties have changed, within the mission of their institutions, to meet the new demands presented by the times.

Leaders of liberal arts colleges should not assume the transformational change taking place in our society means liberal arts colleges must step away from their missions. Instead, leaders should thoughtfully take steps to build the capacity of their institutions so that they might provide better value to students, all within the mission of liberal arts colleges. Capacity building means empowering others to do the daily work at every level of the institution so that it evolves to best serve new generations of students.

NOTES

1. Ferrall, Jr., V. E. (2011). *Liberal Arts at the Brink* (p. 154). Cambridge, MA: Harvard University Press.
2. Zemsky, R. (2013). *Checklist for Change: Making American Higher Education a Sustainable Enterprise* (p. 20). New Brunswick, NJ: Rutgers University Press.
3. Christensen, C. M., & Eyring, H. J. (2011). *The Innovative University: Changing the DNA of Higher Education from the Inside Out* (p. 18). San Francisco, CA: Jossey-Bass.
4. Ferrall, J. (2015). *Breakpoint: The Changing Marketplace for Higher Education* (p. 142). Baltimore, MA: Johns Hopkins University Press.
5. Hart Research Association (2013). *It Takes More Than a Major: Employer Priorities for College Learning and Student Success.* Washington, DC: Hart Research Associates.

6. Humphery, D., and Kelly, P. (2014). *How Liberal Arts and Sciences Majors Fare in Employment: A Report on Earnings and Long-Term Career Paths.* Washington, DC: AAC&U Press.
7. http://www.cic.edu/News-and-Publications/Independent-Newsletter/Fall-2014/Pages/Liberal-Arts.aspx
8. https://www.augustana.edu/Documents/CORE/viking_score.pdf
9. Bureau of Labor Statistics (2015). *Occupational Outlook Handbook.* Washington, DC: U.S. Dep't of Labor.
10. https://www.augustana.edu/academics/academic-centers/upper-mississippi-center
11. College Board (2014). *Trends in College Pricing.* New York, NY: College Board Communications.
12. Balzer, W. K. (2010). *Lean Higher Education: Increasing the Value and Performance of University Processes.* New York, NY: Productivity Press.
13. Bahls, S. C. (2014). *Shared Governance in Times of Change: A Practical Guide for Universities and Colleges.* Washington, DC: AGB Press.
14. Association of Governing Boards. (2009), *Strategic Imperative: New Priorities for Higher Education* (p. 60). Washington, DC: Association of Governing Boards Press.
15. American Association of University Professors. (2001). *Statement on Governance of Colleges and Universities* (1967). In *Policy Documents and Reports,* Ninth Education (pp. 217–223). Washington, DC: Author.
16. Chait, R. P., Ryan, W. P., and Taylor, B. E. (2005). *Governance as Leadership: Reframing the Work of Nonprofit Board* (pp. 86–88). Hoboken, NJ: John Wiley and Sons.

CHAPTER THREE

The Future of the Liberal Arts College, or How to Keep Smiling on the Edge of the Crevasse

BRIAN ROSENBERG
President, Macalester College

Those most invested in the long-term viability of the small, residential liberal arts college sound at times like the fans of the New York Mets with whom I was raised: hope for success is never far from the fear of inevitable disappointment. In a 2013 survey of college and university chief financial officers, "barely a quarter … express strong confidence in the viability of their institution's financial model over five years, and that number drops in half (to 13 percent) when they are asked to look out over a 10-year horizon."[1] College presidents are only slightly more optimistic: a survey in 2015 revealed that "fewer than 4 in 10 college presidents express[ed] confidence in the financial sustainability of their institutions over the next decade."[2] And these are the people who know their organizations the best and who are *paid* to project confidence.

Pause for a moment over those numbers: 87% of college CFOs lack strong confidence in the viability of their institutions until 2023, and more than 60% of presidents lack confidence in the sustainability of their institutions until 2025. Granted, this group includes colleges and universities of all types, but there is no particular reason to believe that the leaders of private liberal arts colleges are any more sanguine than their counterparts at large private universities or in the public sector.[3] If this lack of confidence is justified, most of American higher education could go bust before many current members of those same New York Mets retire from baseball.

Then there are those who openly root for the radical disruption of traditional colleges, of which the small, liberal arts version is perhaps the most traditional example. When interviewed in 2013, Harvard economist Clayton Christiansen, the prophet of disruptive change, offered the following: "I think higher education is just on the edge of the crevasse. Generally, universities are doing very well financially, so they don't feel from the data that their world is going to collapse. But I think even five years from now these enterprises are going to be in real trouble."[4] Billionaires like Peter Thiel and Mark Cuban and a host of politicians—not exclusively from one political party—have in various ways and in various contexts belittled the value of and sounded the death knell for both the residential college and whatever it is we mean by the liberal arts.[5]

The nice thing about being a futurist is that people rarely go back and identify all of the times and all of the ways in which you were wrong: getting one right every once in a while seems sufficient to be declared a genius, or at least to develop a lucrative career as a pundit and prognosticator.[6] In that spirit, I have decided to examine some of the questions most commonly asked about the future of residential liberal arts colleges and to offer some predictions, based both on my experience as president of Macalester College and on my ongoing observations of the sector. I will also offer some thoughts on how the outcomes can be better rather than worse. To paraphrase Ebenezer Scrooge, these are not "shadows of the things that Will be," but "shadows of the things that May be," depending upon the decisions we make within higher education and the broader society.

My fundamental premise is that twenty years from now there will be fewer examples of what is considered today the classic liberal arts college; that this change will not be sudden and disruptive, but, like most change, gradual and evolutionary; and that, if guided by the right decisions, the end result need not be a weakening of the higher education system in the country. Indeed, a more diverse set of institutions could end up educating a larger, more diverse group of students.

Of course, I could be wrong, but I figure that if higher education fails to descend into the crevasse in 2018, I'll at least be a step ahead of Christiansen.

WILL MANY SMALL COLLEGES VANISH?

Colleges are like zombies. They are exceptionally hard to kill, and even when you think they are dead, and by all rights should be dead, they rise again.

People typically underestimate how torturously challenging it is to end the life of a college. Ending a major or a department is difficult enough, so it should not be surprising that attempts to shut down an entire institution encounter passionate resistance not just from employees—totally understandable—but alumni, community members, politicians, and various educational associations and lobbying groups. Lawrence S. Bacow and William G. Bowen have been among many to describe the elaborate attempts to resuscitate Sweet Briar College in Virginia, which included the involvement of the state's Attorney General.[7] Even more agonizing have been the death throes of Antioch College, which has been unsuccessfully attempting to rest in peace since 2007. At the time of this writing, the Board of Governors of the Antioch system had just eliminated the jobs of its five campus presidents and five boards of trustees, motivated by, among other things "a desire to remain competitive."[8]

Thus my predication is that the headline of a recent story in *The Atlantic*—"Farewell to America's Small Colleges"[9]—is wrong, and that far fewer colleges will close during the next decade or two than most experts are forecasting. The most financially vulnerable, typically very small institutions in rural areas serving regional populations, will probably go under, as the weakest have always done. The pace may pick up a bit. But relatively few will actually vanish into the crevasse, and it is important to place the much-publicized closings into context. According to the National Association of Independent Colleges and Universities, there are about 1600 private, nonprofit colleges and universities in the United States, enrolling roughly three and a half million students.[10] The average annual closure rate for the ten years ending in 2013 was five per year and actually declined from 2009 to 2013.[11] It is hard to think of another industry in which so many of the same organizations have continued to do the same thing for so long.[12]

Whether this tenacity is a good or a bad thing for students depends on what colleges do with their determination to survive. If they limp along as diminished versions of their former selves, few will benefit. If, however, they adapt their capacity to educate to the needs of the particular populations that are now being underserved; if even the smallest of colleges stop trying to be all things to all people and become more specialized; if they focus not just on survival but on creative evolution: if they do all this, the refusal of colleges to die might turn out to meet the needs of a country that is at present educating too few of its students. Contrary to the arguments of organizations like the Center for College Affordability and Productivity,[13] we do not need fewer colleges, but we might need less redundancy and more openness to change among the colleges we have.

WILL SMALL COLLEGES STAY SMALL?

One of the more interesting features of the small liberal arts college has been the persistence of its smallness. We have for some time lived in an economic world where bigger is better and *really* big is better still. Why be Kraft or Heinz when you can be both? So too with Aetna and Humana, or Exxon and Mobil. Many years ago, my father owned one of perhaps a dozen small drug stores within a few squares miles in a middle-class neighborhood in Queens. Today all are gone, replaced by Walgreens and CVS and the pharmacy department at Target (which has been outsourced—to CVS).

Given this broader context, there have been remarkably few mergers of small colleges and relatively little growth within individual colleges. Weaker institutions have in recent years seen slight to moderate enrollment declines,[14] while those with the market strength to be more selective have grown, but only marginally.[15] Chiefly this is due to the enormous importance of institutional identity and culture and to the history of shared governance that make a decision to do something like merge with another college or increase the student to faculty ratio next to impossible. While it might make economic sense for the Claremont Colleges to become "Claremont U" or for Hampshire to be absorbed by Amherst, such a move would meet overwhelming resistance from every constituency in every individual college. Nonprofit mergers, moreover, are extraordinarily complex and lack the financial incentives that typically drive mergers in the for-profit sector.

Will this current stasis continue? I do not believe that there will be a rapid increase in the number of mergers, and clearly there is no capacity for growth among the vast majority of small colleges. The single biggest change over the next twenty years, I believe, will come when institutions with the most market strength decide to use that strength to grow. Sooner or later Williams will decide that it can be just as strong academically and better off economically with 3000 students rather than 2100. Why not 2500 at Amherst rather than 1800? Such growth could be achieved simply by saying "no" to fewer, highly qualified applicants for admission. The number of small private colleges with this strength in the market is tiny—perhaps two or three dozen—but given the already small size of the entire sector, significant growth at the top will have a noticeable impact all along the food chain. Students enrolling at Williams will not be enrolling at Macalester, so Macalester will be looking at students currently enrolling at Franklin & Marshall, and so on down the line. This increased access to ultraselective institutions will of course be beneficial to a group of students, albeit a small and highly accomplished one. It will do virtually nothing to increase access to higher education more generally.

The chief argument against the likelihood of growth at the top is the current value placed on metrics like endowment per student. Clearly growth in the range of 20% or 25% would have a dilutive effect on the spending power of endowments and, potentially, on the rankings and reputations of top colleges. I would argue, however, that both the dilutive impact and the reputational risk are small compared to the benefit of significantly increased tuition revenue. Neither the spending power nor the reputation of schools like Williams, Amherst and Swarthmore is likely to be noticeably impacted by moderate growth, particularly if the schools just below them in the rankings follow suit. Decades of evidence suggests that the reputations of elite colleges and universities are virtually impervious to damage, regardless of their actual quality or actions, and the endowments of most of these colleges are massive enough to absorb growth without any need to eliminate amenities, let alone necessities.[16]

While some institutions might be forced into closure by this growth at the top, most will not die, but adapt, chiefly by altering their programs and marketing to appeal to segments of the population for which schools like Williams and Amherst are not competing, especially adult learners, students with less rigorous college preparation, and those seeking various sorts of pre-professional and technical education. In other words, there will not be dramatically fewer small colleges, but there will be fewer small *liberal arts* colleges, as that term is commonly understood. There will also be more programmatic diversity and more specialization within the small college sector. This has been a trend for some time, and it will, over the coming decades, accelerate. Macalester's academic neighbors in the Twin Cities exemplify what we should expect. Thirty years ago, institutions like Hamline University and Augsburg College might have been described as liberal arts institutions. Today they have more nontraditional students, more part-time students, and more programs that fall outside the historical parameters of the liberal arts. Augsburg in particular has made a groundbreaking effort to enroll newly emigrated and first-generation students. I expect both institutions to be around in twenty years, and I expect that an increasing number of colleges will look more like Hamline and Augsburg than like Macalester and Carleton. Though we might mourn the loss of a certain institutional template, this change is not necessarily a bad thing: educating a different, more diverse group of students well is not less valuable, and could in some ways be more valuable, than what is taking place now. This evolution has at least the *potential* to increase access among underserved populations.

In very broad terms, we are looking at a future in which the differences between very well-resourced institutions and everyone else become more stark. This has been happening for some time, and I see no reason for the trend to do anything other than accelerate; whether in endowment returns or fund raising or admissions selectivity, strength begets strength. Macalester is a member of the Associated Colleges of the Midwest, a consortium of excellent liberal arts colleges that collaborate around activities including study away and faculty development. When the consortium was founded in 1958, the ten original members would have been described as quite similar in mission, academic quality, and financial resources. The fourteen current members continue to share important characteristics, but the differences are becoming more and more obvious and relevant. To cite only one, very meaningful metric: the endowment size within the group ranges from less than $100 million to roughly $2 billion. Institutions at the opposite ends of that spectrum effectively operate in completely different worlds. Another consortium to which Macalester has belonged, the Associated Colleges of the Twin Cities, was founded in 1975 by five similar institutions, including Hamline and Augsburg, within a narrowly defined geographic area. Growing differences among the circumstances of its members led to its dissolution in 2015.

WILL THE SMALL, HIGHLY SELECTIVE LIBERAL ARTS COLLEGE BECOME THE EDUCATIONAL EQUIVALENT OF A LEXUS?

The model embodied by the small liberal arts college—close student-faculty interaction, intensive discussion, broad-based learning emphasizing certain habits of mind—has been shown to have better learning outcomes than other models.[17] It also carries higher costs, and no one has yet figured out how the effectiveness of the model can be divorced from these costs: both the outcomes and the costs are highly dependent on relatively large numbers of faculty and staff per student, and personnel costs make up roughly two-thirds of the budget at most small colleges. Since we live in a world in which some people have the ability and the desire to pay more for the quality and prestige of a better car, we should expect that many of those same people will be willing to pay a premium for a more successful and prestigious form of higher education. But the group will get smaller and more affluent: the highly selective liberal arts college will not go away, but it will run the real risk of becoming a luxury good. Assuming an increase of 3% annually, a college costing $60,000 per year will cost $80,000 per year within a decade. Some people will be prepared to pay this amount, but the number will in all likelihood be even smaller than the number prepared to pay the full fare today, barring a dramatic macroeconomic shift. At the same time, the ability of most colleges to attract students through the use of need-based or merit aid will diminish as their costs increase more rapidly than their revenue.

I would add a few caveats to this uninspiring forecast. A very small group of liberal arts colleges, like a small group of private universities, will for the indefinite future have sufficient resources to enroll classes that are economically and racially diverse. Those schools are likely to become *more* diverse as the rest see their ability to subsidize lower income students erode. At some point in the next two decades, I expect universities such as Harvard, Yale, Princeton, and Stanford to eliminate undergraduate tuition, in part as a way to fend off increasing pressure from politicians and the public to tax enormous endowments. Once the first in the group makes the move, the others will quickly follow. This will lead the tiny cohort of liberal arts colleges with whom they compete for students and who have multibillion dollar endowments at least to consider and perhaps to make the same move, or a partial version of the same move.[18] At that point, the ground under every other private college shifts, and the gap between the situation of the wealthiest institutions and everyone else, already wide, grows dramatically wider. In essence, as the wealthiest institutions reach the point where endowment returns and fund raising make them entirely or largely tuition independent, the rest will struggle even more mightily to generate both sufficient revenue and appropriately diverse student populations.

Here is where societal and institutional choices will determine the nature of the outcome. One path—call it the one that leads to Scrooge gazing in despair at his own headstone—would be shaped by continued public disinvestment in higher education and continued institutional inability to make the sorts of choices that will control costs. This appears, right now, to be the path down which we are headed, and it would result in even greater disparities in opportunity than those that exist at present. The other—call it the one that leads to holiday cheer and the salvation of Tiny Tim—would see increased public investment in educational access and increased institutional will to make hard but necessary choices. This latter path, like many other paths to improvement, is not hidden, but it would necessitate a change in mindset both *about* and *within* higher education. The most impactful change in policy would not be something like "free public college for all," which would be a hugely inefficient use of government dollars, but would be to direct more resources to the least affluent students and the institutions that serve them. The most impactful change *within* higher education would be, quite simply, greater openness to change, or what William G. Bowen and Michael McPherson describe as "a willingness to engage in real experimentation, which inevitably entails risk-taking."[19]

WILL THE MODEL OF THE TEACHER-SCHOLAR BECOME LESS WIDESPREAD?

Much has been written about the rapid growth in the number of college faculty who are neither tenured nor on the tenure track. These faculty—variously referred to as "contingent" or "adjunct" or "NTT"—now comprise as much as 70% of college instructors nationwide, more than twice the percentage in 1975.[20] For the most part, liberal arts colleges have resisted this trend, since they almost always have no graduate students and since their chief selling point is student access to full-time, tenured or tenure-track faculty. At Macalester, for example, a slightly smaller percentage of courses are taught today by non-tenure-track faculty than were taught a decade ago. While the data are nearly impossible to obtain, I would suspect that the percentage at most highly selective liberal arts colleges, and even at many less selective institutions, has not varied much over the same period.

At virtually all selective liberal arts colleges, tenured and tenure-track faculty are asked to embody the model of the "teacher-scholar," that is, they are expected to excel in the classroom and to produce peer-reviewed work that can take the form of monographs, journal articles, presentations, exhibitions, and the like. The assumption underlying this combination of expectations is straightforward and largely unchallenged: the two forms of labor are taken to be mutually reinforcing. Typically, the teaching loads are lower and the research expectations higher at wealthier, more selective institutions, though the basic model holds across a wide range of small colleges.

I expect this gradually to change, not because this particular model of the tenured teacher-scholar is broken, but because it is expensive and because its pedagogical advantages are still, after all this time, unproven.[21] Over the past several decades, liberal arts colleges have come increasingly to emulate the model of research universities, with growing expectations for scholarly output and, at more than a few colleges, reduced teaching loads.[22] The impact on budgets of supporting more research and hiring more faculty to teach the same curriculum is obvious; less obvious is the impact of this change on the experience of undergraduate students. The nature of the correlation between teaching and research output (as distinct from research activity) has been much studied and much debated, but "most analyses" come to the same conclusion: "while research productivity does not preclude quality teaching, the two are unrelated at the individual faculty level. Some professors excel at both teaching and research, many excel at one and not at the other, and some are unexceptional in both."[23] Even a major study whose central assertion is that "the teacher-scholar model of faculty professional activity brings important benefits to individual student learners" acknowledges, in something of a self-contradiction, that "little is known about what educational value is gained when effective teaching and productive research occur together."[24] Nonetheless, it is a matter of almost religious faith at many colleges that the quality of teaching and the quality and quantity of research are directly and positively correlated. The human tendency to ignore inconvenient evidence extends even to academics.[25]

My expectation is that fewer and fewer small colleges, faced with both mounting financial pressure and a growing demand to demonstrate value, will be able to sustain the teacher-scholar model in its current form. How the move away from this model is managed will determine the extent to which the change harms or benefits students. Simply replacing tenured and tenure-track faculty with underpaid NTT faculty will be a loss all around. If, however, some small colleges move toward a system of hiring full-time, appropriately compensated faculty members with the expectation that they will be, above all else, outstanding teachers—in essence, more teaching and less demand for published scholarship—the impact on budgets and pedagogical quality could be positive. Another, perhaps less radical option would be to build more flexibility into the process of evaluating tenure-track faculty, so that not all would be expected to excel as both teachers *and* peer-reviewed scholars. (This is not unlike what is happening at some research universities through the creation of positions like "Professor of Instruction.")[26] The present model of the teacher-scholar will remain the dominant one at the most affluent institutions, which face no pressure to change, but one way for less wealthy places to succeed and to differentiate themselves would be to focus relentlessly and openly on outstanding teaching, even if it means that their faculty members will be producing fewer journal articles. This does not mean that faculty members would fail to keep up with the latest developments in their fields or to exemplify for their students the importance of ongoing intellectual inquiry, but that the ultimate success of their scholarly engagement would be measured in student learning outcomes and not publications or conference talks.

Let me not underestimate the difficulty of moving away from the model of small college as small university or the dominant paradigm of the teacher-scholar (with the latter role often more prized). Currently, the preeminence of scholarship is reinforced in Ph.D. programs, in many tenure review processes, and, maybe most important, in institutional self-regard. By some faculty members, it is considered inappropriate even to *ask* whether teaching and scholarly excellence are inextricably linked and positively correlated.[27] But my impression has been that prospective undergraduate students, particularly those looking seriously at small colleges, do not pay nearly as much attention to scholarly productivity as they do to factors like quality teaching, thoughtful advising, and access to full-time faculty members. Sooner or later—maybe only out of necessity—the priorities of enrollment-challenged colleges and the priorities of their potential students are likely to come into closer alignment.

WILL THE TRADITIONAL LIBERAL ARTS CURRICULUM VANISH, TO BE REPLACED BY A STRONGER EMPHASIS ON VOCATIONAL PREPARATION?

Critics of liberal arts colleges have frequently underestimated the degree to which the curricula at those colleges have changed in response to student demand and disciplinary evolution. Today Macalester has a major in Chinese, instruction in Arabic, and concentrations in Community and Global Health, Human Rights and Humanitarianism, and International Development, along with a minor in Data Science. None of this was true when I arrived at the college in 2003. When I began teaching in the 1980s, there were very few departments of Environmental Studies, Media Studies, or Women's and Gender Studies; today they are commonplace. To the extent that there is a "traditional" liberal arts curriculum, it is more fluid than many imagine, though this fluidity has consisted primarily in addition rather than substitution and thus contributed to the increase in costs.

It may be that the next twenty years will see the mass elimination of departments in the humanities, social sciences, and fine arts at small colleges—but I don't think so. Rather, I anticipate two developments, each of which has the potential to make better use of our existing educational resources. First, as I have been suggesting, I expect to see more distinctiveness and specialization and less comprehensiveness among small, financially challenged colleges. There are too many examples today of small, cash-strapped colleges twenty miles apart each attempting to maintain thirty departments and forty majors. If each of those colleges offered fewer, more robust programs, and if the programming at the two colleges were complementary rather than redundant, both students and the institutions would benefit.

Second, I expect to see at least a gradual weakening of the hold on curricula of disciplinary departments. In addition to creating enormously inefficient redundancies and organizational complexity, such a structure fails to match up very well with the needs of most students. Virtually the only places in the world where there is so much division on the basis of discipline is at colleges and universities. In most workplaces, and when dealing with most of the challenges of the current century, college graduates will be met with the need to think and collaborate across subject area. Addressing global hunger is not an economic problem or a scientific problem or a cultural problem: it is all of those things, though it would be easy at times on a college campus to lose sight of this fact. Small liberal arts colleges, because of their size and structure, are better suited than large universities to establish programs that cross disciplinary lines, and if they are smart they will do so as a way of serving students and of offering something valuable and distinctive. The future of small colleges does not lie in being miniature versions of research universities, but in turning their small size into an opportunity to be something other and, in some respects, better. "Despite a good deal of academic propaganda to the contrary," notes Andrew Delbanco, "the fact is that when modern university leaders determine how to deploy resources, which 'fields' to invest in, and so on, undergraduates tend to be of marginal consequence."[28] Small colleges can offer something different. They can also do much to undermine the simplistic distinction between the liberal arts and vocational preparation by offering programs of study that have both a solid foundation in the liberal arts tradition and clear vocational application.

So I suppose, in the end, that I am more optimistic about the future than the majority of college presidents and CFOs, though not in the sense that I believe that small colleges will or should remain precisely as they are today. They will change, either by choice or out of necessity. That change will not be the equivalent of the abrupt departure of the cassette tape or the rotary phone, but will be gradual. And—while this outcome is far from assured—small colleges have the potential to educate an important if different group of students in effective ways, "to do much better than [they are] doing at present in meeting pressing national needs,"[29] if they seize and are not seized by this time of transition.

NOTES

1. "CFO Survey Reveals Doubt about Sustainability." *Inside Higher Education*, July 12, 2013. https://www.insidehighered.com/news/survey/cfo-survey-reveals-doubts-about-financial-sustainability. To be fair, the percentage expressing confidence in sustainability has risen since 2013, but even in the 2016 survey, sixty-three percent of CFOs "said they felt media reports

suggesting a financial crisis accurately reflect the general higher education landscape," up from fifty-six percent the year before. "Foundering Finances, the Faculty Role: A Survey of Business Officers." *Inside Higher Education*, July 15, 2016. https://www.insidehighered.com/news/survey/foundering-finances-faculty-role-survey-business-officers

2. "Economic Angst, Rose-Colored Views on Race: A Survey of Presidents." *Inside Higher Education*, March 13, 2015. https://www.insidehighered.com/news/survey/economic-angst-rose-colored-views-race-survey-presidents
3. On the contrary, they might be less sanguine. A recent conference on the private liberal arts college was reportedly filled with "lots of gloomy forecasting for the sector." "Angst and Hope for Liberal Arts Colleges." *Inside Higher Education*, July 13, 2016. https://www.insidehighered.com/news/2016/07/13/meeting-discusses-challenges-facing-liberal-arts-colleges
4. "Clay Christiansen: Higher Education Is on the Edge of the Crevasse." *Business Insider*, February 12, 2013. http://www.businessinsider.com/clay-christensen-higher-education-on-the-edge-2013-2
5. See, for example, "Back to the Future, with Peter Thiel." *National Review Online*. January 20, 2011. http://www.nationalreview.com/articles/257531/back-future-peter-thiel-interview
6. My favorite definition of a futurist comes from Robert Archibald and David Feldman in their forthcoming book, *Turbulent Waters: The Future of American Colleges and Universities*, to be published by Oxford University Press. "For the most part we are inclined to characterize futurists as people who are happy if you don't read their twenty-year-old books."
7. "The Painful Lessons of Sweet Briar and Cooper Union." *The Chronicle of Higher Education*, September 24, 2015. http://chronicle.com/article/The-Painful-Lessons-of-Sweet/233369
8. "Antioch Eliminates Jobs of Five Presidents." *Inside Higher Education*, July 5, 2015. https://www.insidehighered.com/news/2016/07/05/antioch-university-eliminates-jobs-five-presidents
9. http://www.theatlantic.com/education/archive/2015/10/demise-of-small-private-colleges/408592/
10. http://www.naicu.edu/about/page/quick-facts-about-private-colleges
11. "Closures to Triple." *Inside Higher Education*, September 28, 2015. https://www.insidehighered.com/news/2015/09/28/moodys-predicts-college-closures-triple-2017
12. The rate of closure of rural community hospitals is similar to, though slightly greater than, the rate of closure of private colleges: from 2010 through 2015, seventy-six out of roughly 1850 closed. http://www.shepscenter.unc.edu/programs-projects/rural-health/rural-hospital-closures/ And just for the record, 979 hedge funds closed in 2015 alone. There are presently about 11,000 in the United States. http://www.cnbc.com/2016/03/18/hedge-fund-closing-at-fastest-pace-since-global-financial-crisis.html
13. See Richard Vedder, Christopher Denhart, and Jonathan Robe, "Why Are Recent College Graduates Underemployed? University Enrollments and Labor Market Realities," January 2013. http://centerforcollegeaffordability.org/uploads/Underemployed%20Report%202.pdf
14. "College Enrollment Declines for Fourth Straight Year." *The Hechinger Report*, December 16, 2015. http://hechingerreport.org/college-enrollment-declines-for-fourth-straight-year/
15. Macalester is a fairly typical example. During the past decade enrollment has increased from about 1900 to about 2100, in part to compensate for choppy endowment returns.
16. Worth noting is the fact that Yale has already decided to increase the undergraduate population of Yale College by fifteen percent. http://news.yale.edu/2015/04/17/construction-new-residential-colleges-optimistic-affirmation-yale-s-future-say-leaders
17. See Richard Arum and Josipa Roksa, *Academically Adrift: Limited Learning on College Campuses*. Chicago: University of Chicago Press, 2011, 104–109.

18. See, for example, Roger Lehecka and Andrew Delbanco, "Ivy-League Letdown." *The New York Times*, January 22, 2008. http://www.nytimes.com/2008/01/22/opinion/22lehecka.html
19. *Lesson Plan: An Agenda for Change in American Higher Education*. Princeton, NJ: Princeton University Press, 2016, 70.
20. "More than Half of College Faculty Are Adjuncts: Should You Care?" *Forbes*, May 28, 2015. http://www.forbes.com/sites/noodleeducation/2015/05/28/more-than-half-of-college-faculty-are-adjuncts-should-you-care/#232bf81c1d9b
21. Again, the exceptions will be the small number of very wealthy institutions. While I risk repetitiveness in making this qualification, I cannot emphasize too strongly how important I think this distinction will be going forward.
22. "Faculty members at Vassar College generally agree that teaching five classes per year makes it hard to keep up with research and the one-on-one interaction that students expect." Thus the college plans to reduce the load from five to four without adding any faculty lines, a plan whose benefits to students is difficult to discern. "The Price of Cutting Course Loads." *Inside Higher Education*, July 18, 2016. https://www.insidehighered.com/news/2016/07/18/vassar-faculty-members-want-reduce-their-teaching-load-some-question-plan-would-also
23. Michael J. Prince, Richard M. Felder, and Rebecca Brent, "Does Faculty Research Improve Undergraduate Teaching? An Analysis of Existing and Potential Synergies." *Journal of Engineering Education*, 96 (October 2007), 284. http://www4.ncsu.edu/unity/lockers/users/f/felder/public/Papers/Teaching-Research(JEE).pdf
24. "Student Learning and Faculty Research: Connecting Teaching and Scholarship," May 2007, 3, 12. https://www.acls.org/uploadedFiles/Publications/Programs/ACLS-Teagle_Teacher_Scholar_White_Paper.pdf
25. The most demonstrable benefits of the current model appear in the STEM disciplines, where research work among students and faculty is most collaborative. As evidence, liberal arts colleges are disproportionately successful at sending students to graduate school in these disciplines.
26. See, for example, "Professors of Instruction." *Inside Higher Education*, August 12, 2015. https://www.insidehighered.com/news/2015/08/12/northwestern-us-arts-and-sciences-college-updates-titles-teaching-faculty-and-offers
27. Several years ago, I very tentatively floated the question of whether we should explore the relationship between scholarship and teaching at Macalester. Suffice it to say that the idea was not well received by the faculty and no such exploration took place. I do not plan on floating the idea again.
28. Andrew Delbanco. *College: What It Was, Is, and Should Be*. Princeton, NJ: Princeton University Press, 2012, 85.
29. Bowen and McPherson, vii.

CHAPTER FOUR

Making College Better—for Whom?

TIMOTHY L. HALL
President, Mercy College

I was happily surprised.

In the fall of 2013, the search process for the next president of Mercy College had reached the stage of initial interviews, and I had been invited to Manhattan to meet with the search committee, composed primarily of members of the Board of Trustees. After seven years leading Austin Peay State University, a public regional institution in Tennessee, I was considering a change. There, I had been privileged to work in an academic community which had gained national attention both as a "Great College to Work for" and as an institution devoted to finding innovative ways to support student success. The University was recognized among the Honor Roll of Great Colleges to Work for in my final two years there, in 2012 and 2013, and continued to be recognized after I left.[1] Owing especially to a unique program written and implemented at the University by my friend and colleague, Dr. Tristan Denley, who served with me as provost, the university also won widespread recognition for innovation. The program, called Degree Compass, was spotlighted by the White House, Bill Gates, and numerous national publications for its use of predictive analytics to help inform student choices about course selection.[2]

Now I found myself seated with the search committee in an office building near Grand Central Station in New York City, wondering whether a Southern accent gained from years in Texas, Mississippi, and Tennessee would be understandable to New Yorkers. Among the many things a board looks for in such a search is someone who will lead the college to become "better." But important questions lurk beneath the surface of the word, "better." I was listening closely to discover what this board understood that term to mean. If it was like the boards of many—perhaps even most—colleges in America, the Board of Mercy College would mean "better" as measured, say, by U.S. News and World Report rankings. Central to this concept of improvement would be success at attracting more academically talented students, as represented by standardized test scores. These "better" students an institution attracts will generally be retained at a higher rate, leading to increases in the institution's retention and graduation rates, and to its financial bottom line. Better students will, in turn, attract more talented faculty and inspire more generous support from alumni and other donors. To the extent that better students come from more privileged backgrounds—and they frequently do—the institution will be able to charge more tuition, augmenting its financial resources. More resources will enable smaller classes, another important indicia of institutional quality. The cascade of institutional benefits begins, though, with the successful attraction of "better" students.[3]

EXCLUSIONARY AND INCLUSIONARY EXCELLENCE

"Better" in the sense outlined above is exclusionary—the more applications an institution turns down in favor of those of more academically talented students, the better it is. In addition to tracking average standardized test scores of an institution's students, common rankings also give explicit attention to this exclusionary aspect. The more applications an institution rejects from would-be students, the better it is. The exclusionary aspect of institutional rankings has not been lost on commentators. Michael M. Crow and William B. Dabars, for example, suggest that "institutions have become increasingly exclusive and now define their excellence through admissions practices based on the exclusion of the majority of applicants" (Crow & Dabars, 2015, p. 5). Christopher Newfield argues, similarly, that "The entrenched practices, the deep culture, the lived ideology, the life-world of American higher education all point toward defining excellence through selectivity, and would seek to improve any university regardless of mission by tightening admissions standards" (Newfield, 2010, p. 621). In a context in which retention and graduation rates are given ever-greater national prominence, I have routinely heard college and university presidents complain that the growing emphasis on these statistics would inevitably force them to raise admission standards—that is, to become more exclusive.

I discovered in that first session with the search committee at Mercy College, though, that it meant something different in seeking a president to lead the institution toward improvement. Mercy College has historically been animated by a mission of serving students frequently underserved. It had been founded by the Sisters of Mercy in the 1950s to serve first the women of its order, then young women from working-class families, and subsequently women and men from a variety of races and social backgrounds. Subsequently, the college became a nonsectarian private institution and grew to more than 9000 students with campuses in Dobbs Ferry, Manhattan, the Bronx, and Yorktown Heights (Martone & Perrota, 2013). Animated by a mission of providing "transformational educational experiences to motivated students," the College wasn't interested in replacing its existing students with "better" ones. It was interested in making the College *better for the students it already served*, many of them students of color, most of them students from less-privileged financial backgrounds. These, it believed, were America's hope and its future. Instead of bemoaning whether students were college-ready, Mercy was more interested in seeing that it was "student ready" by making sure it had established the necessary conditions for student success (McNair, Albertine, Cooper, McDonald, Major, 2016; Kuh, Kinzie, Schuh, Whitt, 2005). It embraced an inclusionary view of excellence: it strives to serve as broad a range of students as possible, to create the conditions for student success and then admit those students capable of success under those conditions.[4]

And so was I.

The exclusionary search for "better" students might benefit an institution's reputation, but it is not doing America much good. As observers such as Jamie Merisotis has argued, America needs talent (Merisotis, 2015). In spite of emphasizing the value of access to college, both as a matter of justice and of national self-interest, our nation is falling behind other nations in terms of its talent capital. In 1995, 33% of American young adults had obtained an associates degree or higher from college. By 2015, that percentage had increased to 46% (NCES, 2016). Unfortunately, ten other nations exceeded this percentage, with the Republic of Korea owning first place at 68% of its young adults with college degrees (NCES, 2016). The percentage of college-educated Americans has a clear connection to employment, especially in the wake of the Great Recession. The Georgetown Center on Education and the Workplace estimates that 11.5 million of the 11.6 million jobs created since the Recession were captured by those with some college education (GCEW, 2016). The Center also estimates that by 2020, 65% of all jobs in the American economy will require some postsecondary education beyond high school (GCEW, 2013). Yet, one still finds journalists or politicians willing to ask whether college is worth it. I always wonder whether the same journalists and politicians think college is worth it for *their* children.

Not only has America fallen behind in producing college graduates, but the gap in college attainment by family income is widening. Although the past generation has seen a proliferation of strategies intended to increase college persistence and graduation rates, the gap in college attainment between families in the top quartile of family income and those in the bottom quartile is wider today than it was five decades ago. Then, a 34% gap divided the top and bottom quartiles of family income as to college graduation. In 2015, that gap was 68% (Callahan &

Perna, 2015). All our first-year seminar programs, academic alert programs, and learning communities have inured more to the benefit of the rich than the poor. All our innovations and best practices are, collectively, widening the opportunity gap in America. College graduation is increasingly unattainable for a large segment of American society. Accordingly, the most important question to be asked in a book about making colleges better is the question, "Better for whom?"

A few years ago, I testified before the Senate HELP committee on the subject of innovation in higher education. I was among a panel of higher education leaders invited to address the committee on the subject of what our institutions were doing to make our institutions better. I won't soon forget what Senator Durbin said at the conclusion of the hearing. Noting data suggesting the gap in college attainment based on family income, he asked why we should be focusing attention on innovation unless it helped to close that gap.[5] Do we really favor more educational innovations which have the effect of widening the attainment gap between the rich and the poor, or between students of one race and another? Do we, perhaps, hold to a kind of trickle-down version of higher education innovation, in which we hope—without evidence—that innovations which tend to benefit more affluent students will also "trickle down" to those from less privileged backgrounds. The history of the last generation's innovations might suggest that some trickling is possible, but that over all, the gap between the haves and the have-nots has not been surmounted by most innovations.[6]

Why are we still so far behind in educational attainment and with such stark divides still existing between college haves and have-nots? Perhaps because too many institutions are fixed on chasing the same relatively small pool of "high-performing" students instead of extending the opportunity of college to students who are perfectly capable of earning a college degree if only we will create and sustain the conditions for their success. "Diversity is now a fact of life in U.S. postsecondary education. There are more students of color, first-generation students, full-time workers, students from low-income backgrounds and those who must balance studies with parenting. In this changing environment, educators, policymakers, and politicians should back programs that can accommodate all backgrounds."[7]

Emblematic of the kind of focus that is failing to close the achievement gap is our tendency to concentrate our attention on the problem of "under-matching" (Hoxby & Avery, 2012). We rightly worry that not enough low-income students are reaching our more elite institutions. But this concentration on the highest performing low-income students is leaving out the majority of low-income students capable of completing college and the institutions that serve large numbers of these students. Even if we solved the "under-matching" problem, the gap in college attainment would remain. Elite institutions are simply not serving sufficient numbers of low-income students to overcome the widening gap in attainment (Crow & Dabars, 2015, p. 294; Chingos, 2014).

SCALING COMPLETION SUCCESS

Even in the institutions that serve the most low-income students, we spend too much time focused on small-scale "best practices" that affect only a few students. Though these innovations may be important as pilot efforts, their effectiveness will generally require application to larger groups of students. What our institutions need are scalable practices that offer promise of increasing the chances of success for many of our low-income students. Happily, there are such scalable practices. Think of the innovations implemented at Georgia State University, which have significantly improved graduation rates and closed attainment gaps normally experienced by low-income students and students of color (Kurzweil & Wu, 2015). An alliance of research universities is seeing success in fostering persistence and completion across socio-economic lines (Innovation Alliance, 2016). My own institution has seen significant increases in attainment for all our students through the use of a personal mentoring program referred to as PACT (Durso, 2016). Now, we are laboring to implement scalable strategies such as cohort scheduling and guided pathways.[8]

The importance of scale in college attainment efforts helps to underline the importance of statewide efforts such as those encouraged by Complete College America. CCA champions innovations capable of rewriting the attainment destiny of thousands of students, precisely the kinds of innovations necessary to make college not better for a few, but for the many. I have seen first-hand at Austin Peay State University how redesign of remedial and developmental education along a corequisite model can radically improve persistence of students (Complete College, 2016).

We ought to dismiss out-of-hand the often repeated nonsense that improving persistence and graduation rates for our students inevitably involves lowering standards. If anything, the opposite is true. Increasing persistence and graduation rates normally involves raising expectations for our students' learning and providing the appropriate conditions to support those raised expectations. Those who assert that lowering standards is the inevitable price of supporting greater student success are the equivalent of the student who suggests the only way he can pass a course is to cheat. We must say to both assertions, "No. There are other options available. You appear to be unacquainted with them." As I have suggested, scalable strategies exist which help create conditions for success for low-income students without diminishing academic quality. Institutional leaders can simply not afford to be ignorant of these strategies.

CONTROLLING COSTS

If one of our most significant challenges is closing the attainment gap based by only family income, we cannot be insensitive to higher education costs. Over the past several years, my own board has struggled to contain tuition increases, knowing that significant tuition increases not accompanied by increases in financial aid will inevitably challenge college attainment hopes for our most financially vulnerable. Students who manage to complete a college degree in spite of these increases will inevitably find themselves saddled with student loans that will cripple their ability to prosper, even with a college degree. That fate too often clouds the futures of students from working-class families (Silva, 2013). I am happy to say that since 2009, Mercy College has operated within a range of annual tuition increases from 0 to 2%. As I write, our annual undergraduate tuition is slightly more than $18,000. Significant need-based institutional aid, coupled with federal and state need-based aid, result in students with zero EFC owing a balance of $1100.

Private philanthropy can provide some relief for students facing ever-increasing tuition costs. At Mercy College, for example, we have partnered with donors committed to helping low-income students obtain a college degree without assuming extraordinary debt. These arrangements are designed to see that selected students are able to graduate without any tuition-related debt, and in some cases, without any debt related to room and board or textbook purchases as well. But the numbers of students benefited by these partnerships—at least at the present time—is only a fraction of our student body. If we fail to control the cost of tuition, private philanthropy alone will not shield our students from the barriers to completion such costs inevitably create.

CONCLUSION

America has no lack of great colleges and universities. Its problem is that these institutions, collectively, are not producing sufficient success among students from less privileged backgrounds. Significant increases in college access have resulted in corresponding increases in the number of Americans with some college credential. But our increases have not kept pace with those being experienced in other nations. Moreover, a host of educational innovations over the last generation have not prevented the U.S. from falling from first place in the world in college attainment to eleventh as of 2015. In fact, over the last generation, improvements in educational quality have tended to benefit those from more privileged backgrounds. As a consequence, the gap in college graduation rates between the top and bottom quartiles of family income has grown larger. This gap should alarm all those who believe education to be a gateway to opportunity in America. Nevertheless, although the gap is well publicized, it continues to persist and even expand.

Faced with the stark demographic realities of higher education in America, too many political and educational leaders are inclined either to accept demography or to escape it. We accept demography when we allow our institutions to remain unchanged in the face of strategies known to help overcome gaps in college completion based on income. We attempt to escape demography when we make it our primary aim to attract to our institutions students less encumbered by the results of wealth disparities in America, more insulated by family resources from "the slings and arrows of outrageous fortune." America's future will remain impoverished, however, until more higher education leaders commit themselves to the task of *defeating* demography. Exemplars exist to assure us that this task is within our power to accomplish if we only will. It is not enough to make college better for a fortunate few. The need of our day is to make it better for all of our students, especially those whose attainment of college education is currently frustrated by demographic realities within our power to defeat.

NOTES

1. Great Colleges to Work For. *Chronicle of Higher Education*. Retrieved from http://chroniclegreatcolleges.com/recognized-institutions/.
2. For the reference by the White House, see Fact Sheet on the president's plan to make college more affordable: a better bargain for the middle class. (August 22, 2013). Retrieved from https://www.whitehouse.gov/the-press-office/2013/08/22/fact-sheet-president-s-plan-make-college-more-affordable-better-bargain-. For Gates' reference to Austin Peay, see https://www.c-span.org/video/?c3732111/bill-gates-discusses-degree-compassapsu (June 26, 2012). For media references to Degree Compass, see, e.g., Advising by algorithm, (July 17, 2012). *NY Times*, retrieved from http://www.nytimes.com/interactive/2012/07/18/education/edlife/student-advising-by-algorithm.html. *Inside Higher Ed.* (March 16, 2012). Retrieved from https://www.insidehighered.com/news/2012/03/16/university-builds-course-recommendation-engine-steer-students-toward-completion. The university also received attention for having created an environment hospitable to educational innovation. See Kadlec, Immerwahr, & Currie (November 2013).
3. An instructive example of making a college "better" along these lines is George Keller's account of Elon University. Keller, G. (2004). *Transforming a college: The story of a little known college's strategic climb to national distinction.* Baltimore, MD: Johns Hopkins University Press.
4. Institutions sometimes try to calculate which students are capable of success at the institution without first attending to the issue of whether the institution has created the necessary conditions for success. This mindset is borne of a view which credits colleges and universities with little power to affect the success trajectories of their students. As the text suggests, I believe this view is not sufficiently informed of the conditions an institution can create to support the success of a broad range of students.
5. The video of the committee hearing is available at "Attaining a Quality Degree: Innovations to Improve Student Success" (October 31, 2013). Retrieved from http://www.help.senate.gov/hearings/attaining-a-quality-degree-innovations-to-improve-student-success.
6. Some observers predict that technological innovations will make college more accessible to more students. See DeMillo, R. (2015). *Revolution in higher education: How a small band of innovators will make college accessible and affordable.* Cambridge, MA: MIT Press. To date, however, these innovations have not altered the stark demographics of American higher education.

7. http://www.washingtonpost.com/sf/brand-connect/gates/the-changing-face-of-us-higher-education/.
8. For a discussion of guided pathways in the community college context, see Baily, Jaggars, & Jenkins (2015, pp. 52–80).

REFERENCES

Attaining a quality degree: Innovations to improve student success. Hearing before the U.S. Senate Committee on Health, Education, Labor, and Pensions (October 31, 2013). Retrieved from http://www.help.senate.gov/hearings/attaining-a-quality-degree-innovations-to-improve-student-success.

Baily, T., Jaggars, S., & Jenkins, D. (2015). *Redesigning America's community colleges: A clearer path to student success.* Cambridge, MA: Harvard University Press.

Bill & Melinda Gates Foundation. (2016). *The changing face of U.S. higher education: How students are coping.* Retrieved from http://www.washingtonpost.com/sf/brand-connect/gates/the-changing-face-of-us-higher-education/.

Cahalan, M., & Perna, L. (2015). *Indicators of higher education equity in the United States.* The Pell Institute. Retrieved from http://www.pellinstitute.org/downloads/publications-Indicators_of_Higher_Education_Equity_in_the_US_45_Year_Trend_Report.pdf.

Chingos, M. (January 15, 2014). *Can we fix undermatching in higher ed? Would it matter if we did?* Retrieved from https://www.brookings.edu/research/can-we-fix-undermatching-in-higher-ed-would-it-matter-if-we-did/.

Complete College America. (2016). *Corequisite remediation: Spanning the completion divide.* Retrieved from http://completecollege.org/spanningthedivide/.

Crow, M., & Dabars, W. (2015). *Designing the new American university.* Baltimore, MD: Johns Hopkins University Press.

DeMillo, R. (2015). *Revolution in higher education: How a small band of innovators will make college accessible and affordable.* Cambridge, MA: MIT Press.

Durso, T. (April 2016). *Personalized achievement contract program.* Retrieved from https://www.universitybusiness.com/mox/awards/personalized-achievement-contract-program.

Georgetown Center on Education and the Workplace. (2016). *America's divided recovery: College haves and have-nots.* Retrieved from https://cew.georgetown.edu/cew-reports/americas-divided-recovery/.

Georgetown Center on Education and the Workplace. (2013). *Recovery: Job growth and education requirements through 2020.* Retrieved from https://cew.georgetown.edu/cew-reports/recovery-job-growth-and-education-requirements-through-2020/.

Hall, T. (October 31, 2013). Testimony before senate committee on health, education, labor, and pensions. Hearing on attaining a quality degree: Innovations to improve student success. Retrieved from http://www.help.senate.gov/imo/media/doc/Hall1.pdf.

Hoxby, C., & Avery, C. (2012). *The missing 'one-offs': The hidden supply of high-achieving, low-income students.* NBER Working Paper 18586. Cambridge, MA: National Bureau of Economic Research.

Kadlec, A., Immerwahr, J., & Currie, M. (November 2013). *Seven practices of enlightened leadership in higher education: A case study of Austin Peay State University.* A case study of Public Agenda with support from Lumina Foundation. Retrieved from http://www.publicagenda.org/files/SevenPracticesOfEnlightenedLeadershipInHigherEd_PublicAgenda_2013.pdf.

Keller, G. (2004). *Transforming a college: The story of a little-known college's strategic climb to national distinction.* Baltimore, MD: Johns Hopkins University Press.

Kuh, G., Kinzie, J., Schuh, J., Whitt, E., & Associates. (2005). *Student success in college: Creating conditions that matter.* San Francisco, CA: Jossey-Bass.

Kurzweil, M., & Wu, D. (April 23, 2015). *Building a pathway to student success at Georgia State University.* Retrieved from http://www.sr.ithaka.org/publications/building-a-pathway-to-student-success-at-georgia-state-university/.

Martone, E., & Perrota, M. (2013). *Mercy College: Yesterday and today.* Charleston, SC: The History Press.

McNair, T., Albertine, S., Cooper, M., McDonald, N., & Major, T., Jr. (2016). *Becoming a student-ready college: A new culture of leadership for student success.* San Francisco, CA: Jossey-Bass.

Merisotis, J. (2015). *America needs talent: Attracting, educating & deploying the 21st-century workforce.* New York, NY: Rosetta Books.

National Center for Education Statistics (2016). *Educational attainment of young adults.* Retrieved from http://nces.ed.gov/programs/coe/indicator_caa.asp.

Newfield, C. (September 2010). The end of the American funding model: What comes next? *American Literature* 82(3), 611–35.

Silva, J. (2013). *Coming up short: Working-class adulthood in an age of uncertainty.* New York, NY: Oxford University Press.

CHAPTER FIVE

Rethinking Fit, Choosing to Include, and Educating World Changers

ELIZABETH (BETH) J. STROBLE
President, Webster University

"Give me a lever long enough and a fulcrum on which to place it, and I shall move the world," Archimedes proclaimed. Generations of writers and thinkers have cited his words as they sought the firm and immovable point from which it would be possible to move worlds. Numbered among them are the likes of Descartes, Thomas Paine, Thomas Jefferson, Trotsky, Marshall McLuhan, John F. Kennedy, Robert F. Kennedy, George H. Bush, and Albert Gore ("Lever Quotes," n.d.). Without doubt, college presidents who seek to make their colleges better must identify the place upon which they—with their colleagues, students, alumni, trustees, donors, and community—take their stand.

As I began my presidency at Webster University in 2009, I joined the campus community as a career-long educator with ten years of experience as a public high school teacher, followed by faculty appointments as a teacher educator and in administrative roles at college and university levels. I have lived and/or worked in schools and universities, public and private, in Midwestern cities and suburbs, the Arizona High Desert including the Navajo and Hopi reservations, the Virginia Piedmont, Illinois farm country, and urban and suburban Louisville and St. Louis. As the first generation of my immediate family to be raised outside the South and to graduate from college, I have made my home in at least 12 places, beginning with Newcastle, Wyoming. Generations of my family have always been willing to move to take advantage of opportunity and to make themselves at home in multiple locations, geographies, cultures, and communities. With new homes come new adventures, new learnings, and new growth to be welcomed and relished.

I looked forward to the opportunity to join a university community that, from its inception in 1915, opened previously closed worlds to students. The founding Sisters of Loretto created one of the first colleges west of the Mississippi to offer women bachelor's degrees, preparing them for careers and lives of service. Over its 100-year history, Webster transitioned from Roman Catholic origins, to lay governance, and independence from religious affiliation; welcomed men and women; and took education to students on military installations, U. S. metropolitan and corporate locations, and American-style residential campuses in Europe, Asia, and Africa. Nearly 17,000 students are completing certificates and degrees at Webster campuses and online. Living alumni total 186,000. Here at Webster I found my fit, the place from which to lead making college better, a place whose vision, mission, and values I at once embraced and continue to find enriching, challenging, and expanding in their impact on me personally and professionally. For whom are we making college better? For students and for the world—that is our immovable point.

We seek to help our students be at home in the world. Because the world's peoples are increasingly interconnected—politically, economically, culturally, and ecologically—the answer to the ancient question, "Who is my neighbor?" must be both local and global. Each of us is touched by events continents away, and our future as a world depends upon seeing people everywhere as our neighbors and as fellow members of a human community to whom we express active concern and compassion. Careers of the future with greatest impact on meeting critically important human needs will depend upon intercultural competence and global understandings. That is why Webster's mission commits us to ensuring high-quality learning experiences that transform students for individual excellence and global citizenship. From these convictions flow our actions to make Webster better.

RETHINKING FIT

> Choosing a college because your friends are going there or because of where it ranks on a list does not take into account who you are and who you will become. College is a match to be made, not a prize to be won. Finding a good fit requires time and thoughtfulness.
>
> —MARTHA O'CONNELL (NPR, 2007)

If we approach the topic of making college better from a U. S. perspective, we know that sixty percent of incoming freshmen attending a public university have permanent homes within 50 miles of the institution. While many independent colleges such as Webster attract students from a broader geography, the median distance from home for an undergraduate at a private nonprofit university is 46 miles ("Geography Continues to Matter in College Enrollment Decisions," 2016). We also know that the characteristics of college students are changing as quickly as the demographics of our communities are shifting (Hussar & Bailey, 2016). The

National Center for Education Statistics' data projections to 2023 forecast that increases in postsecondary enrollments will occur in greater percentages among women than men, part-time rather than full-time students, and with greater racial and ethnic diversity. An increasingly competitive market among higher education institutions is heightened by multiple demands: challenged family incomes, fluctuations in supporting revenue sources from federal and state governments, and concerns about student debt levels. Undergraduate students are highly sought and aggressively recruited to "make a class" in number and composition. Successful institutional retention and graduation rates, with resulting perceived prestige and higher rankings, too often correlate with selective admissions policies. Frank Bruni (2015) aptly labels the press to gain a seat in an Ivy League institution "admissions mania." From the point of view of the student, we know that the college-selection decision is not always straightforward and may be driven as much by perceived as real value; and college choices may be further narrowed by sheer convenience and affordability.

As prospective students seek their best "fit" for their college home, they typically seek to duplicate their high school experience. Bruni's (2015) analysis of the sheer diversity in the value and character of U. S. colleges and universities provides a needed antidote: "But too many kids get to college and try to collapse it, to make it as comfortable and recognizable as possible. They replicated the friends and friendships they've previously enjoyed. They join groups that perpetuate their high school cliques" (p. 112). Yet, Bruni exhorts, "Now more than ever, college needs to be an expansive adventure, propelling students toward unplumbed territory and untested identities rather than indulging and flattering who they already are. And students, along with those of us who purport to have meaningful insights for them, need to insist on that" (p. 113).

When the best fit between student and college is framed primarily or solely as similarity—a correspondence between a student's past preferences and experiences and the setting and culture of the college community—both student and college limit transformative learning opportunities for the individual and the community. The convergence of the community and the individual should expand opportunities for both, rather than constrain. Research about fit between a leader and an organization illustrates the positive outcomes that can result from a "dissimilarity perspective" (Hartnell, Kinicki, Lambert, Fugater, Corner, 2016) that instead focuses on the benefits attained when an individual and the community bring elements to one another that are complementary and additive rather than duplicative. As I have built our leadership team at Webster, the dissimilarity perspective has driven the formation of a team diverse in strengths, gender, race, ethnicity, experience, and thought. The composition of this team is a fit for the institution's complexity and mission.

Rethinking fit—seeking complementarity rather than similarity—makes college better by diversifying the community itself. Rethinking fit as a means for the student and the college to round out what is missing, to expand knowledge and relationships, to enrich available perspectives is the foundation for opening previously closed and unknown doors for students as well as the college. To make college better through rethinking fit means that students themselves should be open to choices that have the power to transform because of the institutional mission, the experiences available through academic programs and student life as well as the communities that comprise the college. For colleges, rethinking fit to make college better means building bridges to welcome a variety of students and to embrace the ways those students will challenge the institution to adapt, evolve, and lead in a dynamic environment. Because fit is an evolving concept, a dialectic between individual and environment that impacts both, students are changed by their institutions and institutions are changed by their students. For example, admitting students whose circumstances place them at risk, yet creating value for both them and the community through scaffolding their degree-attainment success, creates opportunity for the institution to grow in mission and identity, to live its commitments to meeting unmet needs with fresh insight.

CHOOSING TO INCLUDE

> Diversity is a fact. Inclusion is a choice.
>
> —Deborah Gillis, Catalyst (2016)

For many years, Webster University has been recognized for the diversity of our student body. *Diverse Issues in Higher Education* (2016) cited Webster as first among all nonprofit public and private universities in the country for the number of graduate degrees conferred to minority students (Sharpe, 2016). Consider these data points for Webster University for fall, 2014:[1]

- Thirty-six percent of Webster's U. S. undergraduates were eligible for Pell Grants.
- Seventy-nine percent of U. S. undergraduates received financial aid in 2014 (grants or scholarships from all sources).
- Forty-one percent of Webster students worldwide describe themselves as white or Caucasian, while 43% of Webster U. S. students describe themselves as white or Caucasian.
- Twenty-seven percent of U. S. students identify as racial/ethnic minorities.
- Fifty-one percent of those awarded graduate degrees in 2016 self-identify as minorities.

Webster has intentionally and naturally become more diverse as a result of educating women and men—traditional undergraduates as well as working adults (including active military, veterans, and dependents) in St. Louis, on military bases and metropolitan locations across the United States, in international residential locations across the world, and robust online certificate and degree programs. Meeting the challenge of inclusion, choosing to support success and community as well as access and opportunity, requires the intention to use talent and resources in purposeful ways.

True to Webster's historic and evolving mission of creating opportunity for an increasingly diverse student body, we welcome students whose talents often exceed their financial capacity and academic preparation. For these Webster students, successful degree attainment isn't something that just happens on a stage with gowns and embossed pieces of paper. For these students, it's made out of one-on-one, intensive academic counseling sessions. It's built out of summer days spent acclimating to the rigor of postsecondary academic work. It's about enrolling a diverse class of students from a wide variety of backgrounds and making it our priority to support them every step of the way to graduation day.[2]

To meet evolving student needs, we have built an integrated system of learning strategies classes, peer advising, and a free residential summer bridge program. The results speak for themselves. Our students are better supported and better prepared for rigorous academic work, and their boosted retention rates have put them on track to graduate at elevated rates. The challenges of closing the educational gaps between rich and poor and of accommodating first-generation students are indeed difficult.

Transfers from four-year institutions and community colleges are growing, and many undergrads enroll on a part-time basis. Like many colleges and universities today, we lend guidance to our students as they address the challenges of their life circumstances while seeking academic success. Our focal point for this endeavor is Webster's academic resource center, an integrated support center geared for student achievement. The center offers academic counseling, tutoring, writing, and assistive technology support, along with services for students with disabilities, and resources for veterans. Connecting components of this system include default-prevention programs, a retention calling program, a new financial resource center, and English-language programs for Webster's international students.

The Transitions and the Transitions and Academic Prep (TAP) programs, which were created by the Academic Resource Center, best exemplify our models of integrated student support. Through these programs, students gain an understanding of successful college behaviors and a roadmap designed to help them thrive. Transitions, created in 2009, serves students who are admitted with conditions typically assessed through at-risk indicators such as ACT scores or grade point averages, and who have completed 30 or fewer postsecondary semester hours. Tailored to fit a student's individual strengths and needs, Transitions provides academic counseling and peer tutoring as well as help with learning strategies, organization skills, and time management. Required weekly sessions establish close relationships with peers and trusted adults.

Prior to implementing Transitions, Webster experienced a gap of 6% between the retention rates for conditionally admitted students versus those without conditions. Since 2009, that gap has disappeared; and the TAP students are now more successfully retained than fully admitted students. Our success with Transitions helped us launch the Webster TAP program in 2011, which was initially created as a non–credit-bearing summer enrichment opportunity for students in the Transitions program. Today, its cohort size has doubled. It is free, residential, and now offers two academic credits and an expanded array of supports for students' success. TAP students explore diversity issues and transition issues, build vital bonds with peers, and leverage new additions, including critical-literacy writing workshops, and financial literacy resources. In this way, Webster is not only diverse but inclusive.

As an institution that has made its home in St. Louis for over 100 years, we have been impacted by the events the world now associates with "Ferguson." In times of challenge for our broader community, reflected on college campuses across the country, we created a two-day conference on February 29 and March 1, 2016, called "Critical Conversations: Embracing Diversity and Inclusion." The conference reflected an inclusive Webster worldview. Webster's Associate Vice President for Diversity and Inclusion worked with university and community colleagues to organize four keynote speakers and several panel discussions on broad and inclusive aspects of diversity, including race, ethnicity, gender, gender identity, ability and disability, nationality, and birthplace. Over 350 individuals joined conversations that were underwritten and, in many cases, moderated by Webster trustees. The response was such a positive learning experience that we decided to convene our second Critical Conversations conference in March 2017.

The Webster initiatives which make college better through strengthening inclusion are many and varied—an international friendship program, women's leadership initiatives, and cohosted summits and speakers by entities as varied as the Committee of 200, Catalyst, the Urban League of Metropolitan St. Louis, the World Affairs Council, and the World Trade Center. The University expresses our commitment to increasing the diversity of talent and leadership in the region through sponsorship of the *St. Louis Business Journal*'s Diverse Business Leaders recognition and partnership with the *St. Louis American* Foundation to provide scholarships to underrepresented undergraduates. Working groups of faculty, staff, and students are preparing to recommend ways to strengthen academic programming, facilities, student life, hiring practices, and scholarship support. Common readings for the first-year experience program now focus on the topics of race, class, and social justice. We have increased donor and institutional scholarship funding for international and minority students as well as providing scholarships with the Rotary Club of St. Louis to the top high school seniors from each St. Louis public school. Leadership at Webster seeks to reach all levels, resulting in trustee membership that is 45% female and 29% diverse in race, ethnicity and/or foreign born.

Because Webster students make their homes in many communities worldwide, our sense of community must be both local and global. Since Ferguson and the tragic shooting at Pulse in Orlando (site of a Webster campus), we have come to associate more and more place names—St. Paul, Nice, Baton Rouge, Dallas, Munich, Istanbul, Tokyo, Hua Hin, Milwaukee—with loss of life, pain, and sorrow. The emotions associated with the name "Ferguson" continue to be present with us and are joined with so many others. These emotions create a bond, a shared identity, and a commitment of the individual to the broader community. At Webster, our mission focus on global citizenship—on developing a global mindset—should open us to be changed by the world at the same time we become world changers.

EDUCATING WORLD CHANGERS

> When we become curious about the dissatisfying defaults in our world, we begin to recognize that most of them have social origins: Rules and systems were created by people. And that awareness gives us the courage to contemplate how we can change them.
>
> —Adam Grant (2016, p. 32)

Webster recently marked the close of its first century and embarked upon the second while launching a new strategic plan, "Global Impact for the Next Century." The four themes of the plan focus on our unique strengths that provide the foundation for a university that is, at once, better for students and better for the world.

- Global Innovation Through Inclusive Leadership
- A Global, Student-Centered Experience
- A Network of Academic and Operational Excellence
- Strategic and Sustainable Development

As a truly global institution that offers distinct learning experiences, we intend, through those experiences, to develop global citizens with the mindset as well as the competencies to lead and to succeed.

Webster's global character is rooted in our history, dating to at least 1919, when the college welcomed two French students as part of the war relief effort. In 1925, Webster created its first scholarship to study abroad; and in 1931, students from other campuses began completing their studies at the Webster Groves campus. During the next twenty years, 200 faculty members and students went abroad or came to Webster. From those beginnings have developed our distinctively global academic programs, policies, and locations as well as the global diversity of our faculty, staff, and students.

The new strategic plan extends Webster's pioneering, capacity-building commitment to global academic and operational excellence. We have established international residential campuses; achieved dual U.S. and international accreditations; developed a global citizenship curriculum; facilitated mobility of faculty, staff, and students among our global network; and forged strategic worldwide partnerships. Each of these components of our institution makes Webster better. But, improving the global experience for all of Webster's students is our intention, which will require a systemic integration of these institutional elements. Making college better requires continuous quality improvements.

Webster's campuses in Europe and Africa are fully residential campuses with full degree programs, educating primarily students native to countries in the region of each campus—Leiden, Athens, Geneva, Vienna, Accra—and from the Middle East and Asia. Thailand is the location for two campuses—graduate students in Bangkok and undergraduates in Cha-am. In China, graduate students complete joint degrees at Chinese partner institutions. Study abroad students from Webster campuses and from our affiliate partners can spend a term, a semester, or a year at other Webster campuses as well as through arrangements with partner institutions around the world.

Our network of campus locations and partnerships means that Webster students can choose to complete an entire degree program outside their home country or can seamlessly transfer credits among campus locations. The curriculum is centrally coordinated, taught in English, and Webster programs are accredited by the Higher Learning Commission wherever they are located. Faculty at international campuses are globally diverse—local to the country or region, recruited internationally, and on assignment from other Webster campuses. In many cases, programs enjoy country accreditation, adding value to a Webster degree achieved in that country.

An increasing number of global hybrid short-term study options have been created to expand opportunities for international travel and study. Webster's many online courses and programs are populated by students from around the world, and our newly developed video classrooms at the European campuses and Webnet+ capabilities support interactive classes taught between and among campuses. While completing academic work when living in another culture has been identified as a high-impact teaching and learning practice (Kuh, 2008) that is notably present for students at independent colleges in the U. S. (Gonyea & Kinzie, 2015), Webster's mission focus especially prizes its significance for a student's personal growth and development. Many Webster students in St. Louis leave their town, their region, and their country simultaneously when studying abroad. And they join a globally diverse community that includes, and is informed by, multiple world views. Recent research (Godart, Maddux, Shipilov, & Galinsky, 2015) posits that breadth of perspective, flexibility and adaptability, and increased creativity can be influenced by an individual's moves to new cities. Living and working for extended times in very different cultures can heighten an individual's originality—and the more different, the greater the impact.

Increasing student, faculty, and staff mobility is key to assuring a global experience for many more Webster students. The impact of international study is enabled by purposeful policies that foster mobility among the campuses. In addition to the portability of credits and the availability of affiliate study-abroad status for partner institutions in the U. S., qualified Webster students at Webster are eligible for the Webster World Traveler Program. This program provides one free airline ticket to study abroad for a term or semester. We are gradually adding scholarships to support international study, in the United States and abroad; and students retain their financial aid. Our commitment to help first-generation, underrepresented, and nontraditional students complete study internationally will require innovative and entrepreneurial approaches and increased financial support.

Assuring a global experience for every student requires that we ensure a global feature in every academic program. Webster students can enroll in programs with intentional global focus. A quick survey of the certificate, undergraduate, master's and doctoral program titles finds at least thirty specific global/international programs spanning all five colleges. Among them is a global M.A. in international relations, requiring cohorts of students to study in multiple international locations during their academic study. Two years ago, our deans created an initiative to further this aspect of comprehensive internationalization through specific curricular content, field experiences, internships, guest speakers, and study-abroad opportunities. This work continues and is designed to extend the foundation created by faculty in the form of a new general studies program called the Global Citizenship Program (GCP). The Global Citizenship Program, recently recognized by the Association of General and Liberal Studies as an exemplary program, is a set of undergraduate degree requirements building students' knowledge in these topic areas: roots of cultures, social systems and human behavior, physical and natural world, global understanding, arts appreciation, and quantitative literacy. Skills requirements occur in courses coded for written communication, oral communication, critical thinking, intercultural competence, and ethical reasoning. Aligned with high-impact teaching practices and 21st-century knowledge and skills identified by the Association of American Colleges and Universities (2007), the GCP is the basis of every Webster undergraduate degree.

The effectiveness of Webster's growing comprehensive and systemic approach to internationalization depends upon investments in the commitment, talent, and capacity of faculty and staff at each of Webster's campuses as well as the quality of their interactions to educate students as global citizens. Faculty and staff mobility has been supported over the years through purposeful exchange and mobility programs for which employees apply. Additionally, faculty who choose a faculty development leave track rather than a more traditional tenure track at the point of hire receive opportunities for leave more frequently in exchange for more frequent reviews. As a result, they often exercise their leave by teaching or conducting research at another Webster campus. This flexibility in leave policies and the ease of our international campus network clearly contributes to mobility.

Efforts to build our own capacities as global citizens take several forms. This year, faculty and staff who lead the First Year Experience program will invite their colleagues to join Critical Conversation reading groups for dialogue about the readings on race, class, and social justice completed by students. They will convene us to learn more about the Crossing Borders Education (CBE) intercultural resources—not only for curriculum integration, but to gain for ourselves a deeper level of transformative learning by linking intercultural learning and diversity training in the CBE curriculum.

Four years ago, the provost and I launched Webster's Global Leadership Academy, an innovative leadership development program designed to enhance our institutional capacity for global work by virtue of the program's impact on faculty and staff leadership. Developing and enhancing the leadership skills of faculty and staff, providing a comprehensive and grounded understanding of Webster's complexity, and creating ambassadors to the communities Webster serves are the three goals of the year-long Academy. In its first three years, these results have been documented:

- Meaningful interactions among faculty and staff from 15 Webster University campuses, including four international campuses and nine metropolitan campuses outside the home campus in St. Louis, Missouri.
- Increased faculty and staff global mobility by providing the first international travel experience for approximately 18% of participants.
- Notable gains appear in participants' (1) establishing of relationships across the Webster network and leveraging them to resolve institutional challenge and (2) recommending innovative and creative solutions to institutional challenges.
- Leadership accomplishments within the project-based framework of the Academy as well as in participants' current roles and new roles as a result of promotions within Webster or at other institutions.
- Key initiatives in the institution's strategic plan have been advanced by participants in areas such as leading major curriculum revisions, developing talent and improved culture within units, building student community, and advancing major facilities and information technology projects. Webster's global impact has been extended by academy participants through new partnerships, faculty scholarship, and campus locations or study abroad initiatives that facilitate greater mobility.[3]

In a comparable leadership initiative for students, the inaugural Global Student Leadership Summit was held in 2015 as part of our Centennial celebration. Twenty-nine undergraduate and graduate students from eight campuses convened in online discussions prior to meeting in person for a week in St. Louis to develop as leaders and share insights and ideas that enhance academic and student life experiences for students. They provided input for ways to advance the four themes of the new strategic plan, with a focus on increased mobility and a more universal global student experience. In summer, 2017, we will convene the second summit at the Vienna campus. The engagement of campus-based student governments with one another, the expansion of the Webster Leads student leadership program across international campuses, and increased interactions among the international campuses in the form of European Soccer (football) Tournaments, humanitarian outreach, and "Webster's Got Talent" competitions are early indicators of the immediate impact of building greater community among our students.

The activities with world-serving and world-changing impact continue to evolve in ways that encourage human needs to continue to grow as well. Instances of human suffering and tragedy have spurred Webster students and colleagues to organize symposia, conduct research, volunteer in community service, launch new courses and programs, participate in sponsored readings and events to remember victims, organize protests, and ultimately to pursue lifelong interests and careers as global citizens. The topics that compel their interest are as varied as the forms of challenges the world faces—public health, global media trends, international relations, human rights and humanitarian issues, international trade, refugees and asylum, literacy, security, human trafficking, leadership development, global entrepreneurship, and equity for women, to name a few.

Will Webster's mission, vision, and values make college better not only for students but for the world? Are our present points of rethinking fit, choosing to include, and educating world changers sufficient to move the world? That ultimate question provides the greatest opportunity and challenge for this global community. The themes and metrics of a mission-based strategic plan both nudge and reflect initiatives to transform students for individual excellence and global citizenship. Yet, our mission's success depends upon our ability to adopt a global perspective (Braskamp, Braskamp, & Glass, 2015) and mindset ourselves—our ability individually and institutionally to "take multiple perspectives into account" (Braskamp et al., 2015). When we are members of communities that perpetuate, intentionally or otherwise, resistance to the uncommon and unfamiliar, we exacerbate the stigma of otherness and inhibit the true sense of belonging that is the "gateway to global learning" (Braskamp et al., 2015).

This lack of inclusion and the desire to feel valued and welcomed cause people to exclude themselves from the larger community and to isolate themselves with small kinship and family groups most like themselves. Even at an institution with

Webster's history, mission, global presence, and diversity, we can feel the ambivalence toward that which is not known and not experienced and, therefore, not valued. We fall short of what Bruni (2015) describes as the purpose of the college experience, to "unveil the complexity and splendor of the world, and prepare students to be thoughtful citizens of it" (p. SR3).

Developing a global mindset opens us to be changed by the world at the same time we become world changers. In her 2014 Webster University Commencement Address, Dr. Koko Tanimoto Kondo reflected on her life as a childhood survivor of the Hiroshima bombing. She has become an international advocate and educator for peace. Her message of reconciliation reminds us that we must first be transformed by the world and then transform the world. Zen Master Kono Taitsu's words resound: "When I change, the world changes." In that wisdom, we find our lever.

NOTES

1. Data provided by Webster University Office of Institutional Effectiveness based on the U. S. Department of Education's Integrated Postsecondary Education Data System.
2. I first described the success of the Transitions and Academic Preparation Program in Attainment = Retention, The Presidency, Fall 2015. While some of the content of this section duplicates that article, I have updated the program description and relevant data.
3. I acknowledge and thank Provost, Senior Vice President and Chief Operating Officer Julian Z. Schuster, for his partnership in advancing Webster's global mission in every way and specifically in launching the Global Leadership Academy. For their exemplary leadership of the Global Leadership Academy and for the contributions of the evaluative data reported here, I am grateful to Director Laura Rein and Co-Directors Holly Hubenschmidt and Erik Palmore.

REFERENCES

American Association of Collegiate Registrars and Admissions Officers. (2016). Geography Continues to Matter in College Enrollment Decisions. Retrieved from http://www.aacrao.org/resources/resources-detail-view/geography-continues-to-matter-in-college-enrollment-decisions

Association of American Colleges and Universities (2007). *College learning for the new global century.* Washington, DC: Association of American Colleges and Universities.

Braskamp, D. C., Braskamp, L. A., & Glass, C. R. (2015). Belonging: The gateway to global learning for all students. *Liberal Education, 101*(3). Retrieved from http://www.aacu.org/liberaleducation/2015/summer/braskamp

Bruni, F. (2015). The lie about college diversity. *New York Times,* p. SR3.

Bruni, F. (2015). *Where you go is not who you'll be: An antidote to the college admissions mania.* New York: Grand Central Publishing.

Gillis, D. (2016, August 11). 10 Steps to Create Inclusive Workplaces. [Web log post] Retrieved from http://www.catalyst.org/blog/catalyzing/10-steps-create-inclusive-workplaces

Godart, F. C., Maddux, W. W., Shipilov, A. V., & Galinsky, A. D. "Fashion with a foreign flair: Professional experiences abroad facilitate the creative innovations of organizations," *Academy of Management Journal* 58 (2015): 195–220 found in Grant, A. (2016).

Gonyea, R. M., & Kinzie, J. (2015). *Independent colleges and student engagement: Descriptive analysis by institutional type.* Washington, DC: Council of Independent Colleges.

Grant, A. (2016). *Originals: How nonconformists move the world.* New York, NY: Viking.

Hartnell, C. A., Kinicki, A. J., Schurer Lambert, L., Fugater, M., & Doyle Corner, P. (2016). Do similarities or differences between CEO leadership and organizational culture have a more positive effect on firm performance? A test of competing predictions. *Journal of Applied Psychology*, vol. 101, no. 6, pp. 846-861.

Hussar, W. J., & Bailey, T. M. (2016). *Projections of Education Statistics to 2023* (NCES 2015-073). U.S. Department of Education, National Center for Education Statistics. Washington, DC: U.S. Government Printing Office.

Integrated Postsecondary Education Data System. (2016, September). Retrieved from College Navigator from the National Center for Education Statistics website http://nces.ed.gov/collegenavigator/

Kuh, G. R. (2008). *High-Impact educational practices: What they are, who has access to them, and why they matter.* Washington, DC: Association of American Colleges and Universities.

New York University Department of Mathematics. (1995). *The Lever Quotations.* Retrieved from https://www.math.nyu.edu/~crorres/Archimedes/Lever/LeverQuotes.html

O'Connell, M. (2007, February 21). *How to choose a college that's right for you* [National Public Radio commentary]. Retrieved from http://www.npr.org/2010/12/08/7506102/how-to-choose-a-college-that-s-right-for-you

Sharpe, R. (2016). The top 100 degrees conferred. *Diverse Issues in Higher Education* 33(15), 33.

Stroble, E. (2015, Fall). Attainment = Retention. *The Presidency* 18(4), 22–24.

CHAPTER SIX

The Soul OF A Christian University

J. RANDALL O'BRIEN
President, Carson-Newman University

A vigorous and important conversation pertaining to the soul of the religiously affiliated university has, for years now, exercised academics, clerics, and laity alike. The issue is at least as old as Tertullian's second-century question, "What has Jerusalem to do with Athens?" The idea of integrating faith and learning logically excludes the elimination of either from the marketplace of ideas, inquiry, investigation and discovery. Along with teaching and publishing, that intellectual bond has long constituted the heart of the American academy. For the religiously affiliated university, however, faith, as soul, accompanies the heart.

THE FUTURE OF THE PAST

The birth of nearly all colleges in America before 1865 came forth from church organizations, or devout Christians, with intentional Christian educational ends in mind:

- Harvard (1636) was established by Congregationalists.
- William & Mary (1693) was established by Anglicans.
- Yale (1701) was founded by Congregationalists.
- Princeton (1747) was founded by Presbyterians.
- Brown (1765) was founded by Baptists, as was the University of Chicago.
- Other church colleges of distinction include Columbia (1754), Penn (1755), and Dartmouth (1769).

Harvard's motto in 1650 proclaimed *Christi Glorium* (Glory to Christ). Her motto in 1692 became *Christo et Ecclesiae* (Christ and Church).[1] Harvard's earliest set of "Rules and Precepts" decreed that each student was "to be plainly instructed, and earnestly pressed to consider well, the main end of his life and studies is, to know God and Jesus Christ which is eternal life … and therefore to lay Christ in the bottom, as the only foundation of all sound knowledge and learning." Yale's stated purpose from the beginning was "to teach and engage the children to know God in Jesus Christ and to love and serve him in all sobriety, godliness, and righteousness of life. …" The first public announcement regarding the University of Chicago read, "The new University is to be a Christian institution. It is to be forever under the auspices of the Baptist denomination." Her first president announced that the "President and two thirds of its Trustees will be Baptists. … In all and above all and under all, the University of Chicago, whatever else it may be, by the grace of God shall be Christian in tone, in influence, and in work. The provisions of this charter … are pledges to you that this shall always remain true."

Dartmouth President, Asa Smith, charged in his inaugural address of 1863 that, "The College … should be distinctly and eminently Christian. … Let the studies which we call moral, have a Christian baptism. … Let Ethical Science … be bathed in the light of Calvary." President's Smith charge of 1863 came as late as 100 years after Dartmouth's founding.

By the early 1900s, however, the secularization of higher education had displaced the dominant Christian intellectual position in state universities and major private universities, and by the 1960s, in most church colleges as well. Aware of the dangers of the secular way, Yale President Charles Seymour, in his inaugural address in 1937, called for a return to our Christian heritage and hope, declaring Yale was dedicated to the upraising of spiritual leaders: "We betray our trust if we fail to explore the various ways in which the youth who come to us may learn to appreciate spiritual values. … The simple and direct way is through the maintenance and upbuilding of the Christian religion as a vital part of university life. I call on all members of the faculty, as members of a thinking body, freely to recognize the tremendous validity and power of the teachings of Christ in our life-and-death struggle against the forces of selfish materialism. If we lose that struggle … scholarship as well as religion will disappear."

Oh, what an uproar William F. Buckley, Jr. created in 1951 with the publication of his book, *God & Man at Yale*! In critiquing his alma mater, Buckley alleged that Yale had lost its way, that she had become incoherent, suffering a loss of mission, that she had drifted so far from her founding ideals in failing to Christianize Yale that the average student attending Yale graduated with a shattered respect for Christianity.

Professor McGeorge Bundy, who would later serve the Kennedy and Johnson administrations as National Security Advisor, published in *The Atlantic Monthly* a scathing response to Buckley, essentially presenting the University's official statement of denial of Buckley's allegations. The battle was joined.

So, where are we today? At a critical crossroads. It is difficult to imagine any of our nation's major private universities, or state universities, being anything but bored with the conversation regarding Christianity's mission on campus. Christianity, along with Elvis, has left the building.

Will Christian faith forever be vanquished from higher education? Or will it be allowed to return from exile? What does Athens have to do with Jerusalem? Tertullian asked. "Much," Duns replied! "Much," sing a chorus of contemporary voices across America! "Everything," say hundreds of history's brightest lights, as well as many of today's leading intellectuals! Paul, Clement, Anselm, Augustine, Acquinas, Erasmus, Calvin, Luther, Orr, Kuyper, Newman, Trueblood, Holmes, Marsden, Noll, Burtchaell, Dockery, Ringenberg, Lewis, Schwehn, Neuhaus, Jacobsen, Beaty, Schmeltekopf, Benne, Plantiga, Wolterstorff, McGrath, Hughes, Evans, and countless other luminaries testify of the inseparable nature of truth and theology. Anselm and Augustine wrote passionately of "faith seeking understanding."

However, Richard Dawkins, a leading spokesman for atheism today, claims, "Faith is the great cop-out, the great excuse to evade the need to think and evaluate evidence."

John Polkinghorne, past Chairman of the Nuclear Physics Board of the Science Research Council in Great Britain, counters: "… we live in a cosmos, not a chaos, so that the world makes total sense. In other words, there is indeed a Theory of Everything. … the name of that Theory is Theology, … the world makes total sense because it is a creation, the unified expression of the Mind and Will of its Creator."[2]

Polkinghorne, fellow of Queen's College, Cambridge, continues: "I believe that theology is of continuing significance in a scientific age and that its pursuit is an indispensable part of the activity of a complete university."[3]

Francis Collins, one of the world's leading geneticists and the former head of the Human Genome Project, the decade-long work to decode the DNA of our species, writes: "… the principles of faith are, in fact, complementary with the principles of science. … In my view, there is no conflict in being a rigorous scientist and a person who believes in a God who takes a personal interest in each one of us."[4]

All of this is well and good, but does anyone believe that Ivy League U., or State U., will rush to become citadels for the integration of faith and learning? Do we really believe our public and major private universities may soon choose to become bastions of Christian orthodoxy? What then is the future of the past? Where then might academies of science, humanities, fine arts, education, professional schools, and faith be found? Good question.

Comes the prophet!

In 1975 Arthur Holmes, influenced heavily by Abraham Kuyper, John Henry Newman, and Elton Trueblood, published, *The Idea of a Christian College.* Holmes argued that only an active integration of faith and learning truly distinguishes the secular and Christian university. Floodgates opened, and out poured volumes of sympathetic works from the ranks of the intelligentsia. The leitmotif of each of their works calls for Christian colleges and universities to reverse their retreat, reclaim their heritage, and to do so by marching boldly into the Promised Land of Christian higher education holding high the banner, "All Truth is God's Truth."

Comes the surprise!

"Distant cousins" are "preaching" a "not-so-distant" message from the halls of secular universities. As William Ringenberg notes, "At least since the appearance of Allan Bloom's *The Closing of the American Mind: How Higher Education Has Failed Democracy and Impoverished the Soul of Today's Students* (1987) and Paige Smith's *Killing the Spirit: Higher Education in America* (1900) … the general modern critique of secular higher education has bemoaned the tendency to replace the character and values education dimension of learning with an intellectualist conformity and anti-religion bias."[5] Ringenberg continues, "Even the traditionally elite institutions themselves are becoming aware of their growing barrenness."[6] As noted by Columbia University professor Andrew Delbanco: "There is a nervousness that may account for the use of compensatory institutions within the institution such as the Center for Human Values at Princeton … or the Institute for Ethics at Duke. But what can it mean that thinking about ethics has become mostly an extracurricular activity?" Add to this critique the work of Harry Lewis, former Dean of Harvard College, entitled *Excellence Without a Soul: How a Great University Forgot Education,* in which he acknowledges that "moral education has withered" in our universities and the testimony of crisis mounts.[7]

All of this is nice, but we in Christian colleges and universities are not simply talking about values and ethics. It is certainly true that we, among others, concur with the need for a renewed focus upon morals. But the cry is for more than that.

If America's colleges displaced historic orthodox Christianity with generic religion and social good, or at best confined Christianity to the office of the campus minister, or a chapel service, or a specially created department of religion, leaving no place for Christian faith in the nerve center of the university and the curriculum; if science became the new orthodoxy in the halls of academe; if our campuses severed the rose from its roots by finding a place for morals in the fields of study but no place for Christian teachings; if our colleges came in time to find morals passé', while manners, whatever that means, became the mark of an educated person, are we really surprised to discover that we are living in communities stuffed with information but starved for values? And if we have fallen over the precipice of civility is the appropriate corrective step to climb part of the way up the slippery cliff during the cultural monsoon and hope we won't be washed away again? Or should we consider ascending to the top of the rock and rest on the solid footing of historic orthodox Christianity? Why was Christianity important in the founding and operation of our institutions of higher education, but, except in sectarian institutions, impotent today? Why the call for a focus on generic morals? Without an authoritative foundation do not morals erode? Isn't that precisely why we have arrived at our point of need?

Perhaps in our secular age state colleges and universities, and most private colleges, will not desire to integrate faith and learning, choosing to go their own way instead. But I would like to join the caravan of sages through the ages, including the company of evangelical confessing scholars today, who hold to the unity of truth, and to the belief that faith and learning, not faith *or* learning, is the best way to attain true erudition.

In our search for knowledge, our quest for truth, why should our learning communities and faith communities remain separate? Let us embrace an open search for truth wherein freedom to think includes permission to ask any question and to analyze every perspective. Open intellectual inquiry may not, after all, by self-definition, exclude thinking "Christianly" across the curriculum. Any search for truth which excludes, a priori, consideration of evidence, or particular views, is at best misguided elitism, mishandled epistemology, or mistaken scientific method, but at worst, missionary secularism intent upon installing the new atheism as the fundamentalist religion of college campuses. Enough of this idolatrous sacrifice of our children![8]

Let us no longer accept the patronizing heresy of compartmentalizing our Christian faith into non-threatening conclaves safely away from the classroom. Rather let us champion both free academic inquiry and committed theological loyalty. We in the academy make much of academic freedom. Then let us in our Christian colleges dare to let truth and error compete for residence in our minds. Let us read widely, listen deeply, reflect critically, observe studiously, present effectively, debate delightfully, write masterfully, analyze keenly, question honestly, dissent respectfully, think "Christianly," and live gratefully in the presence of our Creator-Redeemer-Sustainer God.

The universe is our university; the cosmos is our campus. All truth is God's truth. *Vocatus atque non-vocatus, Deus aderit,* the eminent psychologist, Carl Jung, had carved above the door of his home: "Bidden, or not bidden, God is present."

So, what is the future of the past?

In a story titled, "Christian Colleges are Booming," *Time* magazine reported a U.S. Department of Education survey which revealed an enrollment increase of 67.3% for the decade of 1992-2002 for schools listed in the Council of Christian Colleges and Universities. The increase for all other colleges and universities during the same 10-year period was 2.1%, a 65% differential!

According to the National Center for Educational Statistics, schools associated with the Council of Christian Colleges and Universities experienced enrollment growth of 12.5% in the period 2003–2009. Our Christian university,

Carson-Newman, has experienced 28% growth in enrollment since 2012 with consecutive record enrollments the past three years.

Apparently the longing is for a place where the life of the mind and the shepherding of the spirit might find a welcome home. If so, Carson-Newman's ethos of open intellectual inquiry and a deeper spiritual life—a beautiful tapestry of faith, learning, and caring community—positions us providentially to meet the deepest needs of our neighbor and realize the highest dreams we dare to dream.

I dream of a college where graduates have learned how to think; they have learned what the best and brightest minds throughout the ages have thought and currently are thinking; they have also learned to question, to research, to discover, to think for themselves, which includes permission to think "Christianly."

The college of my dreams features the Christian intellectual tradition as a centerpiece, the integration of faith and learning as the cornerstone, and classroom excellence, inspiring, even epochal research and discovery, cutting-edge scholarship and love of students, all within a caring community.

The college of my dreams stands firmly under the lordship of Jesus Christ where one might unashamedly, faithfully accept our Lord's invitation to love Him with all of our hearts, all of our souls, and with all of our minds."

As Victor Hugo shared, "There is nothing like a dream to shape the future."

THE WAY, THE TRUTH, AND THE LIFE

A Christian university takes upon itself the name of Christ. What responsibility comes with the name! Jesus Christ called Himself the Truth, saying, "I am the Way the Truth, and the Life." His Way, His Truth, equates to Life, according to Him. Do we believe Him? If so, what does it mean to say Jesus Christ is the Way, the Truth, and the Life? Does His truth-claim refer to salvation only? Spiritual living only? Or, to holistic calling? What difference does the matter make to the Christian university?

Christian universities look to an understandable source for the authoritative answer: The Bible. Jesus is no longer with us, incarnate, to address the issue. Christian opinions inevitably vary. We need authority. Of course, even when an authoritative source is available interpretation may differ. Nevertheless, as nations require a constitution to establish jurisdiction, so religions depend upon a sacred canon to provide jurisprudence. A nation which nullifies its constitution will descend into chaos, as will a religion which annuls its authoritative verse. So what does it mean to say Jesus Christ is the way, the truth, and the life? The Bible provides the answer.

Not so fast. Who says the Bible's answer is authoritative? Did Christianity not exist more than 300 years without the Bible we now possess? And did not Paul make clear that Christians are ultimately to follow the Spirit of Christ, rather than the written law? Our answer is yes, and yes.

The outbreak of heresies in the absence of orthodox, authoritative doctrine, however, proved the necessity of a Christian canon. The Old Testament was canonized in 90 A.D. The New Testament was canonized in 397 A.D. Before canonization oral tradition, various sacred writings, and collections carried authoritative standing within the church. Secondly, it is this very body of authoritative writ which privileges a law of the Spirit over the Law. We cannot have it both ways. Is it not this same canon of Scripture, so quickly set aside, which informs us of Paul's revolutionary words (and of course, Jesus's), guiding us to our new favored orthodoxy and orthopraxy of love and the Spirit of Jesus? Dare we surrender so sacred a text, one which not only contains the story of our path of liberation from slavery to sin and the law, but one which converts that law into a wise guide for grateful living now judged by the Spirit of Jesus?

Sadly, a popular modern phenomenon is, in fact, an outright rejection of Scripture as a divinely inspired record of God's revelation, one providing infallible authority of written word and Living Word for the church. In recent decades, modern scholars, whom I will cite or quote, but not name, could not be more clear: The Gospels are not literally true, but history metaphorized. Though there be some history remembered, the Bible is not divine, but a totally human product of two ancient communities. There was no virgin birth and no bodily resurrection. Jesus was a Jewish peasant, certainly not divine. "The Bible is not the word of God in any literal or verbal sense. It never has been!" "There is no God external to life. God is not a being superior to all other beings." The Gospels contain "embarrassing moral and intellectual concepts." So goes the hermeneutic of cynicism.

Some dismiss the divinity of Scripture summarily; others commit bibliolatry, worshiping the Bible; many view the Bible along the lines of grandfather's clock: to be cherished and given a place of honor, but certainly not depended upon to perform the service it once provided. Still others, in my view, get it right. Richard B. Hays, Dean of Duke Divinity School, is one such esteemed scholar, rightly claiming Scripture is *norma normans,* "the norming norm," of the church, which means Scripture is authoritative, normative for the church, whose ethics and practices are Scripture-shaped. Martin Luther, the Father of the Protestant Reformation, cried, *Sola Scriptura*, "Scripture Alone," as the authority for Christian faith and practice.

In his book, *The Strange Silence of the Bible in the Church,* James D. Smart, the late distinguished professor of biblical studies at Union Theological Seminary in New York, argues strongly for the distinction between God's revelation to and through Israel and Jesus Christ versus the *record* of that revelation in writings we call our Bible. That revelation, he stresses, "is not to be equated to a book, but it comes to us *only* through the medium of that book." He warns: "When the book is no longer read and understood by Christians, they have been cut off decisively from the roots of their distinctively Christian existence." He continues, "We create a serious illusion if we leave in men's minds the impression that there is any other way, any direct and unmediated way, for us to find access to this reality of revelation in history except through the reading and the exposition of the text of Scripture itself." In other words, Dr. Smart sounds the alarm, *"No Scriptures, No church! No Scriptures, No revelation!"*[9]

Does Smart mean to say that all revelation is limited to the Bible? He does not! God continues to reveal God's self on the stage of history and to us personally. Christianity is dynamic, not static. Or in the least our understanding of it is progressive. The church's role in civil rights issues regarding races in years gone by, and LGBTQ issues today, offers sufficient evidence of our inability to easily comprehend God's will and our dependence upon a progressive understanding of that will.[10]

Before departing earth Jesus revealed, *"I have yet many things to say to you, but you cannot bear them now. When the Spirit of Truth comes, he will guide you into all the truth"* (John 16: 13). Thankfully, God finds us at our alpha point and takes us to the omega point, or to cite the English alphabet rather than the Greek, God finds us at point A and takes us to Z. Faith is a flowing river, not a stagnant pond. To be sure the river flows faster in some places than others, for some people than others. But surely we will not turn our cracked lips and parched souls away from our God-given streams in the desert. Will we?

Tragically, the move to reject the Word of God as authoritative for our lives dates to our earliest ancestors, as the Garden story of Adam and Eve reveals. Not surprisingly, the words, authority, and author, derive from the same Latin root, *auctor,* meaning, "writer, or progenitor." To rid ourselves of the authority of Scripture is to rid ourselves of its author. Hmmm, who might that be?

Just as no building can long survive without a sure foundation, neither can a Christian university. The foundation of the Christian university is the Word of God, the Bible, which introduces us to the Cornerstone, the Living Word of God, Jesus Christ. Admittedly, the Bible does not purport to be a science book, an algebra text, nor an art, music, psychology, physics, or business manual.

So back to the question.

What does Jesus mean, when he says, "I am the Way, the Truth, and the Life?" Jesus is on the verge of his departure when he speaks these words. His crucifixion is imminent. He reminds his disciples that they can come with him to be with the Father, but only by him. His words speak of eternal life. Next, he elaborates that his followers will do greater works than he, for he, as the glorified Son, will help them do so, as they ask. He then charges them to keep his commandments. He is speaking of godly living. Lastly, he promises the disciples that he will send the Holy Spirit to dwell in them, and the Holy Spirit will "teach you all things." This, I take to refer to holistic calling of becoming all we are created to become—intellectually, socially, spiritually— and to help others do the same.

Jesus had already invited his followers to "Give first place to the Kingdom of God and his righteousness and all other things would be yours as well." They were already invited, as well, to, "Love the Lord, your God, with all your heart, soul, mind, and strength," and to, "Love your neighbor as yourself," unconditionally. Jesus taught his disciples that the secret to greatness was found in serving others. His calling to his disciples, then, was holistic: mind, body, soul, devoted to God, service rendered to others, all wrapped in unselfish, unconditional love. "If anyone would come after me," He challenged, "let him deny himself, take up his cross, and follow me." Self-denial, self-sacrifice, self-surrender, he taught, is the Way of Christ and the Way of his followers.

Since the Bible is the foundation of the church and church college, does that mean that direction comes from the Bible alone? As Professor Smart stated, not at all. The Holy Spirit, our Teacher, teaches us new truths. The way we think, talk, and live is guided by the Holy Spirit of the living Christ, who is Head of the body of believers, and Lord of the Christian university.

In Christ, "… are hidden all treasures of wisdom and knowledge" (Col 2.3). Christ is, "the image of the invisible God. … For by Him all things were created, both in the heavens and on earth, visible and invisible … all things have been created by Him and for Him. And He is before all things, and in Him all things are held together" (Col 1:15–17). Christ is the creator and center of the universe, so certainly, of the university, as well.

All truth is God's truth. In the Christian university, all inquiry, thinking, speaking, behaving, serving, relating, discovery, teaching, learning, integration, application, creating, writing, counseling, playing, coaching, producing, designing, planning, performing, and working serve Jesus, our Lord.

We are called to be Christ-centered, academically rigorous, and service-oriented, especially attuned to the needs of the poor, the marginalized, the needy. While we seek to glorify Christ by reaching our full potential as educated citizens and servant-leaders, our desire and calling is to serve others. Let us remember and celebrate that we are an academic institution, a learning community, a school. Dare any of us waste this God-given opportunity to love the Lord with our minds, to grow, to learn, to become? Heaven forbid! Rather, let us read, think, question, dialogue, research, discover, listen, write, create art, music, and literature, exercise, play, pray, worship, do good work, and make friends.[11]

Although the Bible is our guide we dare not commit the sin of bibliolatry, worshiping the Book rather than the Lord to whom the Book points. That would be akin to eating the menu rather than the food to which the menu points.

The Bible is an antidote to all forms of idolatry. When Jesus becomes Lord there is regime change. Whoever, or whatever, has been king, queen, boss, most significant other, addiction, or god, is dethroned. Jesus is Lord.

New life is ordered by "The Way" of Jesus Christ. His teachings, such as the Sermon on the Mount, which features a radical call to enemy-love, forgiveness and purity of heart, His sayings, parables, and example become normative. The cross of Christ saves us mystically, but also practically. We live in light of the cross, ourselves given to God and others. But there is more than a selfless example in play. There is *empowerment* to live the Christ-life thanks to the gift of the Holy Spirit to believers. Game changer!

Is there a place for God in the Christian university classroom? Should there be compartmentalization of our Christian faith? Rather than confine Christ to chapel, or the religion classroom alone, or the office of the campus minister, might faith and learning be integrated into the curriculum? Or shall we practice what George Marsden calls "methodological atheism?"

Since students read their teachers, even if they don't read the textbooks. How important is the hiring of Christian professors? Important questions, these, aren't they? Might not various disciplines be viewed through a Christian lens? After all, Marxist, feminist, gay-lesbian, capitalist, African-American lenses, and others afford important angles of vision for contemplation and conversation in our fields of study. Why not view a subject through a Christian lens, as well?[12]

The integration of faith and learning are a vital part of Christian critical thinking, but so is the interrogation of faith and learning. Jesus questioned much in His day, especially entrenched religious belief and behavior. Should we not question all things, also? Why not? How else do we separate truth and falsehood? Surely truth will stand. Falsehood will not. Why not ask, "What is good? What is true? What is the common good? What does God desire?" Come, let us reason together. For as one devout scholar noted, "The faith that is afraid to think, is not faith at all, but unbelief hiding behind a mask of piety."

To journey from a non-questioning stage of faith, to a questioning stage is a giant step in maturation. To journey onward to a place of commitment to values, faith and learning, even amidst uncertainty is another leap in development. We are not children. We are adults, thinkers, questioners, disciples, revolutionaries for Christ, courageously confronting falsehood, hypocrisy, ignorance, injustice, oppression, and evil. The daring Christian calling is not one lightly accepted. Jesus sternly warned the curious, to "count the cost." Once He probed, "Can you drink from this cup?" Well, can *you*? Can *we*? Frankly, not everyone can, or will. Yet, Christ is calling each of us personally and communally, to follow Him, learn from Him, die to self, be changed; then, in His power and love, boldly go and change the world.

Harry R. Lewis, Harvard professor of more than 30 years, and former Dean of Harvard College, writes in his book, *Excellence Without a Soul*, "I have almost never heard discussion among professors about making students better people." "College," he adds, "at its best, is where students start to understand themselves and to find ideals and objectives for their lives." But, he laments, "Universities have lost the sense that their educational mission is to transform teenagers. … The role of moral education has withered."[13]

Carl Jung, the renowned psychoanalyst, observed, "Among all my patients in the second half of life—that is to say, over thirty-five—there has not been one whose problem in the last resort was not that of finding a religious outlook on life. It is safe to say that every one of them fell ill because he had lost what the living religions of every age have given their followers, and none of them has been really healed who did not regain his religious outlook."

Did Jung say the healing religious outlook must be Christian? He did not. It is enough to say that Christianity provides a religious outlook which is essential for healing. Therefore, we might conclude that a Christian university which rests on the solid foundation of the Word of God, and features the Way of Jesus Christ in its systemic infrastructure, would yield, for those who wholeheartedly buy-in, a wellness of person. This wellness is one of soul, spirit, mind, purpose, and service. Truly Christ-like persons are well persons.

One would expect students, faculty, staff, alumni, trustees, friends, local-state-national-international citizens, to be better persons, church members, citizens, family members, friends, workers, ministers, and volunteers as People of the Way of Christ, than otherwise they would be apart from their transformational relationship with Christ, Christian education, and their faith community experience.

A FEW PRACTICAL WAYS TO MAKE THE CHRISTIAN COLLEGE EXPERIENCE MORE MEANINGFUL

In his book, *Good to Great,* Jim Collins contends, "Good is the enemy of great." He adds, "We don't have great schools, principally because we have good schools." To counter the merit of his claim, a college cabinet might place on the table a question that is never removed: "How can we do better?" Or, "How can we be better?" Collins, however, noted that his research revealed good-to-great companies focused more on what *not* to do, and what to *stop* doing. Both approaches seem valuable. Humility relieves us from the burden of claiming to have all the answers. Humility frees us to ask questions.[14]

One of the things we may want to discontinue is assuming that everyone knows our university mission. Important questions to ask include: What is our mission? Are we achieving it? How can we better ensure our desired outcomes?

Our school's mission is, "To help our students reach their full potential as educated citizens and worldwide servant-leaders." How do we seek to achieve our mission? By integrating academic and Christian excellence within a caring community. We are academically rigorous and service-minded.

Our accrediting agency requires of our university a five-year Quality Enhancement Plan (QEP). In light of our school's mission, we adopted a plan "to integrate undergraduate students' service experiences into the academic setting." Our QEP has two goals: One, "By the end of the five-year plan, our goal is that 70% of students who graduate from Carson-Newman with an undergraduate degree will have had a developmental service-learning experience within their academic discipline. Two, "Our goal is that 80% of those students will show improvement in identified student learning outcomes." Outcomes are assessed by professors using common assessment tools and data. Service-learning activities are adjusted as necessary to help us achieve our goals. (For the past three years our university has been named a national leader in general community service, as cited by the Department of Education, *Newsweek*, and *Washington Monthly*.)

Christian colleges typically require some variation of chapel services. These gatherings afford ideal occasions for community reflection on the school's core values, Christian ethics, and moral moorings. Why should we not be intentional about the moral development of students? Would not this focus make our colleges better places?

Campus assemblies might be used to focus on issues of justice in society. Other chapel ideas include a series of reflections on truth, beauty, and goodness and an honest examination of questions on suffering, doubt, and faith, as well as issues involving diversity and equality.

Some colleges are building residence halls, sometimes known as "living and learning centers." These facilities provide living space for students, but also feature seminar rooms, an apartment to house a professor-in-residence, a fireplace room for conversation and evening guest lectures, and often a dining hall. Guest lecturers may include politicians, professors, professionals from various fields, authors, and others. This approach combining academic and social interests has much to commend itself.

Many universities like to be known by the students they reject, boasting of exceedingly low acceptance rates, often under ten percent. Christian colleges like to be known by the students they accept. Standardized tests are an excellent predictor of family income and support. But what about disadvantaged youth? Measuring logical and linguistic capabilities primarily, college entrance exams, such as ACT and SAT tests, overlook multiple intelligences, as well as work ethic, motivation, honesty, determination, and perseverance. Along with affordability and accountability, accessibility should be a major commitment of the Christian college.

Realizing that countless persons, for various reasons, cannot move to a college campus for an education, most universities have moved to establish online education opportunities and distance learning centers. Technology broadens the net in our attempt to bring together students and learning.

Christian college administrators value both the 14th and 1st amendments to the United States Constitution. Faced with diversity and equity concerns in a rapidly changing world, administrators will surely advocate for equal rights in society for all, while gratefully practicing freedom of religion. Each institution must find the appropriate balance for her core values in a changing world, while each school that is welcoming and loving of all her students will be a better place than otherwise it would be.

CONCLUSION

Few people would likely argue with the critique of our world today as "messed up," a place where things have gone terribly wrong. Crime, war, terrorism, disease, hunger, poverty, greed, addictions, discrimination, human trafficking, promiscuity, torture, homelessness, child abuse, domestic abuse, rape, and countless other unspeakable expressions of evil spread like aggressive cancer throughout humankind. I am not naïve enough to believe that any one of us in Christian university life, nor the entire Christian university system, will somehow transform earth into a planetary Garden of Eden, where we all live happily ever after in Paradise regained.

But what if we fulfilled our calling as Christian universities perfectly? Not possible. Why not? Because there is no such thing as a perfect person, persons, church, Christian college, nor any other system. All systems are made up of imperfect persons. If, however, we cannot serve God and neighbor perfectly, we can certainly serve imperfectly.

I do believe a Christian university and her people can make a huge difference in this world, as Christ has made in each of us who follow Him. Can we make well the hurting and the hurters everywhere? Can we discover the cure for every ailment? How I wish! So we can't change the whole world? True. But we can change the world for one person. And then another. And another. And another. A student, a faculty or staff member, a child, a minority, a family, a victim, one without hope? Can we? Yes, we can!

The Christian university is a home, however imperfect, for pilgrims of the Way, the Truth, and the Life, a sacred place to come to, to become a transformed, educated child of God. It is Holy Ground to journey from to transform other lives in the Spirit of the Christian university's architect, Jesus Christ, our Lord and hope. May students who enter our gates find education, transformation, and aspiration awaiting them to take them in the power of their life's calling to make the world a better place for all of us.

NOTES

1. The material in this section is so well known it is practically public domain. However, one might consult George M. Marsden, *The Soul of the American University: From Protestant Establishment to Established Nonbelief* (Oxford: Oxford University Press, 1994) for reference. See also William

C. Ringenberg, *The Christian College: A History of Protestant Higher Education in America* (Grand Rapids, MI: Baker Academic, 2006) and William F. Buckley, Jr., *God & Man at Yale: The Superstitions of Academic Freedom* (Washington, DC: Regnery, 1977).

2. John Polkinghorne, *Faith, Science and Understanding* (New Haven, CT: Yale University Press, 2000), pp. 24–25.
3. Ibid., p. 27.
4. Francis S. Collins, *The Language of God* (New York: Free Press, 2006), pp. 3, 6.
5. Ringenberg, *The Christian College*, p. 209.
6. Ibid.
7. Harry R. Lewis, *Excellence Without a Soul* (New York: Public Affairs, 2006), p. 5.
8. Ringenberg, *The Christian College*, pp. 209–210.
9. James D. Smart, *The Strange Silence of the Bible in the Church* (Philadelphia: Westminster Press, 1970), p. 144.
10. Ibid.
11. Ibid., p. 143.
12. Ibid., p. 149.
13. Lewis, *Excellence Without a Soul*, pp. xiii, xiv, 5.
14. Jim Collins, *Good to Great* (New York: HarperCollins, 2001), p. 1.

CHAPTER SEVEN

From Either/Or to Both/And

The Journey of a Lutheran College to Interfaith Living

PAUL C. PRIBBENOW
President, Augsburg University

The intrepid Norwegian-Lutheran pioneers who founded Augsburg College almost 150 years ago to educate teachers and preachers for their immigrant communities likely would not have imagined that today, Augsburg—one of 26 colleges and universities affiliated with the Evangelical Lutheran Church in America—would be a leading institution in the interfaith movement. Some might even consider this fact a turn away from the college's founding values and identity.

I would argue, however, that our journey to interfaith living in the 21st century has been possible precisely because we are a college of the Lutheran church, not despite that heritage. Instead of the "either/or" dialectic that creates chasms between insiders and outsiders, those who share the faith and those from other traditions, we have embraced the "both/and" perspective that enables us to be both faithful to the tradition that shaped us and relevant to the diverse cultures and faith traditions that are present in what theologian James Wallis has called "the new America."[1]

In this essay, I will describe the logic that has guided Augsburg on this journey to interfaith living. First, I will address why our Lutheran Christian faith tradition undergirds our commitment to interfaith work. I then will outline how we have undertaken our interfaith initiatives on campus and in the wider community. Finally, I will describe what we are doing across the college and beyond to live out our commitment to interfaith living in 21st century America.

It is my firm belief that our interfaith work at Augsburg is a clear example of how higher education must be willing to change and innovate to respond to changing demographics, social expectations, and democratic values. Being both faithful and relevant is a challenge all of higher education must address as we equip our students for lives of meaning and purpose in the world.

WHY? THE GIFTS OF OUR FAITH TRADITION

Augsburg University will celebrate its 150th anniversary in 2019. Founded originally as a theological seminary in 1869, the college evolved over the decades to become a comprehensive university, defined by excellence in the liberal arts and professional studies, serving more than 3500 students in traditional undergraduate, adult degree completion, and graduate academic programs. Located in the heart of the Cedar-Riverside neighborhood in Minneapolis—one of the most diverse ZIP codes in the country and home to myriad immigrant communities, including the largest Somali community in the United States—Augsburg has become one of the most diverse private colleges in the country. More than 45% of our first-year undergraduate class in the fall of 2016 was students of color. In the spring of 2016, our traditional undergraduate graduating class comprised 42% students of color.

Augsburg also has deepened its student body diversity beyond racial and ethnic categories. Once a haven for students who hailed from the homogenous towns and churches founded by our Northern European Lutheran ancestors, today Augsburg is an institution that welcomes students of diverse cultural and religious traditions. We no longer have the opportunity to assume that our students share our Lutheran faith, and yet we contend that our faith heritage remains critical to our mission and identity—a foundation of core values and practices that continue to shape our academic mission and community life.

In order to address the inherent tension between the diverse students, we serve and the tradition that has shaped our identity, we needed to return to our tradition and name the gifts that make us who we are. During a presidential sabbatical in 2012, I specifically explored those gifts (or charisms) of our tradition—gifts that make us relevant to the needs of the world. Five particular gifts of our Lutheran tradition emerged in my research.

- We have the gift of the theological concept of *vocation*—the belief that God calls us to lives of meaning and significance in the world. We believe that we are called as an academic institution to help students discern their callings and to equip them to live out those callings.
- We have the gift of *critical and humble inquiry*—the belief that already saved through God's salvific act in Jesus Christ, we are freed to seek knowledge and understanding, to ask difficult questions and to make education a central value of a faithful life. We are grounded in the liberal arts, academic freedom, and the search for truth among competing ideologies.

- We have the gift of *engaging the other*—the claim that God's diverse creation is good. We believe that we are called to embrace diversity and otherness, to learn from each other and to build healthy communities.
- We have the gift of *serving our neighbors and seeking justice* in human affairs—the belief that God calls us into relationship with each other and that our neighbors, individually and collectively, demand our love and service. We educate for service and justice in the world.
- We have the gift of *semper reformanda*—the belief that only God is permanent and that all human forms are imperfect and in need of abiding and loving reform. We are well positioned to build institutions that embrace change and value sustainability.[2]

With these five gifts of our tradition articulated, we then began the important work of translating their relevance for our commitment to serving our students in the curriculum, cocurriculum, and community outreach. This work, we argued, was a form of "evangelism," sharing the gifts of our faith with all of our students. This evangelism was not about converting students to our faith, but rather was grounded in the belief that the gifts of our tradition are in fact relevant to the mission-based commitments of the college to "educate informed citizens, thoughtful stewards, critical thinkers, and responsible leaders."[3]

This belief in the relevance of our faith tradition for our identity and mission is informed by the work of Darrel Jodock, emeritus professor of religion at Gustavus Adolphus College, one of our sister schools in the ELCA. Dr. Jodock has developed a schema that describes a continuum of institutional identities, where on one pole reside "sectarian" colleges and universities, those whose identity is grounded in a particular faith tradition, a tradition privileged in the mission and work of the institution. Leading examples of sectarian institutions include Wheaton College in Illinois or Liberty University in Virginia. On the other pole are "nonsectarian" institutions, where religion might be studied but it is in no way a part of the identity or mission of the university. Public institutions would be prime examples of the nonsectarian model.

Between these two poles of institutional mission and identity, Jodock describes what he calls a "third path" institution:

> I would like to suggest that a Lutheran identity commits a college to a third path—one that is neither sectarian nor nonsectarian. Unlike the nonsectarian model, this third path takes a religious tradition very seriously and seeks to build its identity around it, exploring the riches of that tradition as part of its contribution to the community as a whole. But, unlike the sectarian model, it seeks to serve the whole community and in so doing is ready to work with people of other religious traditions—indeed, welcome them into its midst. The sectarian and the nonsectarian models avoid religious diversity, either by withdrawing from it or by minimizing and sidestepping it. The third model takes religious diversity seriously enough to engage and struggle with it, while at the same time remaining deeply committed

> to the importance of its own Lutheran tradition. Rather than an enclave or a microcosm, the third option is a well dug deep to provide something helpful for the entire community.[4]

Jodock's "third path" describes Augsburg's efforts to combine its particular faith tradition with an openness to critical inquiry, learning from others, and equipping our diverse students for lives of meaning and purpose, no matter their paths in the world. It is upon this foundation that we have built our commitment to interfaith living at Augsburg. As Augsburg professor Martha Stortz has written, this stance allows us to claim that "Lutheran institutions pursue interfaith work, not *in spite of* the fact that they are based in a particular religious tradition, but *because* they are based in a particular religious tradition."[5] In other words, interfaith work is not a luxury for our Lutheran college, it is a necessity.

HOW? AN ORGANIZING FRAMEWORK FOR INTERFAITH WORK ACROSS THE COLLEGE AND BEYOND

Having grounded our interfaith commitments in our Lutheran faith tradition, we then began to explore the form these commitments might take on campus and beyond. We were pleased to work with the Interfaith Youth Core (IFYC), an organization founded and led by Eboo Patel and committed to partnering with colleges and universities to ensure that interfaith work is integrated into all aspects of institutional life. A comprehensive audit of Augsburg's curriculum and cocurriculum, along with a survey of students, was conducted by IFYC staff in 2009–10. Its findings were critical in our strategic planning to integrate interfaith work in the college.

One of the most important contributions IFYC made to our work—complemented by the clear-eyed analysis of our institutional opportunities and challenges—was a framework for organizing our interfaith initiatives. When the IFYC staff provided their analysis and recommendations, it was in the context of three key drivers:

- How do students (and others) gain *knowledge* (and understanding) of other faith traditions on campus? Is the work imbedded in the curriculum? Are there community rituals and conversations that enhance knowledge of both your institutional faith tradition and those of others?
- How do students (and others) develop *relationships* with those of other faith traditions? Does the college community have a diverse array of faith traditions in its midst? If not, are relationships with those of other traditions possible in the surrounding community? How does the institution promote interfaith relationships on campus—in the classroom, residence halls, and elsewhere?
- How do students (and others) develop healthy *attitudes* toward those of other faith traditions? How are unhealthy attitudes challenged and reformed? How are healthy attitudes celebrated and extended?[6]

This framework became both a set of criteria to audit the current state of interfaith work on our campus, and also a set of organizing principles to help set priorities for enhancing our interfaith work together. As the next section describes, our work over the past several years has focused on all three aspects of this commitment—building knowledge, developing relationships, and shaping attitudes toward the other.

WHAT? IMPLEMENTING OUR COMMITMENT TO INTERFAITH LIVING AT AUGSBURG

Our journey as a Lutheran college from either/or to both/and, our efforts to faithfully walk the third path, is well underway, though far from complete. In this section, I want to describe in broad strokes where we have focused our interfaith work across the College. I will not attempt to be comprehensive, but rather to offer a glimpse into the on-the-ground efforts underway in four areas: curriculum, campus life, institutional practices, and community engagement.

IN THE CURRICULUM

We know that we cannot leave the challenge of interfaith living to chance. In an academic institution, the way to ensure that all students are introduced to a concept is to imbed it in the curriculum. At Augsburg, all of our undergraduates take two required religion courses. At least one of the courses introduces all students to the gifts of our Lutheran Christian faith tradition. As our faculty reports, these classes populated with students of diverse faith and humanistic traditions quickly turn into interfaith conversations as students share how the concepts they are learning relate, intersect, and perhaps clash with their own beliefs. That, I believe, is what education is about.

In addition, we have committed financial and professional development resources to further integrate our interfaith efforts into our academic program.

- With financial support from the Council of Independent College's (CIC) NetVue initiative (Network of Vocation in Undergraduate Education), our campus ministry office has partnered with faculty and staff to build an interfaith module into our first-year seminar, ensuring that students understand our interfaith commitments early in their college careers.
- We have created an Interfaith Scholars program, coorganized by our campus ministry staff and religion department, in which ten to twelve students of diverse faith backgrounds are selected in a competitive process to participate in a credit-bearing, year-long seminar that includes study of various

faith traditions, relationship-building, and service-learning opportunities in various faith communities.

- In partnership with IFYC, we also have provided professional development opportunities for faculty members—both those who teach sacred texts and those who are facing, perhaps for the first time, a religiously diverse classroom. We don't assume that faculty members are always comfortable with the religious diversity of their students, and we support them in ensuring that their pedagogical strategies are appropriate for diverse students.

IN CAMPUS LIFE

One example of our firm conviction of our Lutheran faith tradition is our practice of daily chapel during the academic year. Certainly most of the attendees at these brief chapel services share our Lutheran and/or Christian faith, but we also have begun to include on the chapel schedule opportunities for interfaith rituals and explorations. Often these chapel gatherings are organized and hosted by Interfaith Scholars.

In addition, we have engaged faculty, staff, community partners, and our campus space planning efforts to support interfaith living on campus.

- Our residence life staff—those responsible for ensuring healthy community in the residence halls—now receive orientation and training about interfaith issues.
- We have created dedicated spaces on campus for non-Christians to meditate and pray, including making our chapel space available for Muslim prayers on Fridays during the academic year.
- Our dining service provider has been a willing partner in responding to the dietary needs of students from diverse faith backgrounds, including providing late-night dining options for Muslim students who fast during the day during Ramadan.
- We have added a Muslim student advisor to our campus ministry staff, believing that it is a source of strength to ground our interfaith work in an office dedicated to the spiritual life of the community.

IN INSTITUTIONAL PRACTICES

Perhaps one of the most challenging areas of promoting interfaith living on campus has been how we embrace and respect diverse faith traditions in our institutional practices. One simple commitment is to be mindful of the calendar and seek to respect the religious holidays of other traditions. For example, we have changed our employee policies to allow faculty and staff to use flexible personal holidays for religious observances.

We also have engaged important and sometimes difficult conversations about how to integrate the rituals of our Lutheran tradition with the needs of a diverse campus community. We still carry the cross in our commencement ceremonies, contending that the cross is a symbol of the tradition that makes us the sort of college we are. At the same time, we have begun to think differently about how we illustrate our commitment to diverse faith traditions by going beyond simply Lutheran Christian practices. For example, at this year's opening convocation for new students, we complemented the traditional Christian invocation and benediction with prayers and readings from several different religious and humanistic traditions. The impact of this simple change in practice was profound—both for new students who witnessed our commitment to honoring both our own tradition and those of others, and for long-time faculty members who were visibly moved by this embrace of our multireligious community.

I will admit that this effort to ensure that institutional practices honor our interfaith commitments is fraught with complexity. Being both faithful and relevant is hard work. In this effort, we count on a community that is both generous and gentle with each other, knowing that we will make mistakes and counting on each other to both hold us accountable and forgive our failings.

IN COMMUNITY ENGAGEMENT

Our experience of the past decade in seeking to honor our commitment to interfaith living has occasioned opportunities to take our work outside of the campus community as well. Right in our own neighborhood, two local Lutheran congregations now partner with the Muslim imams to host interfaith meals and service projects. The local Jewish federation has partnered with us to send our students to Israel for study trips. Our religion courses benefit from regular visits to non-Christian faith communities, extending our teaching and learning community throughout the city.

Perhaps most meaningfully, our interfaith work—seeking to remain faithful and relevant—has been embraced by our Lutheran church body. We are now leading an effort across the 26 colleges and universities of the ELCA to integrate interfaith living in to their diverse contexts and missions. Lutheran congregations across the country are seeking counsel and support from Augsburg to help them learn how to live alongside neighbors of diverse faith traditions. National foundations are looking to Augsburg to develop programs to support interfaith conversations and projects in Christian churches across the country.

Finally, we are proud to have received national recognition for our work from President Obama, whose Interfaith and Community Service Challenge was launched in 2008 and has continued since. Augsburg's interfaith efforts regularly are noted among the most effective among colleges and universities around the country.

INTERFAITH LIVING IN THE 21ST CENTURY

Today, more and more communities look more and more like the neighborhood around our College. The changing face of America, and of our campuses, means that colleges must seek ways to become better neighbors, to lead by example, to learn from our communities. This is innovation for the common good.

Augsburg University started on this path a number of years ago, and we rededicated ourselves to this work in 2008 following a neighborhood tragedy.

That tragedy involved an Augsburg student who was fatally shot outside a community center in our Cedar-Riverside neighborhood of Minneapolis. The student, a young man who was Somali-American and Muslim, had been at the center for a work-study shift to tutor neighborhood children.

As the campus community—grounded in the Lutheran Christian faith—faced this horrific incident, we wrestled with our grief and fear and sought solace in the familiar rituals of our faith. At the same time, we sought to understand our student's faith traditions, and create space for his family and community to mourn.

Shortly after this event, we gathered to address safety concerns of the community. We intended to talk about security cameras and safety patrols that day. Instead, here's what happened: An Imam stood to speak. His first words were "God is good." Though we were a room of people of very different faith traditions, we together could whisper: "Yes, God is good, and this is not what our God wants for us."

In that spirit, our community came together. We rededicated ourselves to the well-being of our neighbors and to interfaith conversation—to talking and living together. Yes, we also have more security cameras and personnel. But the urgency expressed wasn't about the material. The urgency was to find common purpose in the health, safety, and well-being of our neighbors and neighborhood.

As we consider our interfaith work, we are convinced that dialogue and service must be interwoven in all we do. We believe that what we learned through recent efforts to encourage interfaith dialogue with our neighbors is something we must do each day. We must seek to live side-by-side, day-by-day, on campus and within our neighborhood. Interfaith living is what we must—and do—aspire to teach our students.

Our work at Augsburg University is informed by the 20th-century political philosopher and theologian John Courtney Murray, SJ, who writes:

> *"Barbarism ... is the lack of reasonable conversation according to reasonable laws. Here the word 'conversation' has its twofold Latin sense. It means living together and talking together. Barbarism threatens when men cease to live together according to reason, embodied in law and*

> *custom, and incorporated in a web of institutions that sufficiently reveal rational influences.... Barbarism likewise strikes when men cease to talk together ... when dialogue gives way to a series of monologues; when parties to the conversation cease to listen to one another ..."*[7]

Murray's challenge is clear: How shall we recover our capacity for conversation—both genuine living *and* talking together?

I find inspiration for this important work in the example of the late Henri Nouwen, a Roman Catholic priest who wrote a moving challenge for what we are called to be and do in our interfaith living:

> *Hospitality is not to change people, but to offer them space where change can take place.*
>
> *It is not to bring men and women over to our side, but to offer freedom not disturbed by dividing lines.*
>
> *It is not to lead our neighbor into a corner where there are no alternatives left, but to open a wide spectrum of options for choice and commitment.*
>
> *It is not an educated intimidation of good books, good stories, and good works, but the liberation of fearful hearts so that words can find root and bear ample fruit.*
>
> *It is not a method of making our God and our way into the criteria of happiness, but the opening of an opportunity for others to find their God and their way.*
>
> *The paradox of hospitality is that it wants to create emptiness—not a fearful emptiness, but a friendly emptiness where strangers can enter and discover themselves as created free; free to sing their own songs, speak their own languages, dance their own dances; free also to leave and follow their own vocations.*[8]

This is a vision of faithful living and learning that shapes the sort of education we seek to offer at Augsburg University. This is what we believe it means to be faithful to the tradition that grounds mission and identity and relevant to the changing demographics and needs of the world. We must prepare our students for lives in an interfaith world. The ability of today's students to successfully navigate their futures depends upon being able to navigate a world brimming with diverse people with diverse beliefs. That requires innovation and imagination from colleges and universities whose work is at the heart of a healthy and vibrant democracy.

NOTES

1. Wallis, J. *America's Original Sin: Racism, White Privilege, and the Bridge to a New America*, Grand Rapids, MI: Brazos Press, 2016.
2. Pribbenow, P. *Faithful and Relevant: Five Homilies on Augsburg's Vision*, Minneapolis, MN: Augsburg College, 2013.
3. Augsburg College, *Mission Statement*, www.augsburg.edu/mission, accessed October 2, 2016.
4. Jodock, D. "The Third Path: Gustavus Adolphus College and the Lutheran Tradition," Unpublished paper, 2002. https://gustavus.edu/faith/pdf/Third_Path_Article.pdf, accessed October 2, 2016.
5. Stortz, M. "Why Interfaith Work is Not a Luxury," Unpublished paper delivered at the Vocation of a Lutheran College conference, June 8–10, 2016.
6. Interfaith Youth Core, "Interfaith Triangle," https://www.ifyc.org/sites/default/files/u4/Interfaith%20Triangle%20Poster_Final.pdf2010, accessed October 2, 2016.
7. Murray, J. *We Hold These Truths*, New York: Sheed and Ward, 1960.
8. Nouwen, H. *Reaching Out: The Three Movements of the Spiritual Life*, New York: Doubleday, 1975.

CHAPTER EIGHT

A Case Study

Transforming a Catholic Women's College

PATRICIA McGUIRE
President, Trinity Washington University

"Fix it or close it."

With those words, the chair of the board of Trinity College in Washington, D.C., handed me the keys to the President's Office on July 15, 1989. Sister Regina Finnegan, a Sister of Notre Dame de Namur (SND) and my first board chair, was an experienced educational leader who was well versed in the challenges of sustaining undercapitalized Catholic schools for girls and colleges for women in an age of skepticism about single-gender education and rising consumer demands for amenities and prestige at all educational levels.

Trinity, one of the nation's historic Catholic women's colleges, was suffering low enrollment and fiscal crisis when I became president. Many board members doubted whether Trinity could survive, but underneath her stern warning, Sr. Regina was rooting for the turn-around. She and the board chose for this task a brash young public interest lawyer with a big mouth and great enthusiasm for her *alma mater*, but no real executive experience in higher education. Expectations were low, which proved to be a distinct advantage when I turned the key and entered my new office that day.

Trinity (now Trinity Washington University) is a good case study for *Making College Better*. Like many small private liberal arts colleges struggling to sustain mission amid dramatic changes in higher education, Trinity had to find a pathway through years of declining enrollment and fiscal crisis in order to ensure the vitality of its mission for the future. Guided by a thoughtful strategic planning process that revitalized institutional structures, programs, and services, Trinity refocused its once-national outreach to the educational needs of local students in the Washington region, predominantly low-income women of color. Trinity's goal in the process was not mere survival, which would have been an insufficient reason for so much hard work, but a true paradigm shift that made it possible for the University's mission to thrive long into the future.

FORCES OF CHANGE

Founded by the Sisters of Notre Dame as Trinity College in 1897 because the then-new Catholic University would not admit women at the end of the 19th century, Trinity embodied the idea of responding to social change to educate women leaders for each generation. Trinity flourished in the first half of the 20th century as a very small, elite college for mostly Catholic women from the east coast. Trinity's location in Washington lent itself to attracting politically ambitious young women; the alumnae roster includes such luminaries as the first and only woman to be Speaker of the House and now Democratic Leader Nancy D'Alessandro Pelosi '62; former Kansas Governor and then Secretary of Health and Human Services Kathleen Gilligan Sebelius '70; and Maggie Williams '77, who was chief of staff to First Lady Hillary Rodham Clinton in the 1990s.

Like hundreds of orders of religious women in their own schools and colleges, the SNDs founded and sustained Trinity for nearly a century largely through devoting their free labor ("contributed services") to teach and administer the College. But after the Second Vatican Council in the 1960s, the number of Catholic sisters declined rapidly throughout the United States as religious women sought other ministries and fewer young women joined the orders. Across the country, Catholic schools at all levels experienced fiscal crises as the nuns left and lay people arrived who expected salaries, benefits, leave time, career advancement, and modest perks such as air conditioning in the venerable century-old buildings the sisters had managed to erect through enormous sacrifice and hard work. The sisters left Catholic education everywhere with massive aging infrastructures but virtually no endowments; they had been the "living endowment" and their loss was not only spiritual, but very tangible.

Other external social forces conspired to drive Trinity and similar schools ever closer to the precipice: the massive social shift to coeducation in the 1960s and 1970s rocked the world of women's colleges, and the enactment of Title IX in 1972—the law that mandated equality for women in education—dug the hole deeper as women gained not only access to men's campuses but equal access to their more modern and well-equipped facilities, particularly for sports. At the same time, the rise of NCAA Division I men's sports and the consequent television exposure and revenues made major sports universities household names—publicity and funding that smaller colleges simply could not compete against.

The 1960s and 1970s were also a time of robust Defense Department, National Science Foundation, and National Institutes of Health funding for large research universities; and most of the small women's colleges and Catholic colleges with modest science programs did not receive the federal largesse that built the great university laboratories. All of these movements—changes in the Church and religious life, coeducation, big-time college sports, and massive federal investment in research universities—conflated into the perfect storm that took small private institutions to the brink while, ironically, opening a window of opportunity for dramatic transformation.

CONFRONTING THE IMPERATIVE OF CHANGE

When I took office in that hot summer of 1989, Trinity had fewer than 300 traditional-aged students. A graduate program in teacher education and a Weekend College program for adult working women were providing most of the financial support. However, traditional constituencies among alumnae and the faculty longed for a restoration of the "real" Trinity of fond memories—mostly white, Catholic, middle-to-upper-class residential students eagerly pursing English and History majors.

Many of the faculty I encountered at my first faculty meeting in August 1989 had been my teachers when I was a student at Trinity (Class of 1974), and they expected me to lead that grand restoration. Instead, I stunned them and incurred a good deal of wrath by making it clear that nothing short of wholesale rethinking of our academic model and programs would ultimately "save" Trinity.

Trinity had to accept the reality of necessary change. But what kind of change? Was there any hope to retain our historic mission to women? As we moved through the first tumultuous strategic planning process in the early 1990s, we knew that we had to define *why* Trinity should continue at all. I repeatedly challenged the faculty: if we don't know *why* we open the front door every morning, if we are only doing it out of habit, then we should close. Developing a vision for Trinity's true purpose for the future—a purpose that would distinguish Trinity from all of the other colleges and universities in metropolitan Washington—was essential to moving ahead with a successful planning process.

The result of the planning process was a true institutional transformation that sustained core historic values while embracing a "paradigm shift" in the population of students that Trinity served. While Trinity's student body remains more than 90% female, the profile of the students is completely different in terms of race, social class, academic preparation, and career aspirations. Trinity today enrolls more than 2100 students earning degrees at the associate's, baccalaureate, and master's levels in the liberal arts and professional fields. Early in the 21st century, Trinity College became Trinity Washington University to signify the diversification of academic offerings among five academic schools and across three degree levels.

Perhaps more notable, with a more distinctive focus on local students, Trinity's student body became more than 90% African American and Latina, with more than 80% of the full-time first-year students eligible for Pell Grants. Trinity now serves more District of Columbia residents than any private university in the nation, with most of those D.C. students hailing from the neighborhoods on the eastern side of the city, where poverty levels are high. Once 95% white and Catholic, in 2016 Trinity received U.S. Department of Education designation as a Predominantly Black Institution, opening new avenues of funding for program development, laboratories, the library, and other areas of critical innovation investment.

How Trinity reached this result is a case study in managing institutional change.

SUSTAINING HISTORIC MISSION BY CHANGING EVERYTHING

In my first week as Trinity's president in 1989, I asked the admissions director how many students we had from the D.C. Public Schools. She replied, "None." I asked, "Why?" She said, "They can't do the work here."

And nobody at Trinity at that time saw any problem with that statement.

From that day forward, we began the paradigm shift.

Strategic planning became the backbone for managing the kind of change that Trinity had to embrace if we were to have a future. The process focused on mission, values, enrollment, organizational structure, curricula and programs, services, quality, reputation, and infrastructure—not only in terms of facilities, but also technology and human resources.

As Trinity struggled with questions about its strategic future, some constituents truly believed that the restoration of Trinity was possible "if only" a president would come along who knew what she was doing, and "if only" we could get some competent personnel in admissions who knew how to recruit the same kind of students Trinity had in the past. But the past was just that; there was no going back.

Fortunately, the Sisters of Notre Dame, while increasingly few in number on the faculty and staff, still had moral authority and presence on our board. "Why are we trying so hard to reclaim the past," declared one SND at a board meeting, "when there are thousands of women at Trinity's doorstep who could profit from this education? We founded Trinity to make higher education accessible to women, and countless women still find barriers to achievement. Trinity should be open to them." The call to action for social justice was an SND imperative.

Even as the nuns urged us to open wide the doors of opportunity in our full-time undergraduate college, the adult women who were coming in larger numbers to the new Weekend College that one of my predecessors created in the mid-1980s began to see Trinity as a great option for their daughters. Predominantly African American (many single mothers who worked full-time primarily in government agencies), the women came to Trinity to complete baccalaureate degrees so that they could get promoted at work and improve their economic security for their families—and they discovered the real power of liberal learning as personally, intellectually, and spiritually fulfilling beyond the mere economic incentive. They realized the powerful results of an education focused on making women successful. They brought their daughters, first a trickle and then a great wave, a tsunami of demographic change cresting over the once-impermeable granite walls of Main Hall.

A Middle States reviewer looking at one of the Trinity reports during the 1990s said that remaining faithful to our historic primary mission to women was far more provocative and complex than if we had gone coed, and he was right. But eventually, Trinity began to realize success once again as new populations of women discovered at Trinity the kind of educational opportunities they needed to become successful professionals and leaders for their families and communities.

CHANGING CURRICULA AND PROGRAMS

While refocusing Trinity's historic mission to embrace the educational needs of the women of Washington was certainly controversial, an even more complicated battle loomed when it came to reforming the liberal arts curriculum. As part of the strategic planning process, I shared with the faculty a great deal of regional and national data on population trends, workforce demands, and programs at similarly sized institutions. Some faculty were horrified when I presented to the Curriculum Committee some national data about majors and the workforce; the data showed that business administration was the largest major nationally, and healthcare studies such as Nursing were surging.

"We are a liberal arts college!" sputtered one faculty member, "We don't need to talk about trends. Trinity is not *trendy!*" Another fairly shouted at me across the room, "We thought you came to restore Trinity's mission, not destroy it!"

But Trinity already had programs in teacher education, business administration, and other applied disciplines. Our challenge was to lift up the programs that already were enrolling large numbers of students while finding a way to assure the liberal arts faculty that their jobs were secure even if their major programs might not survive into the future. This is the classic conflict at the heart of the academy in times of reorganization: does loss of a major program mean that the discipline must also disappear, or is there a way to give new life to old disciplines in a reorganized curriculum? English, history, philosophy, mathematics, and art history—we considered these disciplines as central to our entire reason for being and the foundation of general education; whether they could continue as majors was a question for ongoing review. Some made it (English, history, math) and some migrated into robust general education programs (philosophy, art history).

As the curricular conversation evolved, the Washington region was also changing dynamically, and employer demands for a differently prepared workforce were mounting. From the earliest days of my presidency, I was involved with local and regional business organizations such as the Greater Washington Board of Trade, the D.C. Chamber of Commerce, the D.C. Public Schools, the Community Foundation of the National Capital Region, and other business and philanthropic organizations working together to improve the economics and social outlook for the Washington region. As a board member with the Washington Hospital Center, I learned about the healthcare workforce needs of the region, particularly in nursing; this discussion led at long last to the creation of Trinity's programs in nursing and other health professions, a long-overdue evolution of our curriculum.

As I worked with the business community, I learned that CEOs deeply valued the outcomes of a great liberal arts education—corporate executives need workers who can think critically, write persuasively, and conduct deep research and analysis. At the same time, the business community wanted technologically proficient workers adept in all of the modern tools of commerce and communication. Rather than sacrificing liberal learning for some kind of job training, my experience with business leaders taught me that they wanted a better integration of all kinds of knowledge, skills, and values to create a more flexible workforce capable of self-directed learning well beyond the classroom. I shared these insights with the faculty; and by the Year 2000, we were able to agree on a renewed mission statement that acknowledged the importance of integrating liberal learning and professional preparation.

CHANGING STUDENT DEMOGRAPHICS

During the years of the Obama Administration, American colleges and universities heard increasingly urgent demands to open doors wider, to welcome more diverse students, to make more space available for low-income students of color, in particular. While many of the nation's most elite colleges and universities have very small proportions of students of color or low-income students in the total mix of their student populations, Trinity and many similar smaller institutions experienced the dynamics of a changing student body at a much earlier moment in time. Our experience on the front lines of change in the racial and social class composition of the collegiate student body can inform contemporary discussions of how more elite institutions must change to welcome more diverse students.

The real change is not found in the act of admitting more low-income students of color. Rather, the real change that institutions must embrace occurs in the services and programs, the cocurricular activities, and entire campus culture that must embody genuine values of justice, fairness, and equity for all students. To make college better for all students, institutions must live those values in all dimensions of academic and cocurricular life.

As we turned our attention to the "thousands of women at Trinity's doorstep" in the District of Columbia and metropolitan Washington, Trinity learned that welcoming a critical mass of low-income students from previously marginalized populations demanded some big changes in curricula and pedagogy, support services, and student financial aid. The students coming into Trinity had some remarkably different characteristics from prior generations, including:

- *Parenting*: Not only the adult students but even some of the youngest students (in their late teens) arrived with children already in tow. We estimate that more than 25% of Trinity students have children, a statistic that mirrors national data on the changing undergraduate student body.
- *Swirling*: Many low-income students "swirl" among academic institutions, earning credits at community colleges and baccalaureate institutions and online as time and money permit, attending full-time and part-time. Nationally, nearly half of all students transfer at least once, and low-income students are more likely to migrate among multiple institutions across a longer timeframe than the traditional 4- to 6-year timetable.
- *Self-supporting*: About one-third of Trinity's full-time traditional-aged undergraduates are self-supporting and "independent" for financial aid calculation purposes, a significant departure from the more typical expectation that younger college students get support from their parents.
- *Working*: Because they are financially independent even at very young ages, and given the economic circumstances of their families, most Trinity students work many hours each week even while caring for families and trying to do their best in coursework.

These and other "nontraditional" characteristics of Trinity students are emblematic of the vast majority of undergraduate students today. According to the U.S. Department of Education, nearly 75% of all college students have one or more of these characteristics, and these require different institutional policies and programs, as well as different faculty dispositions. Staying engaged, on track, and able to meet deadlines is a huge challenge among students for whom going to class is just one of many tugs on their time and attention.

ACADEMIC CHALLENGES

Too many low-income students also suffer from inadequate college preparation as a result of deficiencies in their K–12 schools. Even very bright students from low-income backgrounds struggle with collegiate basics—critical reading, persuasive writing, and advanced numeracy—not because of any intellectual failing on their parts, but because their high school experiences did not prepare them well for college-level work.

As Trinity welcomed more and more students from local public schools and charter schools, the faculty realized that these students needed different approaches in curricula and pedagogy in order to become successful. Trinity's faculty engaged in an intensive revamping of the First Year Experience to emphasize mastery of collegiate-level skills with a major focus on critical reading. After experimenting with foundational courses for several years, the faculty determined that the students would be more engaged and successful through adopting a corequisite model embedding the foundational skills in substantive courses in the disciplines; this approach has led to success in student persistence into second-year and overall retention.

Pedagogy also had to change to engage new kinds of learners in the more complex material of collegiate courses. While Trinity's faculty have long been practitioners of intensely active learning, giving students many opportunities to participate and present in class, even more creative work on pedagogy became necessary to unlock the talents of students who lacked the framework for academic success.

Faculty leadership emerged in several disciplines, notably in the sciences, where faculty engaged students in undergraduate research and campus-wide public poster presentation sessions putting the students on stage to show off their academic success. The science faculty led Trinity students to a larger national stage on which to demonstrate proficiency through engagement in national meetings such as the Annual Biomedical Research Conference for Minority Students where Trinity science majors have won awards for research presentations. With faculty assistance, Trinity science students also earned prestigious summer research internships at notable laboratories at Harvard, MIT, Georgetown, Johns Hopkins, among others. In 2017 the Howard Hughes Medical Institute awarded a $1 million grant to Trinity to promote even greater success for low-income women of color in the sciences.

Seeing the success of the science faculty and students with undergraduate research, psychology and the behavioral sciences soon followed. More recently, with the support of a Mellon Grant, the Arts & Humanities have also embraced the idea of undergraduate research and public presentation as a form of engaging pedagogy to foster student excitement about learning and ultimate success.

Along with changing pedagogy, Trinity's faculty also embraced the need to offer a new menu of major programs. The addition of nursing, in particular—long sought by the local hospital community but resisted by Trinity for years on the grounds that it was an applied discipline and not part of the liberal arts—boosted enrollment overall, and breathed new life into the sciences. As a result of the enrollment growth in healthcare professions and the sciences, Trinity was able to realize a long-deferred dream to build a new academic center, replacing an 80-year-old science building with new labs and classrooms. In fall 2016, the $35 million Payden Academic Center (named for the family of the major donor) opened to the cheers of faculty and students who have found that a modern instructional environment really does improve teaching and learning.

LISTENING TO NEW AND DIFFERENT VOICES

Race and social class are powerful forces for division and conflict in American life; and no one should be surprised, particularly in the age of Black Lives Matter, that many campuses often find themselves experiencing great turmoil when racism surfaces within the community, or when barriers to affordability and access become clarion calls for change. As Trinity enrolled more African American and Latina students from low-income backgrounds, some constituents mourned a perceived loss of elitism, while others wondered aloud if these new students would ever be as loyal and generous to Trinity as the older alumnae. Trinity had to confront the racism inherent in the resistance that claimed that we were somehow changing our mission by changing the racial and economic composition of the student body. Some of the resistance was masked in concern for religion: "We don't mind diversity," said one alumna to me at a forum on the changing face of Trinity, "But are they Catholic?" We clearly had a lot of work to do!

At the same time, the rising numbers of students of color also had big expectations for Trinity; like Trinity Women across the ages, they were not shy about raising their voices. We had robust discussions about the canon of learning and the voices reflected in the literature; artistic, historical, and scientific role models were presented for student consideration. Over time, with a great deal of dialogue and often urgent argumentation, faculty adapted syllabi to incorporate more voices of black and Hispanic writers, scholars, and actors on the world stage, starting modestly with Maya Angelou and Toni Morrison in literature courses, and the addition of courses such as "Inequality" in sociology—but soon embracing a rethinking of history and the role of slavery in shaping the American experience, and soon on to discovery of Henrietta Lacks (the African American woman donor of HeLa cells used in medical research) and the black women mathematicians whose stories are now emerging as the "Hidden Figures" in the formative years of the NASA space program.

Some of the changes occurred because Trinity also took a deliberative approach to recruiting more faculty of color—scholars who saw in the students at Trinity the opportunity to expand their own approaches to pedagogy and the canon. Changing faculty perspectives—through retirements, new hires, and extensive faculty development—became essential to the ability to adapt curricula and pedagogy for the new student body. Trinity's faculty in 2016 is close to 50% African American, Latino and Asian—dedicated scholars who are eager to develop innovative methods and courses that engage new populations of previously marginalized students.

KEEPING COLLEGE AFFORDABLE

How does Trinity do it? That's the most frequently asked question I get from people interested in Trinity's model but wary of the financial implications. With a very small endowment (about $15 million) and a very needy student population, the calculus is daunting. Over the years, we have learned how to manage finances successfully while making sure that Trinity remains affordable for our students. The keys are a certain habit of frugality—something we credit to the religious women who founded Trinity; a strong business plan without which all good intentions quickly evaporate; and a great network of partners who carry a large share of the financial need of our students.

Transforming Trinity into a modern institution with appropriate academic infrastructure and technologies while also keeping Trinity affordable has been our greatest challenge. The strategic planning initiatives of the early 1990s tackled the challenge in several ways:

- *Diversification of programs*: To mitigate the financial risk inherent in having just one major "product line"—the full-time undergraduate liberal arts college—through the strategic planning process of the 1990s, Trinity fully embraced the fundamental business principle that multiple revenue streams were essential to safeguard against enrollment decline in any particular program. Leveraging existing graduate programs for teachers and working professionals, Trinity created multiple academic units to offer different kinds of programming to diverse student markets in various delivery formats. The College of Arts & Sciences continued as the full-time daytime undergraduate women's college, while, over time, Trinity added four coeducational professional units, including the School of Education, School of Professional Studies, School of Business and Graduate Studies, and School of Nursing and Health Professions.
- *Identification of growth projects*: Trinity's strategic planning process included a disciplined approach to choices about new programs. Trinity's location in a healthcare-rich neighborhood of Washington supported creation of the programs in Nursing, Occupational Therapy, and other health professions. Other new academic programs such as Criminal Justice, Early Childhood Education, and Strategic Communications emerged as a result of market research on workforce projections in the Washington region and estimates

of likely enrollments as well as partnerships with local schools and businesses. The financial template for all new programs required a three-year plan to demonstrate enrollment growth and profitability.

- *Choosing infrastructure projects wisely*: At some point, no matter how committed we were to cost controls, we realized that Trinity had to build-out the infrastructure in order to be competitive in the marketplace for students. Too much frugality undermines institutional success in the long run. In the last two decades, supported by charitable gifts as well as institutional revenues, Trinity made three multimillion-dollar infrastructure investments that were essential to make the living/learning experience better for students and to improve delivery of the academic programs, including:
  (a) development of a modern technology infrastructure to support all academic programs and institutional communications;
  (b) creation of the Trinity Center for Women and Girls in Sports to provide modern spaces for sports, recreation, wellness, and fitness programs as well as added capacity for major conferences and auxiliary programming that bring in additional revenues; and
  (c) building the Payden Academic Center to replace outmoded classrooms and laboratories and to provide a modern teaching and learning environment for all students, with pervasive state-of-the-art technologies in all instructional spaces.
- *Development of partnerships*: The early 1990s planning processes made it clear that the vitality of Trinity's future depended on the College's ability to work in partnership with the city, the corporate and philanthropic communities, and partners in schools, hospitals, and non-profit agencies. By developing strategic partnerships with organizations such as the Girl Scouts, Medstar Health, and the Women's Sports Foundation, Trinity raised its visibility and created programs that widened its circle of friends and supporters. Partnerships made it possible for Trinity to identify new sources of funding for student scholarships as well as the necessary development of new facilities.

As a result of strong planning and careful cultivation of strategic partnerships, Trinity gained financial strength and found new sources of support. Alumnae donations increased, as did donations from new friends who never considered supporting Trinity in the past, but liked what they saw in the "new" Trinity. One major philanthropist contributed millions to scholarships for low-income women in D.C. who wanted to become nurses; another philanthropist contributed an equally large amount for scholarships for Dreamers, undocumented students who have exceptional promise but cannot get federal financial aid. Working with a coalition of the business and political communities, Trinity was able to gain support for D.C. students through the D.C. Tuition Assistance Grant program, the D.C. College

Access Program, and the D.C. College Success Foundation—all programs that Trinity engaged as partners in support of low-income students from the city.

Trinity remains a frugal institution as a matter of longstanding habit, and also as a sign of commitment to keeping college affordable for our students. Trinity strives to keep tuition low while providing an extensive array of grants and scholarships to help students manage the cost of attendance. Nearly all full-time undergraduate students receive Trinity grants worth 40% or more toward tuition; and many receive other grants that, along with Pell Grants, cover the full tuition price.

At a time when the national spotlight is focusing ever more sharply on college affordability and access for low-income students of color, Trinity's model is one that exemplifies the fact that a high-quality private college education can be accessible and affordable for low-income students. Trinity's experience clearly illustrates that "making college better" includes making sure college remains affordable.

At the same time, Trinity also knows that even very low-income students need, and demand, high-quality academic programs, a comfortable learning environment, modern technologies, and a wide range of support services. Ultimately, "making college better" requires continuous active listening to student needs and expectations; careful budgeting to invest in what makes a real difference for students; and development of a nimble institutional culture that can be flexible and responsive as circumstances change.

Trinity's story is far from complete; transformation is never over. The most important test of Trinity's successful model of change will not be found in what has already occurred, but in the University's ability to continue to welcome, educate, and ensure the success of many new student populations far into the future.

PART TWO

Views FROM THE Public Sector

CHAPTER NINE

Learning to Thrive

A Perspective from Texas Woman's—A Large Public University

CARINE M. FEYTEN
President and Chancellor, Texas Woman's University

> *"What I find amazing about the TWU experience is how everything came together in such a way as to alter the course of my life toward success … close connections to faculty fueled academic achievement that transformed my mindset."*
>
> —COURTNEY JOHNSON, TEXAS WOMEN'S UNIVERSITY (CLASS OF 2015)

For at least the last two decades, the overwhelming emphasis in U. S. higher education has been, rightly, on career preparation. As the cost of attending college has risen to unprecedented levels, students and families often see college primarily as the pathway to a good job. Helping support the economy of the nation with new ideas and research-based innovation is part of the reason why universities exist and receive taxpayer support, and preparing our students for career success is central to this public mission. We in public higher education especially embrace that role.

At the same time, however, there is growing recognition on our campuses, among employers, and among our graduates, that job training alone is not what public higher education, at its best, must aspire to offer to America's young people. We in universities run the risk of graduating people with solid technical knowledge and skills but a weak sense of personal direction. Our students may be skilled in business, computing, or nursing, but they may not understand their own motivations, values, or relationships. They know the "what" of their future careers, but they cannot always articulate the "why." They may graduate with only the smallest understanding of how the powerful intellectual and moral traditions of the world have answered such values questions.

A further challenge today is coming from technology: Because abundant information is available through the Internet, and at a time when many universities, including my own, offer substantial coursework online, we must increasingly ask what "value added" does the in-person, face-to-face campus experience bring? We must recognize that higher education has to serve a deeper purpose than merely to produce career-ready graduates as efficiently as we produce widgets.

On my campus, Texas Woman's University, and I believe across the nation, the energy and creativity for making college better is coming from students themselves. They are hungry for purpose, passion, and meaning in their lives. They want to understand the choices and decisions that will affect their future. They do want good jobs, but they also want to understand the pressures they will face and choices they must make in their future lives to keep themselves healthy—physically, mentally, socially, financially, and spiritually. They yearn for multifaceted education of the whole person, and not merely lectures imparting information that is readily obtained on YouTube.

Faculty, too, want to see change: they want their students to have more time for reflection, for deliberation, and to take advantage of a range of opportunities for active learning. College should be a time of intellectual adventure and self-discovery—not a box-checking exercise on the way to the job market. Making college better begins with reclaiming our purpose as educators and seekers, recognizing each member of our community as a whole person, and acting on that recognition.

WHAT GRADUATES SAY: THE GALLUP-PURDUE SURVEY

The 2015 Gallup-Purdue Index brings hard data about what counts in the higher education experience.[1] This index was created from interviews with more than 60,000 U.S. college graduates, and dramatically demonstrates that the character of a student's experiences in college makes a dramatic impact on postcollege success and satisfaction and this far outweighs the impact of where one studies, or even what one earns. The number one influence on graduates' future thriving was feeling that at least one adviser or faculty member cared about them; the index also lends support to active learning experiences, such as internships, capstone courses, and team projects as practices that bring high and lasting impact. As the report says, "Feeling supported and having deep learning experience means everything when it comes to long-term outcomes for college graduates."[2]

The survey identified five key areas of well-being that higher education can shape—purpose, social, community, financial and physical. Sadly, only 11% of university graduates are thriving in all five elements; more than one in six report not thriving in any of these dimensions. These data, supported by the voices and experiences of our students, faculty and alumni, necessitate a call to action and renewal for American higher education: Making college better means helping our graduates learn to thrive, not just for a semester, or a year, but for a lifetime; it means providing a range of choices, connections, and experiences that build a foundation for the growth of the whole person. We in academic leadership must make college better by, first and foremost, listening to these diverse voices on our campuses.

TRACKING THE DELTA: WHAT IS THE REAL VALUE ADDED OF ANY HIGHER EDUCATION EXPERIENCE?

The Economist has taken an intriguing approach to ranking colleges by going beyond average salaries and endowment sizes to focus instead on how much value is added to earning power by each institution, relative to its peers.[3] That is the "delta"—the change in a student by an institution or a program, which the editors calculate through statistical modelling. The results of this analysis were instructive. It found that some institutions made a huge impact on a trajectory of their students' lives. Texas Woman's, I'm proud to say, ranks 45th in the nation on *The Economist*'s list—beating out some of the Ivy League and other well-known and prestigious U.S. institutions. It is clear by these metrics that we make an impressive difference: our students are indeed transformed, and their lives and careers energized by their experience.

We do prepare them well for their careers, but I believe we also earned this ranking because we understand their education in much more expansive contexts. Ideally, we want to see this "delta" for all students, and across all aspects of their lives: to meet them wherever they are, whether A students or C students, and challenge them to reach their full potential and promise as informed citizens, contributing professionals, and compassionate human beings. Seeking this delta, the "before" and "after," in all our students' and graduates' lives, is a particularly powerful imperative for public institutions with their mission of service and adding value to the community. Texas Woman's secret in achieving this result? I think the answer is that we pay close attention to the full range of developmental concerns of our students—in their career goals, in their growth as creative and engaged members of their community, and in becoming healthy individuals.

Failing to do this because we must devote more time and resources to job training is not, in the end, serving our public mission very well. Employers of millennials report that more than half of them begin looking for a new position within just six months of getting their first job. That astonishing and costly turnover comes at least in part because these young people feel unfulfilled and uncertain of their purpose. Clearly, for many of these young graduates, one-dimensional training for the first job alone was not enough. Yet such restlessness is costly, for companies and for communities. Colleges, not workplaces, are the best environments to begin seeking for life's purpose, and to learn to see one's career in larger, and personally meaningful, terms: providing opportunities for such explorations is essential to the overall "delta" of growth that we seek.

Reclaiming this mission requires those of us in higher education to see the student experience as one single whole. We must get beyond the "inside the classroom" and "extracurricular activities" split and see the experience of university from the student point of view, which means blending academic offerings with student support services. This may be a daunting task on many campuses, but I believe this is the central challenge for America's college today.

HELPING STUDENTS THRIVE: MAKING TEXAS WOMAN'S UNIVERSITY BETTER

Every institution will answer this challenge in terms of its own history, mission, goals, and strengths. Texas Woman's University has a particular niche that makes us, perhaps, unique in the United States. We are the nation's largest institution—almost 16,000 students strong—that primarily serves women and one of only two public U.S. universities where the education of women is the primary mission.

This mission for women's education gives us other responsibilities: because we know that, historically, one of the fastest ways to a better quality of life and other social and economic improvements in a community is through educating women. We at Texas Woman's believe we have a particular contribution to make in strengthening the communities we serve. This is heightened by our many degree programs in the health professions, which are pursued by more than half of our students, and a long tradition of committing ourselves to serving others. Our graduates, in turn, will help to educate and influence their patients, colleagues, friends, and neighbors, creating a better future for the state of Texas, the nation, and the world. We also have many connections to other kinds of service: many of our students and graduates serve in the U.S. armed services, for example, and interest in veterans support plays a part in our strategic plan. Some of our alumnae have achieved particular distinction: Major General Mary Saunders, for example, is the first African-American woman to serve as director of transportation for the U.S. Air Force. Such distinguished graduates inspire our current students to delve deeply into the meaning of service in their own lives and careers.

Texas Woman's is also diverse: More than half of our students are first- generation college students, and approximately 20% of our students are African American and 25% Latino. Forty-nine percent are eligible for Pell grants.[4] Except for the large percentage of women (90% of our students are female), Texas Woman's is today, demographically, what all of American higher education is expected to look like in 2040. That means the voices at Texas Woman's are providing a clear signal about where America's universities are heading.

What are these voices saying? Throughout 2014–16, Texas Woman's engaged in a comprehensive strategic planning process, producing a plan that was accepted by our Board of Regents in November 2016. This was a tremendous experience for all of us, involving hundreds of students and faculty at every level and every stage of the plan. The students, faculty, and staff responded with big ideas, enthusiasm, and imagination to every iteration in the process until we achieved consensus.

Our plan, like any good strategic plan, does not attempt to reinvent or turn Texas Woman's into something it is not; rather it builds on the solid strength and special character of our past. The call to active service, which was part of our founding vision as a woman's college, underlines every aspect of our campus culture and educational offerings.

We clearly reaffirmed our commitment to our distinctive areas of focus:

- Women and **leadership**;
- An emphasis on **education** in **health**;
- A commitment to experiential learning, service learning, or "**learning by doing**;" and
- An embrace of our obligation to improving the quality of life for **veterans**.

The task this plan sets for us now is to make Texas Woman's University better by refreshing and renewing our practices and aspirations in each of these areas of distinction. We are now asking ourselves: What does it take to support our graduates in learning to thrive—physically, financially, mentally, and spiritually? What does it mean to help students live a life of purpose?

ALL ARROWS MUST POINT IN THE SAME DIRECTION: SUPPORTING STUDENT HEALTH AND WELL-BEING

To illustrate our approach, consider one area of Gallup-Purdue's five dimensions of thriving, that of physical health and well-being. This is a natural for Texas Woman's, since half of our students major in health-care fields. They understand the theory behind good nutrition. From their coursework and required reading, they also are acutely aware of statistics about the personal and societal costs of poor diets in terms of the national (and even global) obesity epidemic, the impact of diet on disease, and so on. But when it comes to making good personal choices about their own diets and what they are doing in their own homes and families, there sometimes is a disconnect—classroom knowledge does not always translate into healthy decision making.

The task we set ourselves as educators of the whole person, then, is to integrate student self-care education with academic studies. This means creating close linkages between what goes on inside the classroom with what happens outside. It means enhancing our commitment to faculty research, and allowing students to see how research findings can shape their own lives and choices.

Changing culture in this way is a special challenge for us because more than 75% of our students are commuters. By broadening the conversations between students, faculty advisers and instructors to demonstrate this care for the whole person, we want to take on issues of how students make choices in their own trips to the grocery store, the kitchen, or at the fast food restaurant. By demonstrating care and concern for the broader context of student life, we can see that commuter students and graduate students are as engaged as those living on campus.

Such integration requires aligning every part of the university—curriculum, advising, internships, student affairs, dining, design, and facilities—to act in support of this goal. It means adopting environmental policies and sustainability practices that enhance the health and well-being of the planet. All arrows must shoot in the same direction so that we as a university share in living out and acting on our values and commitments to good nutrition and positive health care choices.

To implement these various initiatives, we sought and won foundation funding for a health and well-being initiatives coordinator. This person will be working with all campus constituencies to institute best practices along many dimensions of health and well-being. We are working with vendors to ensure healthier options in dining halls and campus eateries; we want to engage students in making and preparing food. We are encouraging sharing meals as a way of connecting to others and building relationships. We are considering a community garden by repurposing some land near our campus. We hope to add a spiritual dimension, with a meditation garden, cultivating quiet and beauty as another dimension of health. Designing internships that engage students in working on nutrition in the real world is another option. To measure our progress, we will be collecting data through pretesting and posttesting and, above all, listening to our students. We will share these outcomes with all our constituencies. Our goal is that in all dimensions of our university's life, we will reflect our convictions about the meaning of health and well-being. With active and multifaceted engagement around these ideas—in course readings, in assignments, in interactions on campus with faculty, staff, and classmates—TWU's young people will learn by doing and live out values actively and purposefully. Their daily options and choices will reflect what they know about good nutrition, fitness, and health along many dimensions. All of this aligns directly with our core educational goals, both through the state of Texas and through accreditation improvement plans. It also can align with our commitment to policies that enhance the life of the planet, and address long-term sustainability of our practices.

One early success in this respect was in the national Outdoor Nation Campus Challenge, a fun competition to get students outside and active—another feature of health and well-being that is important to us. TWU student, faculty, and staff enthusiasm buoyed us to place #3 in the country—rather good for a commuter school that is relatively small compared to giants such as The Ohio State University and University of Central Florida! I have also instituted what we call "Rolling Meetings with the Chancellor," where students and I bike together around the campus and the community, stopping from time to time to talk, share our hopes and concerns, or noticing something we could improve. It has been a very enjoyable way to conduct meetings and create wonderful relationships with students.

We are also looking to working with learning technologies to motivate healthy choices. Today's young people organize their lives with technology, whether it is managing a shopping list, looking for restaurant choices, or monitoring physical activity on their Fitbits. Students are a great source of ideas for how to use mobile devices and social media in assignments, life skills, and sharing good ideas. Faculty are critical to this success, as they are to everything on our campus. TWU students tell me again and again about "their" faculty members who are caring, approachable, and always encouraging. Faculty led the creation of our strategic plan and are driving its implementation: they are invested in the direction of their fields and of the entire University for the future, and are seeking for ways to connect student academic activity into the broader context of their lives, careers, families, and communities. We are seeking to find resources to enhance the scope of research and creative inquiry across all disciplines. Fortunately for this process, TWU is a very collaborative institution: we are relatively free of siloed programs and disciplines, so the faculty are very comfortable in working with colleagues, both staff and other faculty. We are bringing together, quite intentionally, some activities that fall under the Office of the Provost with the Vice President for Student Life.

AT THE TABLE OR ON THE MENU? THE IMPORTANCE OF LEADERSHIP OPPORTUNITIES

Expanding leadership opportunities for our students is another key goal of our strategic plan and another vital way to make college better by educating the whole person. This takes on special importance given our focus on the education of women. Even in the second decade of the 21st century, it is still true that many young people, especially young women, do not see themselves as leaders; they do not readily recognize that they have what it takes to be in charge of a project or an organization.

Reshma Saujani, founder and CEO of the organization Girls Who Code, an organization devoted to closing the gender gap in technology, theorized in a recent TED talk that girls are less likely to seek leadership roles because they are socialized to perfection, while boys are socialized to bravery. When boys fail, they are brave for having tried and just need to try again to get it right. When girls fail, they are told it is because they just were not good enough and should not have played in the first place.[5]

Showing girls that they can develop a bravery mindset is profoundly important for our nation's future. TWU, like other institutions primarily serving women, has an advantage over co-ed institutions in this respect. Only two percent of women undergraduates in the U.S. today enroll at institutions primarily for women, but consider the disproportionate impact this two percent are having every day:

- 20% of women in the U.S. Congress went to a women's college;
- 30% of women on *BusinessWeek*'s 2016 list of rising business stars went to a women's college;
- 33% of the female board members of Fortune 1000 companies are women's college graduates; and
- 20% of women identified by *Black Enterprise* magazine as the 20 most powerful African-American women in corporate America graduated from women's colleges.[6–8]

The data are overwhelming: women's colleges seem to do better at producing women leaders, simply because women have to do things on our campuses. They are socialized to act, take risks, and be brave. Women-serving institutions, just by their nature, empower young women to step up and take on responsibilities—to learn the bravery, it's-OK-to-fail mindset. Data show that this clearly serves women—and our nation—for the future.

By extension, by the way, this bravery mindset phenomenon likely applies to people who are marginalized because of race, ethnicity, country of origin, religion, sexual orientation, socio-economic status, or any other demographic labels. So this imperative of leadership, at its core, is perhaps to create a space where low-stakes failure is affirmed as leadership development.

What this imperative is suggesting is that this should not be happenstance: it should be integrated into the TWU experience as a whole. We are intentionally focusing on leadership development opportunities that will empower all our students, faculty, and staff.

I like to say to our students: "Either you have a place at the table, or you may be on the menu." They appreciate this idea, especially if they feel like they have been on the menu before. (I usually add that it is also better to be at the head of the table!)

Teaching leadership and the bravery mindset is teaching that it is normal to fail. We do this by offering a continuum of work, in stages: We start with small everyday habits, like learning to speak up in class, and then moving up to being part of a team project, or helping to organize a community or campus event. By encouraging and giving constructive feedback on these efforts at each step, faculty and student affairs staff can align their efforts by encouraging students to take on more ambitious challenges, such as identifying, framing, and solving a problem for a community health clinic, or leading a student organization, or even starting their own companies or NGOs. Also, since no one can be at the head of every table all the time, everyone needs to learn to do what she can from where she is; there are many ways to support a team mission and expand one's sphere of influence in any given situation—whether that is in a family, in a job, in a community, or a nation.

Consider the experience of one recent graduate Courtney Johnson, whom I quoted in the opening to this essay. Courtney entered TWU with marginal grades and not much sense of direction. She was barely motivated to take classes that would prepare her for a good job, and reluctantly began taking math and science, where she admits, she quickly was overwhelmed. She credits a faculty member with working patiently with her to build up her math skills. Working with this faculty member gave her the support and confidence she needed. "I experienced a sudden shift in mindset," she writes, "Not only could I do these things I'd feared, I would do them; whatever it took I would find a way." Courtney's story sums up the TWU growth "delta" achieved through a mix of supportive academic experiences, personal development, and a bravery mindset. Today she is in a Ph.D. program in chemistry at an elite graduate school, and is, in turn, an inspiration to our current students. I am confident she will have an amazing career.[9]

IMPLEMENTING IMPROVEMENTS: IT'S NOT ONLY ABOUT MONEY

As noted above, crucial to the success of our plans is that the University take a fully integrated approach: every part of our operations, our facilities, our organizational incentives, and our educational activities must reflect our drive for the education of the whole person. We need to live out in every way this core commitment to development of the five dimensions of thriving that underpin lifelong success for our graduates.

Funding, of course, is always centrally important in making new things happen at a university, and aligning budget priorities to our goals is definitely part of the picture. Some of our proposed actions do cost more, such as expanding the range of healthy food choices on campus; in those cases, we must get creative with our budgets and even raise additional funds. Not everything can be implemented immediately; phasing in innovations as we can afford them is essential. TWU has generated additional support for these goals from both public and philanthropic sources, and we intend to do more of this as we share success stories with our alumni, friends, and public agencies.

But many of these changes do not require much, if any, additional funding: this is much more about a change in policy, program, and attitude. It does not cost any more to build into our curriculum new opportunities for students to reflect on their learning experiences more intentionally and purposefully and to share these reflections with each other. Making use of existing learning and social media technologies in all our learning processes is clearly important, but there is not much additional cost required to do that. We already have student advisers in place—they can be supported and encouraged to expand their conversations with students to include appropriate discussions about health and well-being. We can offer informal courses on such topics as managing student loans or cooking on a budget that cost little to present. Spreading a mindset of bravery can be done with more intentional coordination and connection between academic offerings and student affairs programs that already exist.

Above all, academic leadership's tone is crucial; acting on our behavior and principles begins at the top. We can insist on policies that respect the dignity of every member of our community, and be willing to discuss these principles as a community. We can find ways for faculty and staff to share thinking about their own health and well-being habits, struggles, and challenges; we can engage with campus constituents over a range of topics in new ways—like my Rolling Meetings do.

All of these new goals present an awesome and exciting challenge for those of us in leadership. Change takes time, patience, many meetings with university stakeholders, and a willingness to experiment with new ideas and approaches; there are trade-offs and, as always, some difficult decisions have to be made.

But it is worth it. Shortly after I moved to TWU in 2014, I met one of our graduates, a nurse in a local hospital. She was thrilled to meet the new TWU Chancellor. She told me about how she came to TWU as a single mother of four with $100 to her name. She was terrified about going to college, but passionately determined to improve her work skills so she could provide for her kids. She told of how faculty helped and encouraged her at every step, and she was bursting with pride over her achievement of a nursing degree. She felt that Texas Woman's recognized and valued her as a whole person, and she told me that attending our University had not only changed the direction of her life, but the lives of her children and every generation after that! *Every generation after that!*

This TWU nurse is absolutely right: positive transformations for our students have ripple effects over time. The university experience can alter the trajectory of many lives and spill over into families, workplaces, neighborhoods, states, nations and the planet as a whole. That is the hoped-for outcome that gives purpose and meaning to our own task as educators and fuels our motivation to keep on making college better.

SUMMARY

While preparation for careers remains a vital role for public higher education, recent research, such as the Gallup-Purdue Survey, confirms that making college better will require university educators to address the growth of the whole person. At Texas Women's University, a new strategic plan is guiding decisions across all University activities and services that address the student experience holistically. While we are building academic skills, we are also looking for opportunities to make measurable improvements in the quality of student lives—in their sense of confidence and positive mindset, in their communications skills, and in their ability to make productive choices for their own financial, physical, mental, and spiritual health. An example at TWU is the goal we have across the campus to support students in making healthy choices in food and nutrition. Such an education, broadly speaking, provides enduring positive impact for individuals, their families, communities, and the world.

NOTES

1 Gallup. (2015). *Great Jobs. Great Lives. The Relationship Between Student Debt, Experiences and Perceptions of College Worth*. Retrieved from http://www.gallup.com/reports/199172/gallup-purdue-index-report-2016.aspx
2. Gallup. (2014). *Great Jobs. Great Lives. The 2014 Gallup-Purdue Index Report: A study of more than 30,000 college graduates across the U.S.* Page 4. Retrieved from http://www.gallup.com/reports/197141/gallup-purdue-index-report-2014.aspx
3. The value of university: Our first-ever college rankings. (2015, October 29). *The Economist*. Retrieved from http://www.economist.com/blogs/graphicdetail/2015/10/value-university
4. Texas Higher Education Coordinating Board. (Spring 2016). *2016 Texas Public Higher Education Almanac*. Retrieved from http://www.thecb.state.tx.us/almanac
5. Saujani, R. (2016, Februrary). Teach girls bravery, not perfection. *TED*. Retrieved from http://www.ted.com/talks/reshma_saujani_teach_girls_bravery_not_perfection
6. Hennessey, R. (2013, February 6). What's in A Women's College? *Forbes*. Retrieved from http://www.forbes.com/sites/rachelhennessey/2013/02/06/whats-in-a-womens-college/
7. Jones, A. (2015, April 29). The end of Sweet Briar College and the problem with women's colleges. *Newsweek*. Retrieved from http://www.newsweek.com/2015/05/08/end-sweet-briar-college-and-problem-womens-colleges-326363.html
8. Salomone, R. C. (2008, October). *Same, different, equal: Rethinking single-sex schooling*. New Haven, CT: Yale University Press.
9. Johnson, C. Personal communication on December 16, 2016.

CHAPTER TEN

Making College Better Through A Reimagined Undergraduate Research Focus

BEVERLY WARREN
President, Kent State University

As president of a large public research university, I am pleased to share my thoughts on the role that engaging undergraduate students in research plays in making the college experience better. While exposure to research experiences and methods at the undergraduate level has long been viewed as a top priority by the most academically talented students—particularly those in the sciences—we are seeing evidence across the curriculum that prospective students (and their parents) from a wide variety of backgrounds are seeking a college environment that promises engaging and distinctive learning experiences. In a public research university, there are many types of learning experiences that meet that expectation; however, research opportunities, including those in the arts, are those we are uniquely positioned to provide. With a renewed focus and energy, we are making college better at Kent State University through expanded access to authentic and meaningful undergraduate research experiences.

THE EMERGENCE OF UNDERGRADUATE RESEARCH

The Carnegie Foundation for the Advancement of Teaching is often credited with significantly advancing the importance of undergraduate research in the U.S. through its sponsorship of the Boyer Commission on Educating Undergraduates in the Research University report titled, *Reinventing undergraduate education: A blueprint for American's research universities* (1998). The Commission asserted that inquiry-based learning is the distinctive obligation and responsibility of a research university:

> Universities need to take advantage of the immense resources of their graduate and research programs to strengthen the quality of undergraduate education, rather than striving to replicate the special environment of the liberal arts colleges. There needs to be a symbiotic relationship between all the participants in university learning that will provide a new kind of undergraduate experience available only at research institutions. Moreover, productive research faculties might find new stimulation and new creativity in contact with bright, imaginative, and eager baccalaureate students, and graduate students would benefit from integrating their research and teaching experiences. (pp. 7–8)

The Boyer Commission's conclusions are echoed by Gonzalez (2001) who suggests the knowledge economy is calling for college graduates with the skills and dispositions that research cultivates. She advocates for greater alignment between the undergraduate and graduate student experiences in U.S. research universities, where undergraduate students require more experience with research and graduate students are seeking more access to mentoring and advice, supports that are typically associated with undergraduate student needs. According to Gonzalez, "Graduate and undergraduate students are usually seen as having very different goals and needs, a view that derives from history rather than from current realities" (p. 1625). She adds:

> The historical separation between graduate and undergraduate education has obscured the connections among the research university's five levels of learning, as well as the university's mission, which is to introduce students to research, to inspire in them a passion for discovery through teaching and mentoring of the highest intellectual and moral caliber at each of these levels. (p. 1626)

According to a study by Hu, Kuh, and Gayles (2007), in the nearly two decades since the Boyer Commission's report, undergraduate research initiatives have expanded not only on the campuses of research universities, but among all institution types. Interestingly, the increases at selective liberal arts colleges exceeded those at research universities. The authors concluded, "If research universities wish to provide enriching educational opportunities consistent with their distinctive research mission, they need to create more inquiry-oriented education opportunities for students" (p. 175).

Other studies have pointed to links between undergraduate research and student success and persistence, demonstrating that research can be an effective form of engagement. The Undergraduate Research Opportunity Program at the University of Michigan, targeted to freshmen- and sophomore-level students, contributed to an increase in the retention of African-American students whose academic performance was below the median for their race/ethnic group, more significantly for sophomore-level students than freshmen. Less dramatic yet positive results were also seen in Hispanic and White students included in the study (Nagda et al., 1998).

A more recent analysis conducted at the University of Wisconsin-Eau Claire reported increases in four-year graduation rates among underrepresented students who participated in an undergraduate research experience as part of the freshman-year experience (Olson-Mcbride, Hassemer, & Hoepner, 2016). Yet another study reflects successful outcomes when undergraduate research experiences are incorporated into the curriculum across all four years of a degree program (Awong-Taylor et al., 2016).

Clearly, there is ample evidence that undergraduate research experiences make a positive difference. Colleges and universities are compelled to determine the best way, with regard to their respective scopes and missions, to embrace undergraduate research as a student success strategy and as a post-graduation portfolio requirement. Webb suggests the expansion of access to undergraduate research opportunities has stiffened competition for graduate school placement and the job market. "Undergraduate research gives students a taste of what a career in science would be like and an edge in applying for graduate schools and jobs. But the edge isn't what it used to be—many graduate schools and employers have come to expect it" (Webb, 2007).

A REIMAGINED PUBLIC RESEARCH UNIVERSITY

Kent State's enhanced focus on undergraduate research is developing in the context of our vision of a reimagined public research university where the priorities for academic excellence, access and affordability not only coexist but merge as critical elements of a high-quality, distinctive learning environment. We have been considering, and actually reconsidering, the essential roles and responsibilities of public research universities: Why do we exist? What do we stand for? Or, expressed in the words of the best-selling author Wes Moore (2016), "Who are we going to fight for?"

Often, research universities commit a good portion of their resources to the advancement of research agendas and academic programs that have the greatest potential to deliver on external funding. While there is nothing implicitly wrong with a focus on boundary-breaking research and the quest for adequate research funding, that approach may not always prioritize the need to provide a high-quality higher education to the greatest number of individuals possible.

This thinking led me to a book by Cornell University's Robert Sternberg that centers on "producing students who want to change the world" (Sternberg, R. J., 2016, p. 3). In his book, *What universities can be: A new model for preparing students for active concerned citizenship and ethical leadership,* Sternberg suggests a new model for preparing students, one he calls ACCEL: Active Concerned Citizenship and Ethical Leadership. He also calls for a different methodology to define university greatness. He defines an ACCEL university's greatness as central to the very core of how we define greatness in American society—the opportunity to make a difference and the chance to make our world a better place. Sternberg believes that in an ACCEL university, the focus should be "not just on how academically smart you are but on how much of your smartness you can give back to the world" (p. 30). Undergraduate research experiences not only provide opportunities for students to give back by potentially creating new knowledge, but they also develop and cultivate skill sets and dispositions that are calibrated on making a difference.

NURTURING A CULTURE OF UNDERGRADUATE RESEARCH

The Council on Undergraduate Research (CUR) has existed for more than thirty years to support and encourage faculty and institutions in the engagement of undergraduate students in research. Among the very helpful resources CUR has developed is a guide for the development and assessment of undergraduate research entitled, *Characteristics of Excellence in Undergraduate Research* (COEUR). Available online, the COEUR begins with guidance on creating a campus mission and culture that support undergraduate research:

> Creating a campus culture that values and rewards undergraduate research is essential for sustaining a robust undergraduate research program. CUR believes that such a culture emerges when institutions have a scholarly faculty and leaders committed to providing high-quality undergraduate research experiences for students; broad disciplinary participation in undergraduate research; and opportunities that are accessible to a wide cross section of students. (Hensel, 2012, p. 2)

Consistent with this advice, and as a result of a comprehensive assessment of research at Kent State, we are pursuing strategic and tactical initiatives designed to enhance a campus culture that values and rewards research. These efforts are specifically centered on enhancing the culture, atmosphere, and administrative support of scholarship and inquiry, including robust opportunities for undergraduate students to be directly engaged in original research. There are direct relationships between our enhanced research focus and our top priorities for student retention and graduation rates, national branding and recognition, local and regional engagement and economic development, and institutional financial stability.

Nurturing a culture of research has involved creating an appropriate administrative structure for the Division of Research and Sponsored Programs, establishing five high-priority interdisciplinary research initiatives and targeted funding. We also formed an Office of Student Research that oversees new programming dedicated to improving the research experiences of our students. We launched the Summer Undergraduate Research Experience (SURE) in 2016, an immersive research experience between an undergraduate student and a faculty mentor conducted over the summer months. We also invested further in our existing symposium for undergraduate research, scholarship, and creative activities. These programs provide two tangible signals of institutional buy-in and support specifically for undergraduate research engagement.

We received nearly 100 applications for our inaugural SURE program and awarded 35 undergraduate research stipends in the program's first year. The intensive eight-week program allocated financial support for student housing, stipends, and supplies. The experience culminated this fall when the participating students presented their research before an audience of faculty and students. Disciplines represented spanned the sciences and also included accounting, geography, economics, fashion design, international relations, public health, and speech pathology and audiology.

Feedback from this inaugural effort has been overwhelmingly positive. When asked to rate their overall satisfaction with the SURE program on a scale of 1—"very dissatisfied" and 5—"very satisfied," the mean faculty mentor response was 4.47. In open-ended questions, faculty provided optimistic observations about the experience, including:

> I really loved this program. It was a huge boost to my research over the summer. I was able to continue recruitment and collecting [data over the summer months] ... the SURE fellow is also writing a paper for publication with me, so it also helped with my publication productivity.

> The mentee made me review basic theory and procedures within my discipline, made me get better organized so that I could train and supervise them, and helped me conduct useful relevant research. We both greatly benefitted from the experience.

Additionally, of the nineteen faculty respondents to the postevent survey, fourteen said they anticipate involving their SURE student as an author on a conference submission. By the end of the summer, one student had already presented at an international conference held in Chicago, Illinois.

Students reflected a similar level of enthusiasm and satisfaction with the experience.

> It was through the SURE program where I discovered my growing passion for sustainability. Through hands-on experience in a research lab and close collaborations with my mentor and colleagues, I discovered what I wanted to do for the rest of my life. SURE didn't just affect me as a student in the lab. I learned how to make mistakes, and more importantly, that it was a natural part of the learning process.
>
> —*Kent State junior, marketing major*

> The SURE program was immensely helpful in fostering a relationship with my faculty advisor. I had already been working with her for several years, but SURE allowed me to really dig deeper into the research process. Because I plan on pursuing a Ph.D. in clinical psychology, having that in-depth research under my belt is going to make me stand out above other candidates.
>
> —*Kent State senior, psychology major*

Table 1. Faculty satisfaction with the SURE program and their experience with the student mentee.

Question	1-Very Dissatisfied	2	3-Average	4	5-Very Satisfied	Mean	Median	Count
Q1. Satisfaction with the SURE program in general	0	0	2	6	11	4.47	5	19
Q2. Satisfaction with the match between your mentee's interest and your interest/expertise	0	0	1	4	14	4.68	5	19
Q3. Satisfaction with the guidance you were able to provide your mentee	0	1	0	7	11	4.47	5	19
Q4. Satisfaction with the quality of assistance that your student mentee was able to provide to you and your research project	0	0	2	4	13	4.58	5	19
Q5. Satisfaction with the amount of time the student was able to work on the research project	1	0	1	4	13	4.47	5	19
Q6. Satisfaction with the amount of time you were able to provide as a mentor	0	0	4	9	6	4.11	4	19

The Summer Advantage Program is an additional high-impact undergraduate opportunity that is part of a comprehensive initiative called DEEDS (Dynamic Education and Engagement of Diverse Students). DEEDS aims to bridge the student success gap between underrepresented students and the general student population. Our data indicate that underrepresented students have retention and graduation rates that range from four to ten percent lower than those of the general Kent State student population. Similar to the University of Michigan and

University of Wisconsin-Eau Claire programs referenced earlier, the Summer Advantage Program engages students in research and other high-impact learning experiences early in their academic careers. The Summer Advantage Program will take place during the summer between the freshman and sophomore years, an important time to enhance the focus on persistence and engagement.

According to the Boyer Commission (1998), "Every university graduate should understand that no idea is fully formed until it can be communicated, and that the organization required for writing and speaking is part of the thought process that enables one to understand material fully" (p. 24). The Undergraduate Symposium on Research, Scholarship and Creative Activity represents one of the ways Kent State is addressing this challenge. The Symposium casts an even wider net across the university system to encourage undergraduate student engagement in research-oriented endeavors. Held annually in the spring, the Symposium is a showcase of student engagement in high-impact learning experiences.

Modeled after a professional academic conference, the Symposium creates an opportunity for students to submit an abstract; develop research and presentation skills; gain experience presenting their scholarly work to faculty judges; and compete for cash awards while sharing the topic they explored with the university community. Entries include a broad array of presentation formats, from traditional poster and oral presentations to video and artistic exhibits.

As was the case in response to the SURE program, student feedback has been enthusiastic, reflecting both intended and unanticipated positive outcomes from the symposium experience. The following are selected and representative postevent survey comments from student participants in the 2016 Symposium who, on the whole, found the presentation and engagement aspects of the experience among the most valuable:

> I learned that my work is really meaningful in the real world! It can sometimes be difficult to feel like you are truly advancing science when conducting research in a laboratory setting, but talking about our findings with other people has reaffirmed my faith in the scientific process to produce meaningful results that can generalize to the real world.

> I came into the event with the intention of developing my presentation skills, which I thought were weak at best. As I placed first in my department, my perspective on my own abilities must have been a lack of confidence. Although I had presented at a national conference prior to this event, it was this particular symposium that really assured me that I have what it takes for graduate school.

> From other students, to faculty mentors, to the dean of the library, hearing their take on my research and the reasons why it interests them was my favorite part of the day. After speaking to more people, I felt like I had discovered more about my research than I had originally realized. I also gained confidence in my ability to present the information in a professional and knowledgeable manor. I realized how much work really needs to be put into a presentation like this.

Participation in the Symposium has grown each year since its founding in 2014, when it consisted of 180 students representing 142 abstracts. The university's enhanced focus on research is expected to double student participation by the time the event reaches its fifth anniversary.

A BRIGHT FUTURE FOR UNDERGRADUATE RESEARCH

Our experience with undergraduate research initiatives to date suggests both interest and capacity to grow student engagement in these and other programs. The fact that nearly half of the inaugural Summer Undergraduate Research Experience projects are slated for presentation at regional, national or international conferences speaks to the quality of this engagement. We are also anticipating the Undergraduate Research, Scholarship and Creative Endeavors Symposium will require systematic curriculum-based integration in order to build upon repeated organic growth in interest and participation each year.

Peer-to-peer engagement is among the undergraduate research areas slated for growth. As an important component of peer engagement, we envision a program where graduate students mentor undergraduate students and offer skill-building workshops, an experience that would provide benefits to both the graduate and undergraduate students. We plan to build teams of researchers in a variety of disciplines where a faculty scholar mentors a team of engaged learners from undergraduate through doctoral studies. Dedicating the resources to jump-start, inspire, and reward strategic leveraging of graduate student talent and other institutional resources will help us to significantly expand engagement in undergraduate research that makes a difference.

It will be worthwhile to also investigate the extent to which undergraduate research can be an effective high-impact learning experience to enhance the success rates of students who are at risk for not persisting to the graduation finish line. There is ample evidence to suggest there remains a great deal of untapped potential for student-centered research universities to transform student experiences and success rates by more fully and comprehensively embracing undergraduate research as a student success tactic.

It is equally important that we better study, understand and articulate the translatable skills that are nurtured and developed through undergraduate research experiences. We know employers, for example, are seeking college graduates with exemplary communication skills, critical thinking and problem-solving skills, imagination and creativity, a strong work ethic, and the ability to collaborate effectively in teams. The transformational experience of creating new knowledge and communicating it effectively can address all of these priorities at once.

According to American biographer Walter Isaacson, "Innovation comes from teams more than lightbulb moments of lone geniuses" (Isaacson, 2014, p. 479). The most intractable challenges of the future are those that will call for interdisciplinary teams looking at challenges and opportunities from multiple perspectives across and between organizations, agencies, governments, and public and private enterprise. Those of us entrusted with the important privilege and responsibility of public undergraduate education are obliged to ensure we are preparing graduates with the skills and dispositions to effectively participate in and lead innovation teams. Undergraduate research exposure can be among the very best ways to accomplish this objective.

REFERENCES

Awong-Taylor, J., D'costa, A., Giles, G., Leader, T., Purcell, D., Runck, C., & Mundie, T. (2016). Undergraduate research for all: Addressing the elephant in the room. *Council on Undergraduate Research Quarterly* 37(1), 11–19. doi:10.18833/curq/37/1/4

Boyer Commission on Educating Undergraduates in the Research University. (1998). *Reinventing undergraduate education: A blueprint for America's research universities*. Stony Brook, NY: The Carnegie Foundation for the Advancement of Teaching.

Gonzalez, C. (2001). Undergraduate research, graduate mentoring, and the university's mission. *Science* 293, 1624–1626.

Hensel, N. (2012). Characteristics of excellence in undergraduate research. Washington, DC: Council on Undergraduate Research. Available at: http://www.cur.org/assets/1/23/COEUR_final.pdf

Hu, S., Kuh, G. D., & Gayles, J. G. (2007). Engaging undergraduate students in research activities: Are research universities doing a better job? *Innovation in Higher Education* 32, 167–177.

Isaacson, W. (2014). *The innovators: How a group of hackers, geniuses, and geeks created the digital revolution*. New York: Simon & Schuster.

Moore, W. (2016, August 26). The work: My search for a life that matters. Speech presented at Freshman Convocation at Kent State University's Memorial Athletic Convocation Center, Kent, Ohio.

Nagda, B. A., Gregerman, S. R., Jonides, J., Hippel, W., & Lerner, J. S. (1998). Undergraduate student-faculty partnerships affect student retention. *Review of Higher Education* 22, 55–72.

Olson-Mcbride, L., Hassemer, H., & Hoepner, J. (2016). Broadening participation: Engaging academically at-risk freshman in undergraduate research. *Council on Undergraduate Research Quarterly* 37(1), 4–10. doi:10.18833/curq/37/1/3

Sternberg, R. J. (2016). *What universities can be: A new model for preparing students for active concerned citizenship and leadership*. Ithaca, NY: Cornell University Press.

Webb, S. (2007, July 6). The importance of undergraduate research. *Science AAAS*. Retrieved at http://www.sciencemag.org/careers/2007/07/importance-undergraduate-research. doi: 10.1126/science.caredit.a0700095

CHAPTER ELEVEN

Public Comprehensive Universities

The People's University at a Crossroads

SANDRA J. JORDAN
Chancellor, University of South Carolina Aiken

In 1824, Philip Lindsley gave a rousing address that foreshadowed the creation and purpose of the state-financed comprehensive universities: "The farmer, the mechanic, the manufacturer, the merchant, the sailor, and soldier ... must be educated."[1] Lindsley, a Princeton graduate, was speaking specifically of a great university in Nashville, Tennessee. The institution Mr. Lindsley envisioned was modeled on the German higher education, which, unlike the early universities in America, was distinguished by meticulous attention to scholarship and research, freedom from the influence of religious denominations, and a focus on student learning. While Lindsley's University of Nashville proved unsustainable, his ideas on education proliferated and continue to reside today in the missions of many public comprehensive universities.

Over the past several decades, the fate of America's public universities has been among the favorite topics dominating professional conferences and publications. There is no question about it: higher education is in the midst of rapid change and the accumulated effects of change are producing challenges that are often difficult to manage. Pressures are coming from all directions: technologies are changing the delivery model, institutions face increasing competition for students and significant changes in student demographics, and public university administrators are frustrated by a cost-to-funding model that is unsustainable. Meanwhile, demands continue for a reformed model for higher education that addresses often competing agendas to increase student access, place greater attention on student learning and achievement, deliver a curriculum that addresses the workforce needs of the region and state ... all at a reduced cost to parents, students, and taxpayers.

Prior to the so-called Great Recession of 2007, criticisms and demands for reform were aimed directly at the expensive elite and/or research intensive universities that were unfairly characterized as being more engaged in research and esoteric topics than in teaching or preparing students for work, whose environment is seen as "faculty-centered" rather than "student-centered," and whose large endowments and luxurious amenities raised questions about why tuition continued to rise. Ultimately, however, no university, regardless of sector, has been shielded from the stinging criticism of reformers. Unfortunately for the state comprehensive universities, baccalaureate institutions, and community colleges, the critics of higher education frequently and blatantly disregard the differences between the various sectors of higher education. And thus, all of higher education is painted with a very broad and coarse brush. This tendency to ignore the various sectors of higher education and to dismiss the history, missions, and achievements of these sectors is a dangerous practice that leads to inaccurate conclusions and prejudices that obscure workable solutions to contemporary concerns.

As a key sector, public comprehensive universities are neither elitist nor research-focused institutions. Rather, they have proven to be highly responsive to their constituents and provide a flexible model of higher learning. The public comprehensive universities were created on the notion of providing greater student access at an affordable price to deliver programs of study that strike a balance between professional training and broader educational ideals. Despite the positive models for education demonstrated throughout this sector and regardless of the fact that the public comprehensive universities enroll and educate a substantial portion of the students attending four-year universities, these universities may constitute the most overlooked and least celebrated segment of higher education in the United States. Perhaps the lack of attention devoted to this sector of education explains why, with seeming indifference, state funding agencies have placed these higher education workhorses at grave peril. Ironically, the state comprehensive universities offer a paradigm that can help reset the direction of higher education in order to better address 21st-century needs. Indeed, with greater realization of the power of this model, this century may be the golden age of the public comprehensive universities, as they finally gain their just recognition as the "people's university."[2]

Before a discussion of specific issues, we must first better understand the history of the public comprehensive state university (PCU). As is true with any history, there are many places to begin; but the story of the public comprehensive university is entwined with the creation of land grant universities, the formation of normal schools, and concerns for the education of women and black Americans. The notion of the power of public education to transform lives is as old as the nation. George Washington's dream of a national university was based on his belief that public higher education was a useful instrument in the shaping of patriotic citizens. So devoted was he to the idea of a public University of the United States that he mentioned it in 1790 during his first annual address to Congress and again in his last address to Congress in 1796.[3] Washington's dream of a national university, along with Thomas Jefferson's and John Adam's desire to design a curriculum that emphasized both practical and lofty content, reflected the post-revolutionary zeal for public education and an education free from religious denominational control.

The spirit of democracy comingling with the values of the Enlightenment appealed to families who recognized higher education as a means of getting ahead. But minds dedicated to public service recognized that higher education was a way to secure the elusive dream of a Republic based on the ideal of a government "for the people, by the people," and the recognition that it would take a citizenry free from ignorance and bias to maintain such a form of government. It was during the American Revolution and the immediate post-revolutionary decade that states began to adopt a more dynamic role in the support of higher education. North Carolina, Georgia, Tennessee, and Vermont all founded state-chartered, state-funded universities before 1800.[4] In addition, Federal land grants, the precedent for which goes back as early as the Northwest Ordinance of 1787, proved to be a major stimulus for the foundation of state colleges. After 1804, every new state west of the Appalachians joining the union was granted two townships for a "seminary of learning" to address the national need for an educated citizenry.[5] Vermont Congressman Justin Smith Morrill was a strong proponent of a practical education. In discussing the desired curriculum he advised "to lop off a portion of the studies established centuries ago as the mark of European scholarship"… and replace (it) by "less antique and more practical value" in order "to promote the liberal and practical education of the industrial classes in the several pursuits and professions of life."[6] This approach to higher education contributed to the growth of institutions on land contributed by individual states. Moreover, the land grant university's role in the support of the nation was clarified by its dedication to providing a service to society. Thus, in addition to promoting practical education, the land-grant colleges were expected to fulfill America's ambitious democratic mission. Established by the Morrill Act of 1862, land-grant colleges and universities were designed to spread practical education, advance democracy, and improve the regions where they were located.

The flowering of state land-grant universities gave expression and form to the Jeffersonian dream of state-supported education. Not everyone was equally supportive of the expansion of public universities. In a speech delivered in 1873, Harvard's president and respected educational leader, Charles William Eliot, attempted to subvert the Jeffersonian concept of state-supported education by making it an issue of class, saying: "There is a skepticism of the masses in Massachusetts as to the justice of everybody paying for the advanced education of somebody's child. The mechanic, the blacksmith, the weaver says: 'Why should I pay for the professional education of the lawyer's son, the minister's son? The community does not provide my son his forge or loom.'"[7] But Eliot's supercilious attempt to scuttle state support was unsuccessful because the state university idea had caught on throughout the United States. In contrast to Harvard's Eliot was the University of Michigan's James B. Angell, who argued that all human beings should be given opportunities to develop talent and character to the fullest. "We need all the intelligence, all the trained minds we can have," he said in an address in 1879.[8] As Frederick Rudolph writes, "President Angell believed that higher education was not a luxury but a necessity that should be made available to all. It would not have occurred to him to make the assumption that came so natural to President Eliot, heir of the wealthy Eliot family of Boston, that the blacksmith's son was destined to be a blacksmith."[9] The establishment of public land-grant universities reflects the conventional wisdom of the time that extolled the public college as a symbol of liberation from the elitist, provincial collegiate traditions of the past. To the hard-working public, the public college was a source of community pride and a concrete symbol of progress, democracy, success, and the promise of even greater opportunities for the next generation.

In the post-Civil War period, the expansion of public universities corresponded with a reform movement sweeping through America. Fueled by a powerful combination of social factors and underwritten by the private fortunes of industrial and railroad tycoons, the new universities would become more secular, more concerned with discovery than the refinement of a gentleman, and devoted to scholarly inquiry and learning, rather than to escalate social connectivity. It is no coincidence that the reform movement parallels a period of boundless technological advances exemplified by industrialization and urbanization. The increasing secularization of society, coupled with a belief that a university education could produce material success, and a certainty that education could assist individuals in finding ways to engage productively with new technologies, made the earlier, antebellum institutions dedicated to the training of the clergy and gentlemen seem outdated. The new model, designed under the influence of the German universities, would be more welcoming to those who were not "to the manor born."

The democratization of higher education and a desire to make an advanced education more accessible to those who had previously been unwelcome, including women and African Americans, led to the desire to create a stronger teacher corps who could prepare their younger pupils for public colleges. Concern for adequate preparation of students in secondary schools paved the way for public comprehensive institutions to expand and refine their mission. The long-standing practice of hiring teachers directly upon their graduation from secondary level classrooms was not proving satisfactory. The Ecole Normale, established in France in 1685 by the Brothers of the Christian Schools, provided a practical model for teacher education in the U.S. The first of the Normal Schools was developed in Vermont in 1823.[10] Soon afterward, inspired by the work in France, a philanthropist in Massachusetts helped the state establish three normal schools.[11] The sensibility of this approach lead to rapid expansion of normal schools in New York, Michigan, Main, and Minnesota. Over the next five decades, state normal schools spread well beyond the northeastern states and were found across the nation. Created to professionalize the training of teachers, the normal school typically accepted high school graduates into a curriculum that concentrated on teacher preparation.

The purpose of the normal school was to establish and disseminate those best practices and teaching standards that would become the "norm" for the teaching profession. The name fell out of favor in the mid-20th century, when many began to support a more descriptive English name of "teacher's college." Ultimately, that name was short-lived and most institutions, cognizant that they were doing far more than disseminating best practices in teaching, opted for "state college" or "state university" in their names.[12] Many public comprehensive universities today began as normal schools, or teachers' colleges, including Appalachian State University, the University of North Carolina at Pembroke, University of Maine at Farmington, the University of North Alabama, Georgia College & State University, Mississippi University for Women, Rhode Island College, Salem State University, Eastern Michigan University, Illinois State University, University of Northern Colorado, and San Jose State University, to name a few. The model continued to be replicated with new institutions formed with a focus on undergraduate education, strong regional ties, and access to a greater cross section of citizens.

Historically, America's public comprehensive colleges and state universities were seen as significant and important social investments. Equally, they were embraced by state and local governments as catalysts for regional economic development. The dominant belief that colleges existed to help develop individuals who would, in due course, become civic-minded and productive citizens and employees was the major defining purpose of a public university education since the very beginning. In 1802, President Joseph McKeen of Bowdoin College reflected this notion when he said: "It ought always to be remembered that literary institutions are founded and endowed for the common good, and not for the private advantage of those who resort to them for education. It is not that they may be able to pass through life in an easy or reputable manner, but that their mental powers may be cultivated and improved for the benefit of society. If it be true no man should live for himself alone, we may safely assert that every man who has been aided by a public institution to acquire an education and to quality himself for usefulness, is under peculiar obligations to exert his talents for the public good."[13] Refined and disciplined by the learning process, President McKeen and his contemporary university colleagues believed that college graduates would be finely suited for service, leadership, and a life of engagement. They would have found it unthinkable to separate the social and civic purposes of a university degree from the academic. This sentiment is even stronger in the state-funded comprehensive universities. The strategic societal function of the state university is to prepare students to be engaged citizens, to educate students who will serve the region's needs, including producing well-prepared teachers, and to leverage talent and resources to help advance the community and wider knowledge.

The historical lineage of public comprehensive universities connects the Jeffersonian dream of public universities, the land-grant institutional desire to offer an accessible and practical education, and the professionalization of teaching devised by the normal school tradition. These attributes combined to shape the contemporary state comprehensive university in a number of significant ways, including creating a segment of public universities that place a premium on the art and practice of teaching and learning. While doctoral institutions with research designations typically garner most of the public attention (especially during the football or basketball seasons), they make up only 7% of the institutions in the United States.[14] Meanwhile, master's colleges and universities, and baccalaureate colleges make up 28% of the numbers of institutions by broad category. In 2015, the number of students enrolled in masters and baccalaureate institutions totaled more than five million.[15]

The nation's public comprehensive universities typically fall within the masters and baccalaureate sector. These institutions are varied and form an unwieldy sector that includes institutions with significant differences in missions, size, scope, degree offerings, and locations. Some of these institutions are urban, while others are purposely located in rural settings. The public comprehensive universities (PCUs) typically focus on the production of bachelor's degrees, but the degree mix with majors in the arts and sciences and in professional fields varies from institution to institution. Moreover, in this sector, there is considerable variation between institutions awarding graduate degrees either in the same fields in which it awards undergraduate, or in special areas. Many comprehensive institutions offer masters degrees along with the bachelors, and some even offer a limited number of doctoral programs. Public comprehensive universities range in size from small, with enrollments under 1000 students, to much larger institutions with enrollments above 15,000 students. Despite the variation between institutions, the historic beginnings have given many of these institutions some commonalities. These include the following:

- Emphasis on the undergraduate experience
- Limited emphasis placed on faculty research
- Prominence placed on interactive and high-quality instruction
- Primarily residential
- Maintains small to mid-size overall student enrollment
- Class size is characterized by higher teacher-student ratios
- Fosters a high level of teacher-student interaction at the center of which are classes taught by full-time faculty rather than graduate student teaching assistants (TAs)

- Accepts a diverse student body with a wide range of abilities, skills, and motivations
- Places a high premium on service, including service performed by faculty as well as service engagement valued among undergraduates

Additionally, state comprehensive universities widely share a series of challenges that unite them in a loose fraternity of sorts. While regional public comprehensive universities educate nearly 30% of America's four-year college students, they are currently at a crossroads. Pressures from changing student demographics, the loss of state funding accompanied by an increase in oversight and regulation, the cost of emerging technologies, the shift in faculty roles, competition, and the impact of the recession on both personal finances and student confidence in the future are reshaping these institutions that were once, and remain today, vital to our nation.

One of the most pressing challenges facing the public comprehensive sector is the shift in philosophy and practices surrounding funding. Many authors have eloquently explained the impact that the seismic shift in funding has on higher education. Less thoroughly examined is the enormous impact the loss of state support has had on the middle-to-small-size public regional comprehensive universities that do not maintain substantial endowments. PCUs fear that if reduced funding is prolonged, it will deteriorate the service mission, erode quality, and grind away at the access mission. The belief that public higher education should be funded by society (through tax effort) has been the prevailing philosophy in the United States and is one of the key aspects of higher education that made our colleges and universities the envy of the world. In fact, the states and the federal government long have sought to provide substantial funding for higher education, but changes in recent decades, stimulated by the recession in the early 1990s and the Great Recession of 2007, have resulted in dramatic drops in state support.

Historically, the states provided a far greater amount of assistance to post-secondary institutions and students than did the federal government, but state support has declined so sharply for public universities that they are, as Fethke and Policano have succinctly wrote, "Public No More."[16] In fact, in states such as South Carolina, some of the private institutions receive more public funding than their sister comprehensive institutions in the public sector. For campus leaders, this is a difficult environment and the shift has serious consequences for public comprehensive institutions. Throughout the last several decades of the 20th century, driven more by fiscal concerns than by nuanced philosophical questions, a shift was taking place in the role of government to support higher education that would ultimately modify the defining purpose of a university education and erode the notion of the university as a social investment.

As King Alexander, currently the President of Louisiana State University, has maintained throughout his career, policymakers involved in the discussions surrounding the inception of the Higher Education Act of 1965 erroneously assumed that the states would provide appropriate funding for higher education through their own volition; thus, there was no need for the federal government to legislate state funding for universities as they had for primary and secondary education. The supposition was that any new federal funding policies, such as federal aid, would simply supplement state funding, not replace it. According to Dr. Alexander, "Many policymakers believed that states would always be the primary funding source for public higher education with the federal government playing only a small complementary role, which is not the case today."[17] That misjudgment was almost immediately obvious as state governments began to reduce funding as early as 1981, less than a decade after the next reauthorization of the HEA in 1972 that outlined the principal programs of today's federal student aid system. What followed next was a series of unimagined state reductions in public higher education funding, the result of which undermined the mission of the public comprehensive universities and placed those institutions in a perilous position. The long-term failure of state policy makers to appropriately fund their institutions is reflected in the fact that state tax effort has dropped precipitously to levels lower than in the 1980s. With the Great Recession of 2007, the transition to redefining the role of the university was complete.

Beginning in mid-2007, the global financial crisis quickly evolved from the bursting of the housing bubble in the U.S. to the worst recession the nation has endured since the Depression of 1929. With the recession came a marked shift in the perception of the purpose of a college education. The entire enterprise was being questioned; pundits and critics emerged like locust on green wheat, finding fault with higher education's business model, the curriculum, wasteful spending, and especially the cost of attendance. Remember, just a few decades earlier higher education was seen as one of the most trusted institutions in the United States. To understand the seemingly sudden shift in perceptions, one has to acknowledge the broad strokes and impact of the Great Recession. Like the Depression, the Great Recession (which officially lasted from December 2007 to June 2009) triggered a loss of wealth combined with loss of confidence in future income, which led to austere cutbacks in consumer spending. Like a domino effect, the loss of consumption, together with the chaos in the financial market, produced a cumulative effect leading to a collapse in business investment. As consumer spending and business investment declined, production slowed and job loss followed. In one estimation, between 2008 and 2009, the U.S. labor market lost 8.4 million jobs, or 6.1% of all payroll employment—again, the most dramatic employment-reduction since the Great Depression.[18]

To compound matters, even after the economy stopped shrinking, recovery was painfully sluggish. Loss of income and confidence, a narrowing job market, failing investment banks, the constricting of business and industry, the end of the construction boom, the loss of business investment and an overall sluggish recovery meant that family incomes dropped, and major family investments and savings and pension investments were lost while poverty rose. Additionally, the public lost faith in government agencies and policy makers and began to doubt the veracity of anything that anyone was saying about the economy. That loss of trust has filtered down to all manner of leadership positions beyond the banking, political, and business sectors. These events, which defined the Great Recession, had an immediate and swift impact on the economy and on all public institutions, including higher education. State budgets were strained, federal dollars for research became more elusive, funding to public institutions decreased, and an increasing number of families could not afford the cost of attending college without significant loans or aid. Families who knew little about the historic loss of state support to higher education over the last three decades suddenly began to notice and complain bitterly that tuition had increased to unattainable levels. Those same families also didn't believe higher education's explanations.

Hearing the frustrations of their constituents, higher education became the favorite "piñata" of both the political communities. Additionally, the rising unemployment numbers and a restricted number of new jobs led some to question whether an investment in a higher education degree was worth the cost of attendance, at least in the short run. Within this troubling environment, accountability became a major concern for both the public and PCUs. Increasingly, policy and regulation entities moved away from input models and probed for proof that higher education was providing a tangible return for the billions being spent on higher education. Complicating that discussion is the absence of readily available, valid, and accepted assessment methods to determine the efficiency and effectiveness of the complex learning enterprise. Meanwhile, echoes of Harvard's President Charles William Eliot's speech are evident in the voices of fiscally conservative politicians who, without the benefit of a national discussion, have continued the attack on higher education by withholding appropriations to the state's public institutions.

Since 2015, several states have begun to restore some of the cuts they made to higher education funding during the recession. But a handful of states, notably in the Southeast, are still reducing appropriations; in almost all states, including those that recently increased their support, higher education funding remains well below pre-recession levels with the average state spending 23% less per student than before the recession. These considerable funding cuts have led to both steep tuition increases and declines in institutional spending that may diminish the quality of education available to students at a time when a highly educated workforce is more crucial than ever to the nation's economic future. Institutions have had to cut back on marketing, limited co-curricular funding, and postponed salary increases already delayed. Within this context of events and reactions, countless speculation about the relevance of higher education, accompanied by no small degree of collective anxiety, public comprehensive colleges, and universities have intentionally focused on the "new realities" and reflected upon, experimented with, and adopted new ways to conduct business, control costs, leverage partnerships, and serve students ... but, then, that is what higher education has done since its founding in the United States. Only today, the work must be carried out in a climate of shrinking state financial support, increased student anxiety over costs, and an atmosphere of distrust of anyone in authority.

It is fair to say that universities tend to respond slowly to changing expectations and emerging demand. A time-honored, yet time-intensive shared governance process; an enterprise that honors tradition; past evidence that higher education policies and trends come and go as quickly as fads in fashion and substantial regulation and oversight—combined with wishful thinking—all tend to act as disincentives to creative and aggressive change. However, with more emphasis on a business model and more reliance on tuition, students will be attracted to universities that keep costs under control and respond to their needs. Public comprehensive universities need not waste any precious time debating whether their institutions will, or can, adjust to different expectations, more accountability, or a business model—because they must. Meanwhile, they need to be creating greater capacity for rapid change so the institutions can respond quickly and sensibly toward solutions. First and foremost, public comprehensive universities need to recommit to their original access and service missions; and in doing so, focus on access, affordability, and exceptional teaching. Many have come to this realization, but have found that one of the "new realities" is that the competition for students is fierce.

Competition for students over the past several decades (especially during the years when the number of students exiting high school declined) has now increased. The traditional population for the PCU base has been eroded by changes outside their control. Large state research institutions have been allowed to add branch campuses in rural regions of the state, not because those regions were not well served, but because the research institutions needed to expand their undergraduate populations in order to finance their large array of masters, doctoral, and professional school programs. As the U.S. stepped away from providing research grants and funding for basic research, the cost of offering a large array of Ph.D. programs became less sustainable. Well-meaning boards and alumni members who held positions in state legislatures approved the proliferation of branch campuses out of a sense of school spirit and without the benefit of a plan or a dispassionate picture of the impact of those branches on the public comprehensives. The large research institutions knew that an effective substitute for research funding was to increase undergraduate enrollment. Bridge programs, branch campuses, and dual-enrollment with high school programs gave these research institutions access to a new population, but not without an impact on their neighbor comprehensive institutions.

In the wake of reduced research grants and funding, a new breed of state research institution has been born over the last two decades … the gargantuan university. Rutgers with 48,378 students; the University of Florida with 49,459 students; Arizona State University with 50,320 students; and Texas A&M University at College Station with 61,642 students provide ample example of this trend (Department of Education, 2015–16).

Legislatures in several states, including California, Pennsylvania, Florida, and South Carolina, have given entirely new missions to the technical schools which, once again, serves to increase the competition for students and dilutes the much needed mission of the technical colleges. Add to the mix that several states have expanded the role of their community colleges by allowing them to provide the junior year of the baccalaureate degree and that private schools are discounting at unprecedented rates, and the enrollment picture becomes increasingly murky for PCUs. The enrollment competition for students who traditionally were the mainstay population for public comprehensive universities is now divided by more types of institutions, making the situation seem even more calamitous for the PCU sector. Thus, instead of recognizing the value of the comprehensive mission and working to expand access through the "People's University," states without a clear plan for higher education have set a path that creates greater challenges. The irony is that the comprehensive institutions, according to the Delta Cost Study, deliver the baccalaureate degree at a cost to the state that is lower than most other sectors, including the technical colleges.

Given the realities of the very real competition for students, PCUs must determine how to stand out in a crowded field through greater differentiation. The recruitment of undergraduate students is an increasingly competitive process and students are not as "brand loyal" within the comprehensive sector as they may be at those R-I institutions with high mascot recognition. Young men and women, particularly those with high test scores and above-average GPAs, have many choices. These students are sophisticated consumers in the commercial and educational marketplace and are shopping for the right institution and fit. Differentiation requires the institution to focus on its individual strengths to determine how to set up authentic opportunities to be distinct. It also requires discipline on the part of the leadership to avoid chasing every alluring idea. To be distinct, institutions must embrace some risk, formulate a plan, be prepared to manage the consequences, and be equipped to assess whether or not the plan is working.

Differentiation can be created through a number of directions, for example: through athletics, co-curricular and extracurricular options, by creating a distinct curriculum, developing a set of programs of distinction, establishing a distinguished academic or honors college, embracing residential colleges, utilizing high-impact classroom techniques, or placing emphasis on leadership, citizenship, and service-learning. Each strategy comes with challenges and PCUs are well served to take time to engage the campus in the development of the focus areas and invest in a narrow set of distinctive agendas that can distinguish the university relative to the competition. Investment in those programs that align with both the mission and the needs of the region, while simultaneously reducing funding to those that do not align, will result in greater differentiation, stronger programs, and a more effective use of resources.

A number of PCUs have developed a liberal arts-focused curriculum as a way of differentiating the university. Truman State University, University of North Carolina Asheville, University of South Carolina Aiken, University of Mary Washington, University of Maine at Farmington, and Georgia College, among others, have done a good job of using the liberal arts curriculum, combined with a significantly lower tuition rate, to compete with private institutions. The Council of Public Liberal Arts Colleges (COPLAC) is an organization that champions and supports the cause of liberal arts education, and institutions accepted into COPLAC must meet a set of criteria to prove that they provide their students access to excellence in a liberal arts education. The political landscape following the Recession of 2007 created a climate that called into question the importance of the liberal arts, especially majors in the arts, humanities, and social sciences. Sobered by the impact of the recession, they sought a relationship between the constriction of business and industry with certain academic disciplines, whose economic value was not immediately apparent.

Despite the fact that individuals in the workforce with college degrees were the least negatively impacted segment of the population during the 2007 recession, and without regard to the fact that a significant number of CEOs of Fortune 500 companies completed undergraduate majors in one of the humanities, those who wanted to justify drastic cuts to education developed a bias in favor of a new model for higher education: education is a commodity, students are customers, universities exist only to enhance current workforce needs, and state politicians are stockholders who see their role as overseers who review university outcomes as if they were a quarterly manufacturing report.

As the economy begins to recover, conversations continue in the public forum around higher education's performance in regards to addressing the need for employable graduates to step into the jobs of the retiring baby-boom generation. Workforce is taking on greater importance as employers are once again hiring, but reporting difficulty finding applicants with needed skills. The question around the need for higher education to do a better job of preparing future workers can be addressed more rapidly and effectively by those many PCUs that have close ties to industry and manufacturing in their region. For the development of the new engineering degree at USC Aiken, a team of twenty engineers from local industry met over several months to design a curriculum that would produce a graduate who would meet their employment needs. Their recommended curriculum was presented to the faculty, who made modifications, determined pre-requisites, and created capstone requirements.

The less cumbersome structure and approval processes at PCUs can translate to the possibility of greater collaboration than in more complex and hierarchical infrastructures. Meanwhile, business and industry need to review the actions they are taking in the area of new hire training and development. Training programs were drastically streamlined or eliminated in many companies as a cost savings during the lean years of the recession. A clear-eyed evaluation and strong return to more robust onboarding for new employees needs to be part of the solution. Micromanaging at an extreme level, a handful of politicians have suggested that states fund only those majors that have an obvious and overt link to advancing the economy. Institutions who have maintained enrollments in humanities, arts, and social sciences majors must work aggressively with their state political leaders, state chambers of commerce, and representatives in the Congress and present a cogent argument to help them understand and rally around the importance of broadly educated students who, in addition to acquiring a depth of knowledge in a major, have a breadth of knowledge across disciplines.

Soliciting the help of business and industry through the chambers or through direct relationships is an imperative. Representatives from higher education are suspect when they defend the status quo, so building alliances with influential business leaders is critical to influencing a more nuanced conversation. Industry and businesses have been vocal about the importance of having students entering the workforce who have skills and abilities in critical thinking, communication, and the capacity to understand and work within a diverse community. At the same time, social agencies, nonprofit organizations, and professional entities such as hospitals, who work with the public, can be allies in the messaging of the importance of graduating students across the spectrum of majors. On the campus, institutions can promote through internal communication the ideals of a liberal arts curriculum and reinforce through examples of alumni the breadth and types of career options that are available across the spectrum of majors.

Additionally, institutions need to remember that today's students are tomorrow's business, political, and community leaders. As eighteen-and nineteen-year-olds, they look to the faculty for their cues. Orientation for new faculty should include the mission of the institution and the rationale for the curriculum. Faculty should also be coached on how to reply to the interminable question asked by students, "Why do I have to take that course?" If the respected science or engineering faculty member can't respond to why a social science or humanities course is included in the curriculum, or if the message conveyed by faculty advisors is that the core courses are those you just need to plow through so you can get to the important classes, then students will not see any justification for the liberal arts. Advocating for a set of articulated university student-learning outcomes and then including in each course syllabus the rationale for how that course contributes to those outcomes is another way of imbedding in students greater appreciation and understanding of the liberal arts agenda.

Comprehensive universities were designed to provide a public university education to those segments of the population that had been historically underserved by the elite private institutions or the large research universities. Often located in rural counties, they serve as economic engines for their regions by creating workforce pipelines in critical areas such as healthcare and education, while providing jobs and often serving as one of the largest employers in their region. Traditionally, the PCU student body draws heavily from a particular region, providing that population with a more affordable, accessible option.

Given that access and opportunity were founding concepts, it follows that PCUs have an obligation to provide proactive and extensive measures to meet the needs of their students. This begins with data-analysis and a clear picture of the demographics of the student body. The demographic groups selected for study should be determined based upon the specific characteristics of the university. For example, an institution might want to know the racial, ethnic, gender, age, geographic, socioeconomic, cultural, linguistic, and religious backgrounds of the student body. Or it might gather information on the percentage of the students who are first-generation college students, veterans, Pell Grant recipients, average SAT/ACT, percentage of honors students, former high school leaders, athletes, average borrowing and debt, and students with special needs (including physical, learning, emotional, or other hidden challenges).

What student activities should be noted? Institutions may track the success of students who go to tutors and seek assistance for academic success, or who are on visas, are working on- or off-campus, or those who volunteer or enroll in the service-intensive courses. Institutions need to understand their campus profile, engagement level of students as well as student retention, persistence, and graduation rates. In the world of big data, the institution should have a clear picture of what it is seeking to know, how the information will be gathered, what techniques and processes will be used to unpack the data, which entity on campus will look for meaning to institutional questions, and how the institution will translate the information into action. The inevitability of demographic change in North America, related to race/ethnicity and generational transition, will significantly affect public comprehensive universities.

Because the mission of the PCUs is to provide greater access and opportunity, they are often highly diverse institutions. Administrators may have noted the shift taking place in student demographics, but few have readily available tools and models to help them navigate the changes already underway, not to mention the changes on the horizon. The growth of non-white, Hispanic, and multiracial populations in America, along with the aging of the white population, will result in rapid increases in diversity at most institutions. Immigration and birth rates among minorities have kept the U.S. growing (unlike many other highly developed economies), but these changes present both complications and opportunities for life in the academy. Those institutions who have struggled in the past to diversify the university will find that it may become easier to meet goals of greater diversity in the student body. Those institutions that are already highly diverse may struggle with how to create a culture of inclusion and empathy at a time when there is growing division over ideas. Demographic experts have predicted that it may take until 2043 before non-Hispanic whites are no longer the majority in the U.S.; but for the racially and culturally diverse PCUs, the shift will be much sooner.

While most public universities understand the benefits of a diverse student body, few go beyond that to deeply understand the characteristics of the student population and determine what and how much action to take to really include students so they become productive campus citizens who reinforce the ethos of the academy. For many leaders in higher education, the increasing racial, political, and social polarization reflected in the nation can be somewhat overwhelming and indecipherable. Campus leaders and faculty recognize and understand that students bring with them a sense of identity, opinions, ways of communicating, and a sense of purpose shaped by their parents, their communities, their religions, their experiences, etc. These influences are critically important to the individual student's persistence, development, and success; understanding the complexity of those identities contributes to productive human interactions across the campus community.

Typically, the unanswered question and dilemma lies in determining how much of a resocializing agent the university should attempt to be. Most institutions of higher learning have not clearly decided whether or not they should merely reflect society or whether they should consciously enculturate the microsociety living, working, and learning on the campus into academe's values. Moving a diverse population of students toward a gradual acquisition of the characteristics and norms of university life will take intentional programming, delivered over time. Recent research on the impact of campus climate on the success of students suggest that university leaders can significantly improve the support of students on a diverse campus. Universities can purposefully and strategically strengthen the climate on their campuses through deliberate socialization. This process begins by designing and implementing systematic and comprehensive educational programs to help all members of the campus community to identify and confront the stereotypes and myths that people have about those who are different from themselves.[19]

Because perceptions of discrimination and unfairness have consequences for all students, including student persistence in college, institutions should do all within their power to ensure that policies are fair to all. To accomplish this goal, universities must be aware of best practices, clearly state their policies and the formal judicial processes, and establish mutually agreed upon and published institutional values and expectations. As with most values-driven education, communication from the campus leadership reinforcing the agreed upon institutional values is important. Both formal and informal processes to deal with infractions should be published to help the campus community confront and resolve incidents. Opportunities for cross-racial and cross-cultural interactions—through academic classes, co-curricula events, clubs and organizations, and special programs—all help to build understanding, reduce racial tensions between students, and improve perceptions of campus climate.[20]

One of the best ways to make certain that the voices of students with differing perceptions of inclusion are heard is to execute regular assessments of campus climate for diversity. Concurrently, institutions should review the most recent research relevant to racial and ethnic campus climate to help determine the most effective ways to support and socialize students into university life, including the role of student services, faculty, peer group education, residential life, advisors, and student organizations. The administration, focusing on the demographics of the institution, will need to review and determine if the initiatives to support a positive campus climate have enough resources and staff to serve the students successfully and attain the institution's goals.

Contemporary researchers writing on institutional climate highlight the impediments to student success: poor socialization of diverse students into the culture of the institution and academic departments, faculty indifference to mentoring students beyond the academic sphere, little or no training in cross-cultural communications, and conflicting priorities for time, resources, and development. A crisis or incident that interrupts harmony on the campus may change the priority of social inculcation on the list of initiatives, but the institution is well served to ask the questions and plot a course in a manner that enhances discussion on campus and to address relevant issues prior to an incident. Assumptions may be made around the question about resocialization in various quarters of the university; until the university asks and answers the basic questions, it will struggle with inadequate codes of conduct, value statements, responses, and judicial processes in the face of the challenges that are created when diverse people live, work, and learn in close proximity.

Beyond the issues of campus climate, universities must also focus on the success of their diverse students. In order to address the desire to produce more graduates and increase undergraduate populations, institutions must recognize that they will likely be enrolling more first-generation students and more students emerging from high schools with less than adequate preparation for college. To address a wide assortment of learners, the university is well served to consider those practices that yield positive results and support students as they progress through their studies. At USC Aiken, this includes clustering more student support services closer together under a single roof so students can easily shift between various support activities. This cluster of support services includes the Career Services

Office. Emerging research indicates that engaging students early in the discussion about their career aspirations can enhance student motivation, focus, and satisfaction. Several institutions have implemented an early intervention program that includes individual appointments between freshmen and career counselors during their summer orientation program. Vincent Tinto's research on retention indicates that students who do not possess a clear academic focus and career goals may be at higher risk of swirling, stopping, or dropping out.[21] Career Services that are proactive around targeting, tracking, and engaging students in conversations about careers can also be useful to the university's retention efforts. By assisting students in the exploration of majors, aiding students in the process of linking their individual strengths to career paths, and demonstrating how to set goals to achieve their dreams, Career Services personnel are critical to the process. One thing seems clear: if universities are unable or unwilling to address the inevitability of the shifting demographics within their campus populations, then their relevance, funding, and ability to meet the needs of their students will be at risk.

Adding to the complexity of an increasingly heterogeneous campus population is the impact of technology on the ways young people think about belonging. Technology is shifting the way people gather. Students attend classes with other students, or they may sit alone in their rooms and interact with students in their class online. Attending class, even electronically, is a way of gathering and participating. On campuses all over the nation, students gather daily for their meals, or to attend a music or athletic event. But gathering and belonging are not the same thing. Belonging is much deeper; helping students to shift in and out of multiple groups to which they belong and assemble around areas of interest, not exclusively by race and ethnicity, has the potential of deepening a sense of connection and belonging. Institutions can use technology to assist with this, creating clusters of online spaces around interests and coaxing students to "meet-up" through an app connection. This more loosely assembled form of gathering could minimize student isolation. Marketing expert, Kyle Sexton, writing for membership organizations, reminds us that only a fraction of members show up for anything. But measuring the effectiveness and value of the institution through attendance (gathering) is unreliable and nearly meaningless.[22]

The ways people learn and acquire information have expanded. While institutions may cling to semester structures and rigid course schedules for content delivery, individuals can cluster for support, create personal connectivity around areas of interest, and enhance belonging through high-quality, two-way video and virtual meetings. One doesn't have to look far for good examples. Fantasy football combines human connectivity through team spirit, drafts, and bowl game parties, with real-time web site information and tracking software. Using the same model to support and engage students in a political science class, or around a university's basketball team, can expand students' sense of belonging to the campus.

In addition to finding ways to help students on a heterogeneous campus to feel a sense of belonging, there is a need to recognize that greater numbers of students currently enrolled in institutions need assistance beyond academic tutoring. The decline in resilience among students can be verified by Counseling Services and low success rates across the service sector. *The Chronicle of Higher Education*'s recent article by Robin Wilson describes a generation of students who are overwhelmed by their own everyday life problems.[23] Faculty do not tend to see providing emotional support for students to be within the realm of their expertise. Furthermore, there is a sense of helplessness among the faculty who are conflicted about how much "coddling" should be done, along with the feeling that the administration's attention on retention and graduation rates compel them to lower the pressure on students by lowering standards. Students who are emotionally frail or whose maturation is delayed may well benefit from being assigned an advocate who provides trusted advice, encouragement, and coaching. Having an advocate who is not a faculty member or advisor, who will not be writing the student a reference or grading student progress, provides a level of personal support not typically found in universities.

The idea of assigning individuals with advocates is not new to the service sector and has been used effectively by hospitals and community health organizations. In those settings, patient advocates are those who support, encourage, translate, and smooth communications between the patient and the other members of the healthcare team. What would a student success advocate do? Naturally, roles will vary by institution, but in general the advocate would serve, much as the healthcare advocate, as the support person for students. In this role, she would help steer students through the red tape and jargon of the university. She would be the trusted support person who would have ongoing discussions with students about their future goals, provide encouragement, clarify options, connect to campus and community resources, clarify institutional expectations, and respond to questions. Over time she will help the student decide what the student is able to handle on his own and what he may need help with. In short, the advocate will be helping the student to build a greater capacity for resiliency and to become an effective self-advocate. Given the advancements in technologies, student meetings with the advocate can be enhanced by electronic meetings and social media, rather than always relying on face-to-face contact. This would allow the campus to utilize well-trained volunteers or retired staff and faculty, instead of diverting funds from existing initiatives. As in all things, the university is best served if decisions are made and clearly articulated about what the advocate must know, the expectations for consistent communications and the tone of communications, and what kind of decisions and actions they can be involved—in contrast to those that may be in the purview of the faculty or other campus support offices. Few would debate the importance and centrality of the faculty to the creation of a climate of inclusion and student success. The struggle is to find ways to effectively socialize faculty into the institutional culture, continuously develop the faculty so they can effectively share in the design and implementation of initiatives beyond their disciplinary expertise, and to adequately reward those who successfully advance institutional goals. Most PCU faculty evaluation processes continue to focus on teaching, scholarship, and service without clearly defining any of those areas and to the exclusion of additional institutional goals that may fall outside those three categories.

From the very beginning of the movement to create more higher educational access, including the design of the Morrell Act and the establishment of the normal school movement, comprehensive universities were seen as key components in a plan to provide greater support to their regions. For some PCUs, this aspect of institutional work takes the form of continuing education, economic development, employment, or strategic partnerships. At this moment in time for the PCU, it is important to consider which strategic partnerships might advantage both the institution and the community. Engaging in more partnerships on a broader set of university endeavors than in the past can help the university build greater support across sectors: local government, industry, business, nonprofits, and public services. Seeking partnerships is important for numerous reasons because partners can bring new perspectives to the campus, make available additional financial and human capital, and be new sources for student internships and jobs. Additionally, forming alliances and partnerships provides the campus community with powerful, real-world examples of the importance of collaboration.

Partnerships, however, necessitate both institutional stability and long-range thinking. Meaningful and strategic partnerships require correspondingly strategic planning, communication, and sustainable effort. Institutions have a variety of reasons for seeking partners, but they must understand that 21st-century problems are highly complex. Creating partnerships and working collaboratively across sectors creates many opportunities to hone the institution's purpose and self-awareness. Collaborating requires the institution to articulate, refine, and deliver results around stated competencies. Thus, collaboration can contribute to a clarification of purpose across the institution. Institutional collaboration can also provide a platform to address organizational goals more effectively, and outcomes may be greater than if working alone. Twenty-first-century problems are big and complicated, so working with corporate, community nonprofit agencies, and businesses expands upon the old adage, "two heads are better than one," and demonstrates to students how to go about solving problems in the real world by combining the talent, experience, finances, and infrastructures beyond the campus.

While engaged in collaborations to address local and regional issues, the educational and social organizations thrive when complimentary organizations unite to find solutions. Among the PCUs, the most frequent examples of partnerships fall within three areas: stewards of place, asset leverage, and knowledge exchange partnerships. Potential partners may be attracted to a collaboration with a university because they perceive that it is affluent, or it shares similar values, or because it is seen as a repository of human and intellectual capital. In any case, it is important for all participants in the collaboration to be clear about their expectations and reasons for partnering. Given the close and ongoing relationship that PCUs typically have with their communities, collaborations around the "stewardship of place" provide opportunities for natural partnerships to emerge. A PCU outside of Cincinnati, Northern Kentucky University shaped its identity around service learning and community collaboration. Others have partnered with nonprofits to advance volunteer opportunities or collaborated with local schools or healthcare providers to support educational or public health. Those PCUs that are leveraging assets may be working on mixed-use developments or melding and meeting community and campus needs through their partnerships. Examples of leveraging assets abound among the comprehensive universities: Georgia College partnered to renovate the façade of a vacant movie theatre to preserve the historic look of Main Street while repurposing the structure to serve as the new bookstore; the University of Mary Washington worked with the city of Fredericksburg, Virginia, to develop a hotel for the community that also provided event space for the University; and USC Aiken partnered to create an event center for the community that also serves as a basketball arena for the campus. Knowledge exchange partnerships are typically collaborations between state and federal government and universities that augment basic and applied research, provide teleconferencing networks, and bring new discoveries to the marketplace. Throughout the collaborative process, regular communication, persistence, and a willingness to calibrate the project along the way will help support success. Time and practice are necessary to navigate collaborations, but with each collaboration, the university and its partners will build a greater capacity to succeed.

For centuries universities have provided a forum for communities to come together to explore and expand upon common concerns, emerging social trends, and new knowledge. PCUs open their campus facilities to their community members, provide continuing education and K–12 educational programs, and, among other things, host entertainment and athletic events that are open to the public. The current political and social landscape in many of our regions is fragmented. The inability or unwillingness of those groups to listen to each other, to respond with civility, and to work together to solve very real issues presents universities a unique moment in time to step up and serve as both conveners and moderators. This role, which may be a challenging one for other entities to play, can highlight several of the university's strengths that are demonstrated daily by the campus community. University faculty are skilled in looking at issues from multiple perspectives, leading discussions around complex issues, structuring opportunities for a range of diverse voices and opinions to be heard, and teasing-out productive solutions. Universities have a history of nurturing mutual understanding, fact checking, and negotiating compromise in order to shape creative and valuable resolutions. PCUs can initiate partnerships with their community and step forward to act as the fair and impartial convener to create a better model for working together.

To remain relevant in our current environment will take leadership and a bit of courage. We need to call on our flexibility and rethink how we expand our educational enterprise to new populations. New demands require change on our part. As Leon C. Megginson notes: "It's not the strongest or most intelligent species that survives. It's the one that is the most adaptable to change."[24] The same can be said of universities. But, unless more is done within the academy, the next challenge to face PCUs will be a crisis of leadership. The Council of Independent Colleges released a study in 2010 that reported that fewer than one-quarter of chief academic officers aspire to be presidents.[25] What is troubling about that finding is that ascent to the presidency is often through the role of the provost or the chief academic officer (CAO) position. The reason? The CAOs don't like the internal job responsibilities or the external demands of the presidency. In addition to duties on campus, presidents spend much of their time in fundraising, meetings with boards and legislators, alumni and community relations, risk management, and strategic planning.[26] University presidents serve many constituents, are under heightened scrutiny, and juggle many responsibilities. University stakeholders, from trustee boards to faculty senates and alumni groups, are either advocating for change or resisting change; they are becoming more vocal, and less predictable. Couple that with greater state and federal oversight, more vitriolic opinions from every corner, entitled students, hovering parents, and a 24 × 7 news cycle, it is no wonder that veteran presidents feel the position has become more challenging. The *American College President 2012* report found that the average age of a U.S. college president in 2011 was 61 years old. The council's Center for Policy Analysis also reported that the average length of service in 2011 for a president was seven years compared to 8.5 years in 2006.[27] At a time when PCUs need experienced leaders who can anticipate trends, adapt to change, define, and implement innovative strategies with courage and purpose, there may be a shortage of qualified individuals who aspire to the job.

The times have changed. Today's PCUs are presented with competitive challenges and shifting social, technological, political, and economic variables that are rapidly transforming the environment in which they operate. The nation's founders supported a system of public education because they knew that a government "of the people" could not be sustained "by the people" without an educated populace. If the opinions of our nation's founders seem irrelevant in the new landscape of the 21st century, then contemporary research on this topic should provide the needed verification. In a recent and expansive set of research studies by the Pew Charitable Trust, entitled *The Economic Mobility Project*, the overwhelming evidence confirmed that the power of a college education to both promote upward mobility and prevent downward mobility is substantial.[28] The conclusions contained the startling fact that the chances of moving from the bottom of the family income ladder all the way to the top are three times greater for someone with a college degree than for someone without one. Moreover, the study confirmed that, when compared with their less-credentialed counterparts, college graduates can count on much higher earnings and lower unemployment rates. In addition, the Georgetown Center on Education and the Workforce recently published a significant document entitled, *The College Advantage: Weathering the Economic Storm.*[29] That publication, which is frequently quoted, states that more future jobs in all industries will require more college preparation. Projecting to 2018, and assuming a labor force of 166 million, the research revealed that only 10% of future job opportunities will be available to high school dropouts while 33% of those jobs will be open to individuals who complete both a bachelor's and graduate degree.

Is college still a good buy and worth the investment? The only possible conclusion one can draw from the recent research must be yes, it is. Thus, it is time to move to more significant and relevant discussions to secure a healthy future for higher education, and especially for the public comprehensive sector that serves rural regions, closes the achievement gap, and provides access and teaching excellence to a diverse American demographic. Thus, the time has come for states and the federal government to create a plan to help individuals and families achieve the "American Dream" by supporting higher education. A half a century after the Higher Education Act, the nation is still waiting for a comprehensive and sustainable agenda that provides predictable and appropriate funding for the public comprehensive universities so they can continue to advance their mission as the "People's University" through affordable access to an excellent education.

A significant example to note in the United States: none of the original top thirty industries listed on the Dow Jones Industrial Average in 1928—the year before the great stock market crash—are on that list today; yet, all thirty of the major universities in the country in 1928 still exist. This is important, for a long list of business articles have suggested to their readers that those in business understand their missions as well or better than colleges. They claim that if colleges would just adopt a business model, all would be well. However, it is clear that higher education not only understands the mission … our planning model has allowed us to adapt to the changing milieu, the evolving needs of the student body, and new expectations placed on college graduates when they enter the workforce. And, colleges adapt better than many businesses and industries.

> "Oh, Henny Penny, the sky is falling and I am going to the King to tell him about it." "How do you know it?" asks Henny Penny. "It hit me on the head, so I know it must be so!" says Chicken Little. "Let me go with you." says Henny Penny. "Run, run!"[30]

The folk tale of Chicken Little has been retold for centuries. So common is the story in our consciousness that the mere use of the phrase, "The sky is falling!"

reminds us of one of the lessons of that parable: fear-mongering and catastrophic conjecture can actually precipitate paralysis or ruinous outcomes. In the case of Henny Penny and Chicken Little, while obviously the sky could not and did not fall, their collective anxiety hurried their own calamitous demise. There may be a lesson for higher education in this children's fable. Is the sky falling for the public comprehensive universities? Those who are predicting doom for higher education have forgotten their history. Universities adjusted to survive the depression; they adapted quickly when the first GI bill brought a new population, with radically different needs, to the campus; they modified to meet the demands of the baby-boomers, echo boomers, and the so-called me-generation. PCUs changed their curricula to address national needs during WWII and the atomic and space races, as corporations rose to dominance in the 20th century; and they shifted again when facing the challenges of global and knowledge-based economies. As new technologies became available, PCUs retooled delivery methods and created more flexible pathways so student access could accelerate. All of us who have made higher education our profession recognize that change is in the wind. Some of the recent criticisms of higher education have been centered on the question of whether academe—a system that can trace its roots to the 13th century—can radically reimagine itself in order to serve the needs of future students, industries, and businesses. My response to that is—well, of course, we can!

NOTES

1. Halsey, L. J., ed.: *The Works of Philip Lindsley, D. D.* Philadelphia, 1866, p. 81 Referenced in F. Rudolph, *The American College and University: A History,* Athens, GA: University of Georgia Press, 1990, pp. 90, 117, and 219.
2. Henderson, B. *Teaching at the People's University*, Boston: Anker Publishing, 2007, title page.
3. Rudolph, F. *The American College and University*, Athens, GA: University of Georgia Press, 1990, p. 42.
4. Tewksbury, D. G. *The Founding of American Colleges and Universities Before the Civil War*, New York: Bureau of Publications, Columbia University, 1932, p. 64.
5. Knight, G. W. 'Higher Education in the North West Territory,' *Annual Report of the US Commissioner of Education for 1888*, Washington DC: U.S. Bureau of Education, 1889, pp. 1039–1047.
6. Eddy, E. D., Jr., *Colleges for Our Land and Time: The Land Grant Idea in Education*, New York, NY: Harper, 1956, pp. 31–32.
7. Quoted in Rudolf, F. *The American College and University*, Athens, GA: University of Georgia Press, 1990, pp. 278–279.
8. Angell, J. B. *Selected Addresses*, New York, NY: Longmans, Green and Company, 1912, pp. 42–56.
9. Rudolph, 1990, p. 279.
10. The Forty-First Vermont School Report by the Superintendent of Education to the General Assembly, Montpelier, VT: Capital City Press, 1910, p. 24.
11. Lucas, C. J., *American Higher Education*, 2nd ed., New York, NY: Palgrave Macmillan, 2006, p. 140.

12. Henderson, 2007, p. 23.
13. Hatch, L. C. *The History of Bowdoin College*, New York, NY: Loring, Short & Harmon, 1927, p. 19.
14. Carnegie Classifications of Institutions, Facts and Figures, 2015.
15. Ibid.
16. Fethke, G., and Policano, A. *Public No More: A New Path to Excellence for America's Public Universities*, Stanford, CA: Stanford University Press, 2012.
17. Alexander, F. K. Prepared Statement to the U.S. Senate Committee on Health, Education, Labor & Pensions, http://www.help.senate.gov/imo/media/doc/Alexander3.pdf, 2007.
18. Mishel, L., et al. *State of Working America*, Economic Policy Institute, 12th ed, Ithaca, NY: Cornell University Press, 2012, pp. 11–15.
19. Pascarella, E., et al., 1996, p. 185.
20. Pascarella, E., et al., 1996, p. 190.
21. Tinto, V. *Leaving College: Rethinking the Causes and Cures of Student Attrition*, Chicago, IL: University of Chicago Press, 1987.
22. Sexton, K. *Remembership: New Thinking for Tomorrow's Membership Organizations*, Salem, OR: IncPlant, 2011, p. 24.
23. Wilson, R. "An epidemic of anguish: Overwhelmed by demand for mental-health care, colleges face conflicts in choosing how to respond," *Chronicle of Higher Education*, August 31, 2015. Updated article retrieved from http://www.chronicle.com/article/An Epidemic-of-Anguish/232721
24. Bryan, J. C., and Megginson, L. D. "Lessons from Europe for American Business," *Southwestern Social Science Quarterly* 2012, 44(1): 3–13, p. 4.
25. Hartley, H. V. III, and Godin, E. E. Council of Independent Colleges, 2010. Retrieved from http://www.cic.edu/Research-and-Data/Research Studies/Documents/CICCAOSurvey.pdf
26. Bryan, J. C. *The American College President Study: Key Findings and Takeaways*, American Council on Education, Washington, D.C., 2012.
27. *Economic Mobility Project, 2012. Economic Mobility of the States*. Washington, DC: Pew Center on the States. http://www.pewstates.org/research/datavisualizations/economic-mobility-of-the-states-interactive-85899381539
28. Carnevale, A. P., Jayasundera, T., and Cheah, B. *The College Advantage: Weathering the Economic Storm*, Georgetown University, Center on Education and Workforce, 2012. Retrieved from http://cew.georgetown.edu/report/the-college-advantage/
29. *American College President*, American Council on Education, 2012. Retrieved from www.acenet.edu/news-room/Pages/American-College-President-Study.aspx
30. Gladone, P. *Henny Penny*, New York, NY: Houghton Mifflin, 1968, pp. 3–5.

REFERENCES

Alexander, F. K. Prepared Statement to the U.S. Senate Committee on Health, Education, Labor & Pensions. Retrieved from http://www.help.senate.gov/imo/media/doc/Alexander3.pdf, 2007.

Angell, J. B. *Selected Addresses*, New York, NY: Longmans, Green and Company, 1912.

Carnegie Classifications of Institutions, *Facts and Figures*, 2015.

Carnevale, A. P., Jayasundera, T., and Cheah, B. "The college advantage: Weathering the economic storm," Center on Education and Workforce, Georgetown University. Retrieved from http://cew.georgetown.edu/report/the-college-advantage, 2012.

Christensen, C. M., and Eyring, H. J. *The Innovative University*, San Francisco, CA: Jossey Bass, 2011.

Cook, B. J. *The American College President Study: Key Findings and Takeaways*, Spring Supplement, 2012. pp. 49–50. Retrieved from http://www.acentet.edu/the presidency/columns-and-features/Pages/The-American-College-President-Study.aspx

DeVitis, J. L., ed., *Contemporary Colleges and Universities*, New York, NY: Peter Lang, 2013.

Eddy, E. D., Jr., *Colleges for Our Land and Time: The Land Grant Idea in Education*, New York, NY: Harper, 1956.

Fethke, G., and Policano, A. *Public No More: A New Path to Excellence for America's Public Universities*, Stanford, CA: Stanford University Press, 2012.

Forty-First Vermont School Report by the Superintendent of Education to the General Assembly, Montpelier, VT: Capital City Press, 1910.

Halsey, L. J., ed.: *The Works of Philip Lindsley I*, D. D., Philadelphia, 1866.

Hartley, H. V., and Godin, E. E. "CIO Survey," Council of Independent Colleges. Retrieved from www.cic.edu/Research-and-Data/Research Studies/Documents/CICCAOSurvey.pdf, 2010.

Hatch, L. C. *The History of Bowdoin College*, New York, NY: Loring, Short & Harmon, 1927.

Henderson, B. *Teaching at the People's University*, Boston, MA: Anker Publishing, 2007.

Holmes, D. O. W. *The Evolution of the Negro College*, New York, NY: Columbia University Press, 1934.

Kerr, C. *The Uses of the University*, Cambridge, MA: Harvard University Press, 1963.

Knight, G. W. *History of Land Grants for Education in the Northwest Territory*, 1885, New York, NY: G.P. Putnam, 1886.

Knight, G. W. "Higher education in the North West territory," *Annual Report of the U.S. Commissioner of Education for 1888*, Washington DC: U.S. Bureau of Education, 1889.

Lederman, D. 'A College Friendly Take on Rising Prices,' Inside Higher Education, November 2, 2007. Retrieved from https://www.insidehighered.com/news/2007/11/02/costs

Lucas, C. J. *American Higher Education*, 2nd ed., New York: Palgrave Macmillan, 2006.

Merginson, L. D. "Lessons from Europe for American Business," *Southwestern Social Science Quarterly* 44(1): 3–13, 1963.

Mishel, L., et al. "State of Working America," *Economic Policy Institute*, 12th ed., Ithaca, NY: Cornell University Press, 2012.

Pascarella, E., Whitt, E., Nora, A., Edison, M., Hagedorn, L., and Terenzini, P. 'What have we learned from the first year of the National Study of Student Learning?' *Journal of Student Development* 37(2): 1996.

Pew Center on the States, "Economic Mobility Project: Economic Mobility of the States," Washington, DC Retrieved from http://www.pewstates.org/research/datavisualizations/economic-mobility-of-the-states, 2012.

Rowley, D. J., and Sherman, H. *From Strategy to Change*, San Francisco, CA: Jossey-Bass, 2001.

Rudolf, F. *The American College and University: A History*, 2nd ed., Athens, GA: The University of Georgia Press, 1990.

Sexton, K. *Remembership: New Thinking for Tomorrow's Membership Organizations*, Salem, OR: IncPlant, 2011.

Tewksbury, D. G. *The Founding of American Colleges and Universities Before the Civil War*, New York, NY: Bureau of Publications, Columbia University, 1932.

Tinto, V. *Leaving College: Rethinking the Causes and Cures of Student Attrition*, Chicago, IL: University of Chicago Press, 1987.

Veysey, L. *The Emergence of the American University*, Chicago, IL: University of Chicago Press, 1965.

Wilson, R. 'An epidemic of anguish: Overwhelmed by demand for mental-health care, colleges face conflicts in choosing how to respond,' *Chronicle of Higher Education* August 31, 2015. Retrieved updated article from http://www.chronicle.com/article/An Epidemic-of-Anguish/23721

CHAPTER TWELVE

The Role of Public Regional Universities in the 21st Century

ELSA M. NÚÑEZ
President, Eastern Connecticut State University

INTRODUCTION

Public regional universities[1] have a special place in higher education, one that positions them well for continued relevance and value in addressing the educational needs of U.S. citizens and the workforce requirements of the 21st-century economy. For institutions with a strong identity, shared values, a clear sense of direction, and a commitment to growth and change, the next few decades can be golden years within the public regional university sector.

I share this perspective based on my own experiences over the past decade as the president of a medium-sized state university in Connecticut. In this chapter, I will be using the lessons learned and the successes realized at Eastern Connecticut State University[2] to illustrate what I believe are keys to student success and effective campus operations. In some cases, our efforts have been part of broader collaborations—either as a member of our state system of public colleges and universities or through regional and national pilot projects. In other situations, we have depended on our past experiences or research on best practices to inform our work.

I have no doubt there are other schools in our country that are also doing what we are doing at Eastern. In this chapter, in instances where I am aware of best practices elsewhere, I have mentioned initiatives at other schools. I am most familiar, however, with the changes we have made on my own campus, and they serve as the primary examples of strategies I believe can help other universities prosper. I am hopeful that this "sample of one" provides insights into how America's public regional universities can best respond to challenges facing higher education.

State University Beginnings—A Focus on Local Residents

Most regional state universities have their historical roots in the normal school movement of the mid-1800s. My own campus opened in 1889 as the Willimantic State Normal School. The first normal school in Connecticut—what is now Central Connecticut State University, our counterpart in the Hartford, Connecticut area—opened in 1849.

The normal school movement was launched in New England by such visionary educators as Horace Mann and Henry Barnard, who understood the importance of preparing primary school teachers to provide quality instruction in the nation's emerging public school system. Creating standard texts, instructing in common pedagogical methods and establishing teaching standards were all part of the process of ensuring that publicly supported teacher preparation schools were consistently providing the tools young teachers needed to join the workforce of a nation that was growing at every turn.

The normal school foundation of today's public regional universities has served to guide our institutions' missions and also presents us with renewed opportunities for growth and relevance. For one thing, from our beginnings regional state universities were clearly tied to the educational needs of local residents. Unlike the international scope of liberal arts colleges and national universities ranging from Williams College to Stanford University to the University of Texas, public state universities were created to support the people surrounding our campuses.

At the time of its creation, the Willimantic State Normal School served young women from surrounding towns who wanted to become primary school teachers. Today, as the state's only designated public liberal arts university, Eastern draws students from 160 of Connecticut's 169 towns. Our three sister institutions have a more regional focus, drawing most of their students from the towns and cities closest to their campuses. All four universities have a commitment to serving the residents and workforce needs of Connecticut, with upward of 95 percent of our students coming from within the state, and the vast majority of students staying after graduation to live, work and raise their families here.

Over time, as normal schools transformed into teachers colleges, later becoming comprehensive state universities, their role expanded from concentrating on teacher education to providing career preparation in a variety of occupations. In keeping with the mission of public regional universities, Eastern and its three sister institutions in Connecticut have developed curricular specializations in response to local and regional workforce needs. Like other state universities across America, Eastern focuses on serving the people of our home state, knowing that the majority of our students will stay in Connecticut after graduation. This commitment is at the heart of the public mission of regional universities, and impacts everything from the majors we offer to classroom instruction to other activities that occur on and off our campuses.

New Challenges

A variety of issues confront public higher education today, any one of which could command our full attention. How can we address the changing demographics in our nation so that underrepresented populations gain the social and economic mobility that a college degree promises? How do we ensure that our curriculum is relevant to the needs of employers? How can we enhance academics and student life so that students persist and graduate well prepared to be successful professionals and engaged citizens?

In addition to these challenges, public universities are confronting a variety of financial issues. To a greater or lesser degree, all of us face tight state finances that have resulted in budget cuts: families who are finding it increasingly difficult to pay for a college education; students focused on finding jobs after graduation; and everyone from accrediting agencies to politicians demanding more accountability of the public's investment in our campuses.

On the face of it, this list of challenges may appear to be daunting. However, I firmly believe that public regional universities are in a favorable position to respond. With our historical focus on meeting the needs of our local and state constituencies, state universities have the tools to prosper in what might otherwise appear to be an adverse environment.

Reaffirming Institutional Identity

The first step in tackling today's challenges is to reaffirm our institutions' core identity. To me that means having a clearly articulated mission and core values—both developed and owned by the campus community, kept fresh in the campus and public consciousness, with strong alignment between the university's identity and institutional actions.

Mission. Every university has a publicly articulated mission statement. How recently has your mission been examined and reframed? Is it grounded in your historical commitment to your local and state communities? Does it reflect current economic and social conditions? Does it align with your core values and vision? Is it flexible enough to allow for innovation and growth? Do you routinely share it with key stakeholders? Revisiting your institution's mission can be an important opportunity to reaffirm your identity as a public university serving your region and state.

Core values. The challenge in having meaningful core values is not in their creation. Through group process and open-ended feedback, any university can develop a set of core values that are shared by members of the campus community and other stakeholders. The challenge is in taking the time to measure your university's major initiatives against this set of guideposts and keeping them alive and in front of people's consciousness.

Institutions faced with creating or updating their core values should take the time to validate alignment between who they say they are and the steps they are taking to serve their students and other major stakeholders. At Eastern, when we updated our strategic plan in 2008, more than 250 faculty and staff were part of the planning process; one committee was charged solely with reviewing and updating our mission, developing a vision statement and reaffirming our core values. The time invested in this process was well spent, because it resulted in a heightened sense of purpose and commitment shared across the campus community.

I would be surprised if most public regional universities do not share and support the principles that constitute Eastern's six core values—Academic Excellence, Engagement, Social Responsibility, Inclusion, Empowerment and Integrity. While each campus must go through the exercise of confirming its own identity, as public institutions of higher learning we all share two fundamental commitments—one to our students and the other to the communities we serve.

Regardless of what their core values may be, it is critical that public regional universities take the time to confirm their identity. If you do not know who you are, how can you present a compelling case to prospective students, legislators, donors, and other key stakeholders? When clearly defined and shared by the campus community, institutional identity not only drives strategic planning, it serves as a stabilizing influence on campus while inspiring innovation and progress. A shared identity is also a source of pride for alumni and other donors and a selling point to prospective students, who are seeking a place where they can belong.

Aligning Campus and System Identities

While I have focused my perspective on institutional identity based on what I know best—the activities taking place on my own campus—Eastern is part of a system of seventeen state colleges and universities.[3] Not only is the Connecticut State College and University System larger than the University of Connecticut System, most of our students come from Connecticut communities, and most of our graduates stay in Connecticut to provide leadership in their workplaces and neighborhoods.

We are a relatively small state compared to Texas, California, and Minnesota. Those states also have state university systems but I suspect their size makes collaboration among institutions and statewide planning more of a challenge. California has more than twenty state universities in addition to a number of campuses of the University of California and Texas has six separate public state university systems!

With many state systems in New York, Florida, Georgia, Illinois, Tennessee, Louisiana, Michigan, Massachusetts, North Carolina, and other states, few public state universities can seek to improve student learning and campus operations without taking state priorities and initiatives into consideration. In Connecticut, we have attempted to brand our four state universities with areas of distinction, in addition to each providing comprehensive educational offerings. For instance, Western Connecticut State University is only an hour from New York City and its theater, art and music industries, hence Western's focus on the performing arts. Southern Connecticut State University is known for its graduate programs, while Central Connecticut State University has an outstanding engineering program. Eastern, in turn, is the state's designated liberal arts college. Providing such campus-specific areas of specialization while also respecting campus autonomy has been critical to ensuring institutional viability in a time when competition for students is fierce and public funding is declining.

In addition to this strategic positioning of the four state universities, we have been able to create a number of initiatives in Connecticut's system of seventeen state colleges and universities to enhance student learning, improve campus operations and find economies of scale. For instance, our state college and university system has developed collaborative partnerships among the four state universities and our twelve community colleges in the areas of advanced manufacturing, health sciences, nursing, and other high-demand occupations. Of particular note is the Transfer and Articulation Program, which allows associate degree graduates from Connecticut's twelve community colleges to seamlessly transfer their credits towards more than twenty degree concentrations in the four state universities; more articulations and career pathways are being developed as the program continues.

At the same time that public regional universities face budget constraints and declining state revenues, stakeholders expect us to continue to seek cost efficiencies while expanding educational access to underserved populations. In such a climate, state universities must be proactive in aligning their institutional goals and operations with system-wide initiatives, especially in states that have significant system operations.

Prepared for Progress: A Living Strategic Plan

Assuming a public regional university has a clear sense of its identity—taking its role in its state system into account—what approaches can be pursued to enhance student learning, relieve the financial burden facing students and their families, and better serve local residents and our state economies? How can we ensure that underserved populations have access to the promise of a college degree? How can we improve retention and graduation rates?

At Eastern, we posed these and other questions during the first year of my presidency. It was an opportune time, because we were due to update our Strategic Plan. We seized that moment as a chance to create a plan that reflected the best thoughts on campus, with the goal of making it a living document that would inform our decisions in the future.

The 2008–13 Strategic Plan and the updated 2013–18 plan that guides our current work were created through a campus-wide collaborative process. More than 250 faculty, staff, and administrators worked to develop our Strategic Plan. We formed committees, convened focus groups, conducted research, and held campus-wide forums on key issues. We surveyed students and each other. We created feedback mechanisms to communicate progress to the campus. After the Strategic Plan was finalized, we reconvened in new groups to monitor implementation of the plan.

All of the examples of innovation and institutional success occurring on our campus that I will be sharing in this essay have come from our commitment to planning a principle-centered approach to fulfilling our mission. The plan drives annual objectives, guides budgetary decisions, and serves as the basis for assessing institutional progress.

If your own campus is nearing a point in time when updating your central planning document is in order, I would ask you to consider the following questions: Do you need to readdress your mission, vision or core values? How can you best involve interested faculty, staff, administrators, students, alumni, and other stakeholders in planning your future? What are the internal and external forces you must consider? What best practices on other campuses can you borrow to improve your own institution?

A comprehensive strategic plan, created through campus-wide involvement by all stakeholders, is the best recipe for systemic change and sustainable progress on your campus. If you are about to embark on a planning exercise at your university, I would offer five working principles that might serve as guideposts in the process.

KEYS TO THE FUTURE: RESPONSIVENESS, RELEVANCE, ENGAGEMENT, ACCOUNTABILITY, AND ADVOCACY

What approaches can be pursued by public regional universities to enhance student learning, relieve the financial burden facing students and their families and better serve local residents and our state economies? How can we ensure that underrepresented populations have access to the promise of a college degree? How can we improve retention and graduation rates?

In considering these questions, five guideposts for action come to mind: responsiveness, relevance, engagement, accountability, and advocacy. Institutions that are responsive to the local and regional needs of their state; relevant to current student and employer interests; committed to engaging students on their campuses; and willing to be proactive in meeting stakeholder expectations can find opportunities for success in the coming years. Let me share what we are doing at Eastern Connecticut State University to follow these five guideposts.

A Responsive Campus

As a public university, Eastern has a primary responsibility to prepare its graduates to enter the state of Connecticut's workforce. As part of our commitment to the state economy and the quality of life in Connecticut, we are also determined to provide educational access to more residents from underrepresented populations.

Workforce development

Developing new majors in emerging occupations is a critical element of our Strategic Plan and mirrors the priorities of the Board of Regents, the governing body of our system of state colleges and universities. In response to the needs of the Connecticut economy, Eastern has recently developed new majors and/or ramped up programs in health science; computer science/business information systems; bioinformatics; new media; insurance/finance; and environmental health. To support students in these areas, internships and field experiences are giving students important hands-on experiences as well as networking opportunities with potential employers.

In fall 2014, Eastern launched a Health Sciences Major in recognition of the growing health care sector in the state of Connecticut; just two years after its creation, the program has 275 student majors. Our Business Information Systems major has a statewide reputation, with students winning national awards for their pro bono work at local nonprofits. In fall 2016, we added a bioinformatics minor. At a time when demand for computer science is growing by almost 25%, four of the fifteen top job-growth areas are in business information and healthcare information systems, and we have several major companies in Connecticut using bioinformatics and computational biology in their work.

One of five new majors introduced at Eastern in fall 2014, the New Media Studies major is unique within Connecticut's state universities. Demand for digital media employees in Connecticut is three times the number of available candidates, so students have excellent job opportunities into the future. The finance major and related insurance minor were launched in fall 2014 and spring 2017, respectively, to respond to needs of Connecticut's large financial services and insurance industries. Job growth at banks, brokerage firms and other financial services is projected to exceed overall job growth; the insurance industry alone has expanded 25% in the past five years.

These new programs are just a few examples of how we are responding to Connecticut's workforce needs. Every public regional university has a local or regional economy to address. Regardless of their unique local workforce needs, there are four takeaways I would offer to universities seeking to develop new programs.

First, use your alumni to keep you apprised of trends occurring in the local economy. On my own campus, with most Eastern alumni living in our state, we benefit from alumni serving on advisory committees, placing interns and hiring our graduates. These relationships span decades and result in curriculum modifications, on-campus recruitment of students seeking employment and the expansion of internship opportunities.

Second, focus on working with companies and industries that actively support student internships. It is critical that students have the opportunity to apply their learning before they are employed. When a company is willing to support student interns with an ongoing program and a significant number of placements, it demonstrates that they understand how students learn best, and are willing to invest in those students and your campus as precursors to hiring your graduates.

Third, in cases where your campus is part of a statewide system of public universities, developing new programs in response to state workforce needs must be strategic and coordinated. Avoiding redundancies, optimizing investment of public funds and sharing knowledge and resources across the state will result in a stronger state workforce.

Finally, when new programs can address local, state and national workforce needs at the same time (e.g., health sciences), students have significantly more options in pursuing job opportunities. Graduating students with portable skills in occupations such as health care, computer technology, and digital media make a university even more attractive to prospective students in today's mobile society.

Access for underrepresented populations

At the same time that public universities must be responsive to the workforce needs of their regions and state, there is another reality that we must address. I refer to the changing demographics in our nation that has seen a significant increase in ethnic minorities over the past few decades.

According to U.S. Census projections, Caucasians will be in the minority by 2050. Yet even as minority populations have grown, they continue to be disproportionately underrepresented on our campuses. Public regional universities are well positioned to respond to this challenge. Perhaps only community colleges have been more committed to reaching out to underrepresented populations than public regional universities over the years. With a commitment to inclusion and a recognition that local residents from a variety of backgrounds deserve the opportunity to go to college, we have historically worked hard to ensure educational access.

At Eastern, 53% of our student population is either an ethnic minority, a first-generation student or someone from a low-income family. We share this commitment with other public regional universities, and it puts us in position to respond to an ever-pressing need to expand educational opportunity.

Apart from the moral imperative of helping people gain social mobility, there is an economic reason why is it so critical to enroll and graduate more minorities from our nation's colleges and universities. The Center for Education and the Workforce at Georgetown University projects that two-thirds of jobs in the future will require at least a two- if not a four-year college degree.[4] To ensure that our economy has the skilled workers it needs to prosper, we need to increase the number of first-generation, low-income and minority students going to college and completing their education.

At Eastern, we have several programs in place to promote educational access, including our Dual Enrollment Initiative with high schools in Hartford, in which we partner with our local community college to prepare and then enroll inner-city students who deserve access to a college education; our Summer Transition at Eastern Program/Contract Admissions Program, an alternate admissions opportunity that provides access and freshman-year support to high school graduates who are either the first to attend college, are from low-income families or are from groups traditionally underrepresented on college campuses; and our Summer Proof of Ability program, which provisionally accepts students not meeting traditional entrance criteria and provides intensive summer instruction to promote successful transition.

As much as ensuring educational access is a critical strategy to achieving economic and social mobility for all sectors of our society, recruiting minority students is only a first step. It is no longer simply enough to get underrepresented students in the front door. We need to support them so they leave our campuses with a degree, ready to succeed in the workplace.

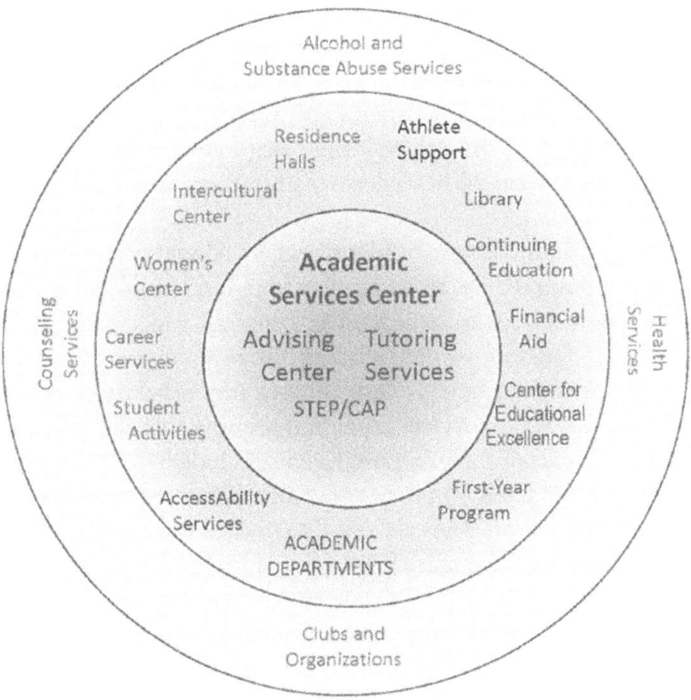

Retaining and graduating minority and first-generation students requires new investments on campus. One key strategy of Eastern's Strategic Plan was the creation of our Student Success Model. It features many programmatic elements, but the enduring effectiveness of the model has been due to the cross-functional collaboration of academic and student support units.

Among the new initiatives put into place to support this Student Success Model was a predictive data system to better identity incoming students who were likely to be at-risk academically. Using a multivariate analytical tool developed by our faculty, we use different factors—Pell eligibility, minority status, first-generation, high school GPA, declared major—to assess and place new students into one of four Targeted Advising Cohorts (TACs). Students in the highest risk cohort are targeted for tutoring and other proactive interventions. Interestingly, we found that one of our best predictors of academic success at Eastern is whether or not a student attended our library orientation. This indicator of motivation and self-discipline has provided new insights into how best to assess potential academic success or failure.

An initiative related to our TAC model is our enhanced advising system. In addition to hiring more full-time professional advisors, we created a four-tier advising program that includes pre-enrollment advising, first-year advising, major advising, and career counseling. An example of the system's proactive approach are workshops on declaring a major and exploring careers that are conducted in freshmen residence halls. Our own data mimics national statistics that show declaring a major early on is a positive factor in improving retention and graduation rates.

A physical addition to campus was our Academic Services Center, which we opened in 2008 to bring support services that were scattered across campus under one roof. The center uses faculty experts and trained peer tutors to provide supplemental instruction in math and writing, discipline-specific tutoring and other support services. More than 2000 students visit the center more than 10,000 times each year.

Another key initiative in our Student Success Model is the "Six Week Challenge," a program designed to assist all first-year residential students during the transition from high school to college. The program was created in response to national data that indicates freshmen students are most at risk during their first six weeks. Integrating students quickly into campus life, providing access to campus resources to improve college survival skills, and keeping students on campus during the weekend are all goals of the program. Events include hall and floor socials, dinners with students attended by resident assistants (RAs) and resident hall directors, roommate contracts, one-on-one conversations held between RAs and individual students to build connections, and RA-initiated programs in the residence halls that focus on academics, life skills, and current events. Running parallel to the Six-Week Challenge is our at-risk notification program, which sends notifications to faculty, residence hall staff, and advisors when at-risk behavior, that is, skipping class, is noted, so that follow-up interventions can be initiated.

While all of the aforementioned strategies support our entire student population, we are also sensitive to the special needs of minority students. One way to address their needs is through faculty hiring practices; we are proud that Eastern has the highest percentage of minority faculty in Connecticut.

Implementation of our Student Success Model has resulted in significant improvements in retention and graduation rates. Eastern has the highest retention and graduation rates in our state university system. In addition, retention of African American students is higher than that of our overall student body. Of particular note, in 2012, the Education Trust found that the improvement in the six-year graduation rate of our Latino students was the highest in the country. From 2004 to 2010, that rate improved from 20% to 57.8%, an increase of 37.8% that dwarfed the average growth of 3.5% found among public institutions in the study.

Leveraging financial aid

I cannot discuss increasing educational access to underrepresented populations, who often come from low-income neighborhoods, without talking about the issue of affordability. While individual public regional universities can only indirectly impact the national issues of student loan debt and federal and state financial aid support, we certainly can make decisions regarding how we package and offer financial aid on our campuses. At Eastern, we are using academic data and a family's estimated financial contributions to predict student persistence as a function of their ability to afford a college education. The decision point on financial aid awards evolves around which students needing financial assistance are most likely to return to campus each year to complete their education. Saddling a family with loan debt that they cannot repay is a recipe for failure—not only are those students likely to drop out, they do so with financial burdens they do not deserve and cannot manage. Counseling such students to attend a more affordable community college during their first two years or stopping out to work and save money is in the students' and the University's best interests. Using our admissions rating system, historical data, and new analytical tools, we are making progress in identifying students with moderate financial need who are most likely to persist and graduate, and awarding financial aid accordingly.

Summary

Using their historical focus on serving local needs, public regional universities are ideally situated to meet emerging workforce needs in their communities and the changing demographics of their states. Mindful collaborations with state university systems, programmatic change, and curricula renewal are all important steps that state universities can take in ensuring that they are responsive to the 21st-century challenges they face.

Relevance in the 21st Century

Being responsive to workforce needs and demographic changes occurring in our nation is critical to public regional universities meeting the needs of local constituencies. Being relevant in the 21st century is another important challenge. When I consider how public regional universities might work to ensure relevance in the global, technology-based society in which we live, two key stakeholders come to mind—**young people** and **employers**. It is a simple equation—one group will provide the energy, knowledge, and skills sought by the other. And the role of college campuses? We are the matchmakers who can groom and prepare young adults for successful careers by listening to employers.

The new generation(s)—a numbers game

Like many other northern tier states, Connecticut has witnessed an outward migration of young people for years. According to the U.S. Census, 5.8% of young adults ages 20 to 34 left Connecticut in 2014, paralleling similar figures in Vermont, New Hampshire, and Rhode Island. In addition to a general outward migration of young adults, high school graduates in Connecticut go out of state to college at a rate exceeded in the nation only by Vermont. Half of all Vermont students go out of state to college; Connecticut loses 45% of its students to out-of-state colleges and universities. Compare these figures to California, where 90% of the students stay in state; Utah, where 92% state in state; and Mississippi, where 93% stay in state.[5] The students leaving our state graduate from out-of-state institutions and often do not return to Connecticut to live.

Another emerging challenge is the decline in the number of students graduating from Connecticut high schools; high school graduating classes in Connecticut are projected to decline 1.2% a year through 2024.[6] This trend is also occurring in other states, especially those in the northern tier.

Attracting the newest generation of college students—even as the number of those students is shrinking dramatically—is a challenge that is being faced by most public regional universities, not only to safeguard their future as institutions, but to ensure that they contribute to a well-prepared workforce for their state economies. That means having majors and campus life opportunities that interest young people.

The good news? When you consider the individual interests and social dynamics of today's "millennial" and "Gen Z" generations, it is clear that public regional universities have a tremendous opportunity. The values and programs that are the hallmark of state universities have the potential of responding directly to the collective consciousness of today's young adults. In a highly competitive market, we can hold our own in competing for new students.

The Last of the Millennials

The last few years of the "Millennial" generation is on our campuses today. Born between 1981 and 1997, they consider themselves to be global citizens, and are able to connect to the rest of the world through a variety of digital technologies and online platforms. They favor collaboration over competition, and champion innovation and change. They respect diversity in all its forms—gender, sexuality, and religion—and expect college campuses to demonstrate that same commitment. Millennials are also committed to the environment and want to participate actively in stemming the effects of climate change. Millennials are altruistic and willing to invest their time in volunteering for causes intended to improve the quality of life in their communities.

These characteristics speak to a student population that is eager to engage in the challenges facing the world, willing to work together on a variety of issues and possessing a broader worldview than previous generations. College campuses that offer majors in emerging occupations while providing on- and off-campus engagement opportunities, including those that support the environment and local community initiatives, can have great success in attracting today's millennial generation.

"Gen Z"

The next generation of college students is right around the corner, and it bears equal and careful consideration. Gen Z comprises young people born after 1997. More than clothing, more than food, more than sleep, members of Gen Z cannot exist without the ever-present mobile devices that are the center of their lives. Communicating with friends; watching movies, concerts, and television shows; shopping online; and accessing every piece of information known to mankind are just some of the daily activities of the next wave of college students.

They don't just accept differences among themselves—they celebrate them. Diverse sexual identities and ethnic backgrounds are common in their social circles. The traditional nuclear family is foreign to many of them, although they are very close to their parents. They are more global in their perspective even than millennials, and equally committed to the environment, addressing world hunger and other pressing social issues. They have a strong work ethic even as they are suspicious of social institutions and traditional employers.

Gen Z values education—half are projected to go to college as they reach adulthood. They also are keenly aware that colleges and universities consider them to be a "market" to be cultivated. They would rather find a student at our schools on Facebook to get the "word" on our campuses than listen to the institutional messaging refined and delivered by our university relations offices.

Nothing about these two profiles should concern college administrators and faculty who are committed to responding to new generations of students. Campuses that have a clear identity grounded in values shared across the faculty and staff are positioned to provide a principle-centered, engaged experience to students dedicated to making a difference on campus, in their local community and across the world. Inclusive campus communities that foster multicultural experiences for their students can nurture the global perspectives of today's millennial and Gen Z students. And faculty who focus on meeting the workforce needs of their state economies will find that our newest generations of college students are very interested in careers in health, computers, the media and the nonprofit/public service sector—the same areas of our economies that seek well-prepared workers.

What do employers want?

At the same time that we must work to be relevant to today's newest group of college students, we must also ensure that our curriculum is relevant to the needs of regional and state employers. I have shared a number of examples of new majors on my own campus that have been launched in response to the workforce needs of Connecticut. Each of those majors includes core courses that delve deeply into their respective professions. Health science majors take classes in genetics, nutrition and anatomy and physiology. Media studies students master the latest digital communication technologies. Business information systems students learn the intricacies of computer programming. All these skills are essential to the future career success of students. Nonetheless, more important than job-specific or occupation-specific skills are the broad-based intellectual skills sought by America's employers.

In the past decade, a series of employer surveys commissioned by the Association of American Colleges and Universities (AAC&U) has consistently found that employers want to hire college graduates who can think critically, communicate clearly, solve problems, work together, and possess ethics and integrity. These broad intellectual and life skills are considered fundamental to career success by the vast majority of American employers. These same surveys indicate that employers value college campuses that provide applied learning opportunities—for example, internships—so that students can relate their classroom learning to practical situations.

Eastern has a mission-driven focus on the liberal arts. As Connecticut's only public liberal arts university, we pride ourselves on a sequential, integrated liberal arts core curriculum, with all Eastern students taking classes in science, math, art, the humanities, and social sciences. Within this curriculum are embedded four core competencies—critical thinking, communication, ethics, and information literacy—that speak to the broad intellectual abilities sought by employers across our nation.

Eastern is not unique in understanding the importance of developing a student's broad academic skills. Every public university offers some form of liberal arts or general education curriculum. Given the value placed on broad intellectual skills by American employers, we need to ensure the effectiveness of our general education programs. Staffing these courses with more full-time faculty; aligning general education courses with our majors; developing applied learning opportunities across campus; and improving the way we assess the effectiveness of our general education core are some of the ways that universities can ensure that we are providing students with skills that are relevant in today's workplace. There is no greater measure of our institutions' success than the ability of our graduates to fulfill their career aspirations. Making sure they have the skills most valued by U.S. employers will be the linchpin of that success.

Summary

We live in a world of constant change. Each succeeding generation of college students comes to campus with a new cultural perspective, new career interests and new technology tools to use in learning more about the world. Addressing the special needs and lifestyles of each new generation, while also responding to the skill requirements of the 21st-century workplace, are essential strategies for public regional universities seeking to remain relevant in the higher education arena.

Engagement: Motivating Today's Students

We can develop majors and other academic programs in response to our state and regions' workforce needs. We can respond to our nation's changing demographics by expanding access and improving services for underrepresented populations. We can align our campus programming to meet the interests of today's new generation of students as well as the needs of local employers. However, if we do not effectively capture the enthusiasm of our students, they will not stay to graduate from our institutions.

Data over the years—from the National Survey of Student Engagement (NSSE) to research conducted by the Association of American Colleges and Universities—has conclusively shown that students who are fully engaged on campus persist and graduate at higher levels. Yet the most recent NSSE survey showed that only 54% of college freshmen feel challenged by their institutions. While students drop out for many reasons—finances, personal challenges, poor academic performance—we cannot afford to have students leaving campus because we did not engage them and make them feel that they belong. That is a factor we **can** impact!

Residential life

Campus engagement can come in many forms. At the most basic level is campus residency—students who live on campus have better retention and graduation rates and higher GPAs. This is not hard to understand—common sense says that being near the library, computer labs and faculty advisors helps a student succeed. At Eastern, 90% of freshmen and 60% of all students live on our campus. We are the smallest of Connecticut's four state universities but are still the most residential. Not all state universities have an emphasis on residential life, but it is clearly one way to immediately engage students.

Clubs and organizations

Another way to engage students is through cocurricular clubs. Not all clubs are grounded in an academic discipline. However, those that are can provide a strong connection between a student's academic program and student life activities, ensuring that the skills they learn in both settings inform their personal and professional growth moving forward. We have more than eighty student clubs at Eastern, a number that grows each year as students create new clubs to explore shared interests. Our "Warrior Cup" provides a friendly competition between our thirteen residence halls that combines academic, social, and recreational contests. In the end, our data has consistently shown that students who participate in club activities have higher GPAs than our campus average.

Civic engagement

Another important way for students to be engaged both on and off campus is through community service and civic engagement. Social responsibility is one of Eastern's six core values, and students express this value by providing important services across the community—working in after-school programs; in middle school mentoring programs; at the local food pantry; in social service agencies; and in many other public and nonprofit organizations.

Central to this service commitment is the Center for Community Engagement (CCE), which was established in 2009 as part of our Strategic Plan. Prior to that time, resident students were required to perform eight hours of service in the community each year, yet with little attempt at coordination. Other volunteer activities occurred in a random, unorganized fashion. Since the CCE was created, volunteerism has increased, and service performed by students has been aligned with clearly defined community needs.

By coordinating our campus's commitment to the local community, the CCE has greatly expanded our presence and has resulted in national recognition (President Obama's Higher Education Community Service Honor Roll; Carnegie Foundation Community Engagement Designation) as well as the satisfaction of knowing Eastern is making a positive difference in the lives of local residents.

Our faculty has also created "service learning" courses where students apply skills learned in class to perform specialized community projects. One English class created business plans for local Latino businesses. Another group of students from the Psychology, Social Work and Education programs created a mentoring program for local middle school students. Business Information Systems students created a website for the local soup kitchen. Mentored by their faculty, graphic design students have performed pro bono design work for a local dairy and Paul Newman's "Hole in the Wall Gang" camp for children with serious illnesses. All of these are examples of where students applied their classroom learning to support community causes. It is no surprise that these are some of our best students!

Eastern is certainly not alone among public regional universities in teaching students social responsibility. What we have found, and I encourage other public universities to consider, is that coordinating all service to the local community through one central operation maximizes our resources and provides the greatest good in meeting pressing community needs. In addition, when faculty create service learning classes that link academic learning to community service, students have additional opportunities to apply their classroom experiences. Finally, in using the expertise and enthusiasm of their students to effect positive change in local communities, public universities can strengthen their identity and public image as socially responsible institutions serving local and regional constituencies.

Environmental stewardship

Another aspect of Eastern's commitment to the local community and state is our Institute for Sustainable Energy, which provides environmental education and service to municipalities (free energy audits), school districts (sustainable curriculum), and fellow college campuses (as cochair of the Connecticut Alliance on Campus Sustainability with Yale University). The Institute works closely with our Environmental Earth Science Department to provide on-campus internships for students in our sustainable energy program, and also collaborates with our Facilities Department on a variety of green campus initiatives. All of these efforts have resulted in Eastern being named one of the nation's top green colleges for the past seven years in a row by *The Princeton Review* and the U.S. Green Building Council. This list of green colleges includes many other public regional universities, whose focus on serving their state provides impetus to pursue sustainability initiatives to protect the local environment.

On-campus internships

One of the more innovative strategies we have in place at Eastern to enhance student engagement is our on-campus internship program. Such a program is different from developing and encouraging students to take internships off campus. Most if not all public regional universities support off-campus internships. At Eastern, those include placements at ESPN, Aetna, Pfizer, United Technologies, and many other sites in Connecticut and elsewhere.

Even though these off-campus internships (for credit) and co-ops (paid internships) are important aspects of applied learning at Eastern, our on-campus internship program provides a unique opportunity for students while strengthening our ties with major state employers. It began in fall 2011 when Eastern partnered with Cigna, the international health care provider headquartered in Bloomfield, Connecticut, to open a "Work Hub" on campus as part of Cigna's Technology Early Career Development Program. The facility gives students an on-campus location to develop practical skills by completing real-time work assignments without having to travel off campus, while providing Cigna with a secure computer network and dedicated facility where its staff delivers on-site guidance to Eastern student interns.

Since the Work Hub's inception, more than seventy Eastern computer science and business information systems majors have held paid internships in the program, and fifty-four have continued with Cigna as full-time employees after graduation. Eastern's relationship with Cigna has opened opportunities to work with other major employers in the state. One is the Jackson Laboratory (JAX), a major biomedical research facility based in Farmington, Connecticut. A summer program at JAX to provide Eastern interns with opportunities to conduct bioinformatics and computational biology research has been so successful that plans are underway to bring JAX to Eastern to be part of the on-campus Work Hub. Other additions to the Work Hub include Horizons, a local nonprofit organization, and most recently, the Connecticut Department of Energy and Environmental Protection (DEEP). Students studying geographic information systems in the Environmental Earth Science Department have been tasked with developing a searchable database for all state land holdings (state parks, forests, and other properties) under DEEP jurisdiction.

While hosting employers on campus to provide students with convenient internship opportunities may not be unique to Eastern, I have not found a great number of other schools employing this strategy. For instance, Brigham Young University has an excellent on-campus internship program for private sector and other off-campus clients. However, most public regional universities have a more traditional approach, where on-campus internships are limited to internal academic and administrative departments.

I would encourage more universities to consider using the Work Hub model we have implemented at Eastern in supporting off-campus organizations. The key takeaway is that such opportunities represent true partnerships with employers, where students learn skills that are preparing them for clearly defined career pathways. At the same time, employers like Cigna are gaining more insight into the comprehensive liberal arts education provided on our campus and developing important relationships with our faculty. With students interning for a major economic player knowing that they have an opportunity to prove their worth and be gainfully employed at the company after graduation, we have created a powerful career development strategy and an example of how engaging students in active learning can maximize their college experience.

Summary

Current NSSE data suggests that American colleges and universities are being challenged to motivate and engage today's students. With their historical focus on serving regional constituencies, public regional universities are well positioned to use their campuses and local communities as laboratories for social change while addressing community needs and other regional concerns. Engaging students and developing their leadership skills through cocurricular clubs, addressing environmental issues and providing applied learning opportunities through on- and off-campus internships are additional approaches to engage students on our campuses. All of these strategies align with the historical mission and strengths of public universities. Engagement is not simply adding value to the undergraduate experience. When we can engage students' hearts and minds, we can increase retention and graduation rates and meet our public mission in the process.

Accountability: Turning Compliance into Opportunity

Our campuses need to be responsive to changing conditions in our states, and relevant to the global society of the 21st century. We also need to ensure that our students are fully engaged in and out of the classroom on our campuses. A proactive response to these challenges can put public regional universities in position to prosper and grow in the coming years. However, in addition to these challenges, we also face expectations from a host of stakeholders. And whereas curricular renewal, expanding educational access and enhancing student life opportunities on our campuses keep us internally focused, effectively responding to stakeholder expectations is inherently an outward-directed, public experience.

Some expectations are formal—self-study reports and five-year updates to our accrediting agencies; statistical reports to state governing agencies; and annual data reports to national clearinghouses. Other levels of accountability are less formal and represent an ongoing dialog with taxpayers, parents, donors, and other constituencies who expect us to provide a quality education at an affordable price that prepares students for gainful careers and productive lives.

In addition to responding to these expectations, we must also address other criticisms. Many people in our country question the need for a college degree at all in today's economy. Others insist that a college education has limited public merit and should be entirely paid for by students. Those who appreciate the value of a college degree nonetheless insist that we are doing a poor job of teaching the right subjects to prepare students for the jobs that exist in our local and state economies. Or they look at our institutional metrics and challenge us to do a better job of retaining and graduating students.

Such complaints are born from tough realities we must be willing to confront. The cost of a college education has skyrocketed. State legislators face the unenviable task of allocating limited funds to many deserving public agencies. Across our nation people are concerned about lost jobs and a static economy. We cannot ignore these concerns.

Too often in the past we have viewed the issue of accountability as a matter of compliance. If we completed a report, submitted data or answered a survey, we hoped that "they" would go away. On my own campus, we have struggled in the past to assign sufficient time and resources to the task of monitoring and assessing the progress made toward meeting our goals. Some departments have been very good about evaluating their effectiveness, but others have not. I suspect this scenario plays out on every public university campus in America.

What can we do?

How can we best demonstrate that public state universities are accountable and deserving of the public's trust? First, I believe we need to understand what accountability issues are best left to advocacy groups at the national and state level, and which ones are best approached on our own campuses. While we focus on that which we can directly impact, our campuses can certainly participate as actively as we can in the national dialog surrounding the perceived value of public higher education.

Two issues of particular note on the national stage are student loan debt and the overall cost of higher education, and the related issue of tuition relief for students attending public institutions. These issues continue to be debated by political candidates and in the halls of Congress. Organizations such as the American Association of State Colleges and Universities, the Association of American Colleges and Universities, the American Council on Education and others are best positioned to lead the discussion on how to make college affordable for more families in this country. What can individual institutions do? We can provide data, alumni testimonials, student success stories and other anecdotal information when asked, stay apprised of the issues, and do what we can back on our campuses to help students manage their finances while seeking cost efficiencies in our operations.

We should also be actively engaged with our partner institutions in any state initiatives within public higher education systems to address the interests of local and state stakeholders, including legislators and other policymakers. In Connecticut, for instance, our system of state colleges and universities is currently engaged in a collaborative planning project to improve student outcomes on our seven campuses while seeking cost efficiencies and economies of scale. Committees composed of faculty, administrators and system staff are looking at purchasing, financial aid, human resource issues, and other strategies to improve our state system and demonstrate to legislators and other stakeholders that they are making a sound investment in our institutions.

We are also expanding use of data to demonstrate our success. Data collected by the Integrated Postsecondary Education Data System (IPEDS) limits graduation data to first-time, full-time students graduating from their native institution. When a student transfers to another school and graduates, neither the campus they leave nor the institution receiving them gets credit. Our Connecticut system of public colleges and universities is looking at the Voluntary System of

Accountability and the Student Achievement Measure, both of which measure and aggregate the graduation success of students attending multiple institutions.

Back on our campuses, I believe all public universities should be about the task of improving their ability to assess and enhance educational offerings and programs. Regional university campuses can point to the success of their students and the services they provide local and state constituencies as symbols of their ultimate value. We need to be as strategic in responding to accountability concerns as we are in developing new curriculum, improving on-campus services to students and responding to shifting social demographics and economic realities. If we can do that, we can reaffirm the value of state universities and advocate for more public support of our institutions.

On my own campus, we are committed to a campaign to improve how we assess student and institutional success. This campaign is being led by a Faculty Senate-approved Assessment Committee tasked with creating an assessment climate on campus and coordinating an ongoing, standards based, comprehensive program of programmatic and institutional assessment. Using the work of Truman State University in Missouri as our model, we are planning an annual Assessment Day to conduct campus-wide assessments while engaging in an intensive dialog on how best to gather and evaluate assessment data. And we are not limiting the scope of our assessment culture to academic majors and our liberal arts core

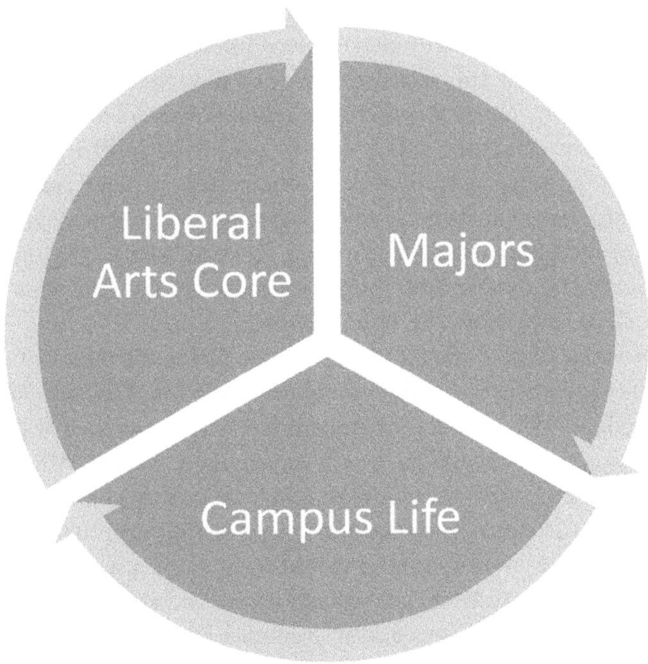

A Campus-wide Commitment to Assessment

curriculum—everything on campus will be part of the new assessment paradigm. Creating a culture of gathering and assessing data while aligning program and institutional effectiveness measures are central to our goal of making assessment everyone's business on our campus.

Assessing student learning outcomes in the liberal arts core

Following our most recent reaccreditation site visit, our accrediting agency—the New England Association of Schools and Colleges—asked Eastern to develop a more comprehensive strategy for assessing student learning in our liberal arts core curriculum. We are not alone. Colleges and universities across the nation are being asked to prove that students in general education courses are learning the broad intellectual competencies sought by employers. In addition to accrediting agencies, this expectation is shared by governing boards, legislators, students, and their parents.

Eastern is involved in a major project to address the issue of assessing broad intellectual competencies—the Multi-State Collaborative Project (MSCP). The project is cosponsored by the State Higher Education Executive Officers Association and AAC&U. Connecticut is one of nine states in the MSCP pilot project—Utah, Massachusetts, Oregon, Kentucky, Minnesota, Missouri, Rhode Island, and Indiana being the others—and Eastern was one of eight institutions in Connecticut involved in the pilot project. The AAC&U's VALUE rubric (Valid Assessment of Learning in Undergraduate Education) was used to assess the broad intellectual skills of critical thinking, written/oral communication, and quantitative literacy.

The project assessed the actual artifacts of student work—the portfolio of a graphic art student; an award-winning educational video produced by early childhood education students; and a robotic prototype built by a computer science student. By focusing on student work, the project avoided standardized tests, something faculty have consistently told us cannot properly evaluate the diversity and richness of individual student learning. Another key to the model was that the review process was undertaken by out-of-state faculty reviewers who did not assign the work or come from the same campus.

Eastern was one of fifty-nine institutions involved in the pilot, with more than a thousand faculty members across the nine states using the AAC&U VALUE rubric to assess more than 7000 products of student work. If you looked at the exit survey data from the project, you would have to be encouraged. Almost 90% of participants said the VALUE rubric was useful in measuring the quality of student work.

With 20% of the states in our country now having experience in the MSCP student outcome assessment model, it would seem to be a wonderful opportunity worth pursuing more broadly at the national level. And at the state level, with half of our Connecticut state colleges and universities involved in the MSCP, we are leveraging this national project to develop statewide assessments. We kicked this initiative off with a statewide assessment conference in May 2016.

Assessing student learning in the majors

The faculty involved in the Multi-State Collaborative Project certainly see implications for assessing the work of students in their majors, especially in assessing portfolios, artifacts, and other outcomes of capstone projects. Another project we are working on is the LEAPS Challenge, a project sponsored by AAC&U involving eight colleges and universities in New England. Running through 2018, the three-year project aims to improve experiential learning by helping faculty modify their courses to enhance capstone projects as well as freshmen research experiences. By engaging students in "signature work" that impacts real problems facing local communities, the program seeks to enhance student engagement, deepen their learning and assess the impact of experiential learning on student progress in their major. Two of our newer majors—Health Sciences and New Media Studies—are involved in the project.

An additional example of how our academic departments are assessing major-specific competencies is our Psychology Department, which uses American Psychology Association guidelines to assess knowledge among freshmen and seniors. In response to these assessments, the department has expanded its research methods sequence from one to two courses and created a one-credit "introduction to the major" course to give students a clear understanding of the essential skills they will be learning.

Assessing student affairs and other campus life operations

On a small campus like Eastern's, every department has a role to play in student success—including the groundskeepers, food service workers, clerical help, and the bursar's office. As we continue to implement a campus-wide assessment culture, all operations on our campus will benefit from improvements in how we evaluate their effectiveness. One area of the campus that has been conducting self-assessments for years is the Division of Student Affairs. From collecting data on student life activities on campus (clubs, events, and community service) to having its own Assessment Committee and schedule of assessing individual offices, to using the Student Affairs Program Assessment System developed by Educational Benchmarks, Inc., the division has become a model for other nonacademic departments.

Summary

Public universities are facing expectations from a host of stakeholders, as legislators, accrediting agencies, donors, alumni, parents, and students seek greater accountability for the significant investment America makes in its public higher education system. Even the inherent value of a college degree is under attack. Advocacy groups at the national and state level are working diligently to find ways to make a college degree more affordable, at the same time they present evidence of the important contributions public colleges and universities are making in this country. Back on campus, public university administrators and faculty should be about the task of assessing student learning and institutional operations, not only to strengthen the public trust, but to improve the quality of education our students receive. Taking our role in demonstrating accountability seriously will go a long way toward regaining the public's faith in the importance of public higher education in the United States.

The Role of Advocacy

As universities continue to stretch limited resources in the face of new demands for educational programs and services, the role of advocacy in educating the public has never been more important. There are certainly valid criticisms of higher education that must be addressed. We need to improve retention and graduation rates. We need to expand educational access. We need to make higher education more affordable. As we address these issues, it is imperative that we make a case for renewed support of public higher education. When we can show our boards, legislators, accrediting agencies, and others that we are developing assessment tools that they can support, they become partners in our efforts rather than critics.

Crafting a message that combines verifiable data with the experiences of students and alumni—through anecdotes and testimony—is critical in advocating for more support from state legislators and higher approval from taxpayers, parents, and other important constituencies. We can never assume any constituent knows enough good news about our institutions!

We have a strong message to share, both in terms of the fundamental need for public higher education and our value in meeting the career aspirations of our residents and the social and economic requirements of our democracy. We know—with certainty—that a college degree is the best avenue young people of all backgrounds have of economic prosperity and social mobility. We know with equal certainty that the viability of our local, state, and national economies depend on a future workforce that will require more, not less education. We know that liberal arts and general education core courses are a fundamental component of any successful college student's education. We know that the public's investment in higher education can continue to pay dividends for students, for employers and for society-at-large.

In 1990, America was number one in the world in the percentage of adults with a college degree; we are now no better than fourteenth in the world. Not only do economists continue to cite our need for a more educated workforce; data from multiple sources have historically shown that a college degree increases a person's earning potential over their career. These facts should not be presumed to be widely known or accepted by our constituencies. Restating the need for a college degree and for an educated citizenry must be a central part of our advocacy.

The second part of what must be a heightened campaign to articulate the value of public higher education is to insist on renewed public funding of our institutions. The best way to do that is to show a return on the public's investment, using both the personal stories of our graduates and data that show improved metrics—better retention rates, higher graduation rates, lower student debt, increased alumni philanthropic support, and other measures of exemplary educational programs and sound fiscal management.

Certainly university presidents must be central to this advocacy effort, whether hosting breakfasts for legislators, speaking publicly to civic organizations, or appearing on radio talk shows. However, expanding the messenger corps is an important consideration. On my own campus, we have found it very effective to have faculty and students testify in legislative hearings and other public forums. Not only do they speak to their own personal experiences, but we provide them with data so that they can also demonstrate statistical proof of our progress.

CONCLUSION

Public state universities serving regional constituencies face many challenges today. Especially in our northern states, high school graduating classes are declining, and students are leaving to attend colleges out of state. There is intense competition for those students staying in state, at the same time that the state appropriations needed to fund essential educational services is declining. Employers are concerned about finding enough trained employees and students are stressing about finding gainful employment. Legislators are demanding greater accountability while parents are fighting the rising cost of education.

These are difficult times for college administrators, but our response need not be despair. In particular, public regional universities are uniquely positioned to respond to these challenges with educational programs and operational improvements that will garner increased support and approval from key stakeholders. In reaffirming our historical mission to serve our local communities and residents and taking the time to plan their future, we can demonstrate the critical need for public higher education in this country and the value our institutions can add to our economic vitality and the social order.

By truly being responsive to the workforce needs of our state economies and changing demographics; by ensuring the relevance of our academic programs to the new generation of students; by teaching the broad intellectual skills being requested by employers; by engaging students and making them feel at home on our campuses through a wide range of student life and applied learning activities; and by treating assessment of student outcomes and campus operations as an opportunity not a burden, public regional universities can take a leadership position in today's higher education arena.

It is time to step out of the shadow of land-grant institutions and national universities. No doubt those institutions will continue to elevate our stature as the world's most advanced nation. However, it is our public regional universities—working hard to serve the majority of college students—that are preparing the future citizen leaders of their states. We need to vocally declare the need for public education, insist on the financial and other support needed from state legislators and taxpayers to ensure our success, and articulate the value we add to our society to every one we can reach with this message.

There is one more reason why public higher education continues to be the best investment we can make in the future of our great nation. Since the days of our founding fathers, America's leaders have understood the importance of education in protecting our freedoms. Thomas Jefferson wrote that publicly supported education was necessary "to enable every man to judge for himself what will secure or endanger his freedom."

In September 1938, President Franklin D. Roosevelt renewed that belief when he said, "Democracy cannot succeed unless those who express their choice are prepared to choose wisely. The real safeguard of democracy, therefore, is education." In a presidential election year in which personal attack has replaced policy discussion, Jefferson's and FDR's words have never been more meaningful. Education has and will continue to be the safety net to protect the democratic freedoms we enjoy. And public regional state universities have a central role to play in protecting those freedoms.

NOTES

1. Most public regional universities in the United States have a similar history. Today they principally serve residents and employers of their home state, often with a regional focus, especially in larger states. They are publicly funded by state appropriations to varying degrees, and usually organized and governed by a statewide system structure.
2. Eastern is one of four state universities in Connecticut and part of a system of seventeen state colleges and universities. We are located in Willimantic in northeast Connecticut.
3. Our Connecticut State Colleges and Universities system includes twelve community colleges, four state universities and an online college.
4. Anthony P. Carnevale, Nicole Smith, Jeff Strohl, "Help Wanted," a report by the Georgetown University Center on Education and the Workforce, Georgetown Public Policy institute; June 15, 2010.
5. U.S. Department of Education, National Center for Education Statistics; Table 259; 2012.
6. U.S. Department of Education, National Center for Education Statistics; April 2016.

CHAPTER THIRTEEN

How Transformational Change Can Prepare HBCUs and MSIs to Be Competitive in the 21st Century

JAMES A. ANDERSON
Chancellor, Fayetteville State University

While I continue to be hopeful, I feel uneasy as I review the statements and summaries of others as they discuss the current state of affairs and/or the future prospects of Historically Black Colleges and Universities and Minority Serving Institutions in the United States. Many of these stated positions are generally factual and well intentioned; however, they suffer from similar shortcomings: the focus is too broad or primarily conceptual; they emphasize a limited MICRO range of strategies as opposed to a broad MACRO institutional analysis; many comments are not grounded in the best research, best models, and best practices; they do not stress a transformational vision; they do not offer evidenced-based suggestions; and they fail to calculate the real cost of transformation. I have been very fortunate over the last twenty-five years to serve as a consultant for over 300 two- and four-year institutions, including thirty-five HBCUs, and I was able to apply a critical lens to each.

HBCUs and some MSIs (Minority Serving Institutions) face multiple issues that are complex and often confounded and are shared by other U.S. institutions. However, they are also confronted by challenges that are unique to them. Many HBCUs/MSIs are attempting to stay true to their historical mission and core values while also developing secondary identities that are shaped by new pressures that are inescapable. Among these are (a) introducing new demographics into traditional enrollments; (b) confronting new fiscal constraints; (c) performance-based funding; (d) developing new revenue streams; (e) adopting online and distance education; (f) enhancing their research identity; and (g) marketing for the competitive edge. Utilizing both a survey and face-to-face interviews with HBCU CEOs, The Association of Governing Boards of Universities and Colleges issued a report (2014) titled: "Top Strategic Issues Facing HBCUs, Now and into the Future." The report identifies seven pressing priorities for HBCUs: enrollment management, academic quality, infrastructure, federal and state policy, governance and leadership, and threaded throughout all of these was the issue of ensuring student success. As a data gathering report, this is an excellent tool but it is only the starting point for the development of working models for any HBCU.

HBCU EDUCATIONAL DESIGN: INTENTIONAL, COHERENT, AND EVIDENCED BASED

Integrated transformative change at HBCUs/MSIs begins with and will be driven by institutional and educational design that is intentional, coherent, and evidence based. This represents the overarching umbrella for 21st-century change and preparedness on individual campuses. Over the years, as I have worked with HBCUs and MSIs, I often begin by asking the campus community, and especially institutional leaders, whether or not they are a learning-centered institution, and if so, describe what that means. Invariably they struggle to answer and many campus members simply state that they do not know. Additionally, their answer becomes less confident when I ask what evidence is utilized to justify their answer. My analysis of learning-centered institutions suggests that they are characterized by a seamless integration of the following:

- A Commitment to Institutional Effectiveness and Accountability
- The Utilization of a Strong Conceptual and Strategic Model
- The Utilization of Appropriate Goals and Measurable Program Outcomes
- The Incorporation of Effective Teaching-Learning Outcomes
- The Integration of Co-Curricular and Academic Support Outcomes
- The Application of Outcomes That Influence Success Strategies
- The Committed Support for Faculty Development and Renewal
- A Commitment to New or Reallocated Resource Support
- Evidence of Transformational Leadership

With these same institutions, I follow this discussion with another probing exercise that asks a similar question about the presence or absence of a "student-centered" learning environment on their campus. This refers to a student success effort, which is characterized by:

- Clearly defined and measurable outcomes in the areas of teaching, learning, retention, and student social-psychological development
- Front-loaded activities which engage the student, as soon as possible, and introduce him/her to the academic and social expectations of the institution
- An ongoing assessment effort associated with student development and program improvement
- A community of faculty and staff who are deeply committed and who are well trained to deliver the appropriate services

While institutions may vary in terms of the amount of commitment to each of the above at any given point in time, the first step to transformation is the realization that these, and others, are vital factors. Such critical awareness must become a badge of leadership and accountability among HBCU/MSI leaders. University of Pennsylvania scholar Mary Beth Gasman (2013) identified the need for "forward thinking presidents" to tackle the major challenges facing HBCUs. Other presidents lament the significant turnover in CEO positions at HBCUs in the last few years. During the 2015 convening of the White House Initiative on HBCUs, a panel of HBCU presidents reiterated the importance of innovative and effective leadership to address institutional challenges (Arnett, 2015a). Yet my experience is that many of these same leaders do not translate their words into effective action for their institution. Perhaps part of the problem may be that they do not surround themselves with highly competent leadership (staff/administrators), and then empower them to produce successful efforts. When their power is unleashed, we find that they often begin their efforts by identifying the appropriate questions that will drive their thinking. For example, in an attempt to address the question of the efficacy of an institution's student-support program, an empowered leadership team might begin with the following questions:

1. What institutionally based information on student needs and characteristics is utilized by student support personnel? Is this the correct information?
2. What specific information about student subpopulations (women, students of color, nontraditional students, first-generation students, etc.) is utilized by student support personnel to foster their success?
3. What information about student culture, campus climate, faculty attitudes, and concerns is gathered periodically and shared with the appropriate audiences?
4. Describe a profile of the students who utilize student support services the most/least. What accounts for their respective behavior?
5. Based upon this profile what is the impact of your responses to the previous questions on (a) grading (b) classroom participation and performance,

(c) persistence, and (d) a reduction in the percentage of D, F, W, and incomplete grades.

Institutional leaders must ask themselves: in the absence of such probing questions, what information is utilized and shared to promote transformational change and student success?

MONITORING PROGRESS IN ACHIEVING GOALS

All colleges and universities gather and analyze some of the same data, often because they have to report on it. But the real value of data gathering and analytics to the institution is that it allows us to monitor our progress in achieving our goals. This is especially true if the institution operates under a model of performance-based funding. An unsophisticated approach to data gathering and analytics can lead to false conclusions or a picture of institutional health/effectiveness that is not supported by data. Poor data cannot and should not inform resource decisions. The aforementioned AGB report (2014) suggests that as HBCUs build sustainable enrollment management models, they should share information with their respective Boards that brings the Boards into the critical dialogue.

My tenure as a member of the Executive Council of SACSCOC, the regional accrediting body, allowed me to conduct site visits and/or review the portfolios of several HBCUs. Invariably their problems fell into two categories: institutional effectiveness and fiscal issues. HBCU decision-making must be guided by evidenced-based decisions. For example, among the data that we collect for target populations at Fayetteville State University (FSU) are the following:

- Enrollment of target populations (first-time freshman, transfers, students of color, commuters, on-line students. Pell Grant students, etc.). Targets can be achieved by improving retention and, if not, the campus will need to increase enrollment.
- Earned credit ratio: Percentage earning at least 80% of attempted hours (students falling below this threshold will not likely complete a degree).
- Credit accumulation threshold: Percentage earning at least 30 credits per calendar year (students who fall below this threshold will likely not complete the degree in four years and thus increase indebtedness).
- GPA threshold: Percentage earning minimum cumulative GPA associated with degree completion.
- Gateway courses: Percentage earning at least a C in gateway courses (those that influence movement into a major or degree program and that often have high failure rates or incompletes).

- Persistence: annual percentage of students that re-enroll or earn a degree.
- Undergraduate Degree Efficiency: a better metric than persistence because it shows the true relationship of enrollment and graduates more fully. This metric is the percentage of all enrolled degree-seeking undergraduates that complete a degree in a year—first-time freshmen and transfer students.
- Loan indebtedness: Monitor indebtedness on annual basis to determine if loan indebtedness puts student in future risk.
- Work hours: Monitor impact on other metrics.
- Utilization of academic supports: Weaker students need to assertively use them more. If Pell recipients are falling behind other students in completion of Gateway courses, we would look at the utilization of academic supports and perhaps discover that (1) we need to increase the amount of supports that are offered (additional funding), and/or (2) we need to mandate that Pell students participate in academic supports

What is the responsibility of the President/Chancellor, Chief Academic Officer, and Board Chair concerning the dissemination of this data and any subsequent discussions? First, it must be shared with every appropriate constituency group, and second, it must be reviewed on a consistent basis. At FSU, we update our Board of Trustees at every meeting on any significant changes in the data, and whether the results portend any changes in the existing resource investment. In my cabinet meetings, I and the Vice Chancellors discuss the data several times a semester or as often as need be. What can be said about campus leaders and Board members who do not receive this information or don't know how to interpret it? They are not engaging in evidence-based decision-making and, most likely, find it difficult to operate in the absence of such critical data. These institutions also will not attract transformative leaders to positions that are open as part of a search process.

When I arrived at Fayetteville State University in 2008, I asked for a summary of the varied types of data collection that was occurring at the University. In particular, I wanted to examine the data related to the predictors of persistence and effective academic performance. The target group that we chose to examine were high school students and first-year transfers who were slightly below FSU's admission standards and who had to participate successfully in a Summer Bridge program to be admitted in the fall semester. Most were low-income African American students. We examined the structural relationships of four constructs on academic performance and persistence for a Summer Bridge Learning Community (SBLC) versus the non-SBLC students. Constructs included: (1) student background variables, (2) academic confidence, (3) desire to finish college, and (4) the intent to transfer to/from Fayetteville State University. I placed an additional burden on the staff who were conducting this research by indicating that I wanted a high-quality research report that could be submitted to a refereed journal. The finding was that there was a significant direct effect of academic confidence on academic performance for SBLC members. This finding then influenced the design of many of our first-year initiatives (Allen & Bir, 2012).

EFFECTIVE TEACHING AT HBCUs AND MSIs

Because the demographic characteristics and level of preparedness often differ when we compare HBCUs/MSIs to Predominantly White Institutions (PWIs) the assumption might be made that the quality of teaching must also differ such that it is more accommodating in a negative sense. In fact, the reality is that the teaching/learning model must be more rigorous and grounded in the best research, best models, and best practices. Returning to the earlier theme of intentionality and coherence in educational design, the teaching/learning model should be aligned at the MACRO level with:

1. Overarching institutional goals (example: retention and degree efficiency)
2. Divisional and department goals (example: success in the major or a reduction in the percentage of student Ds, Fs, and Ws in gateway courses)
3. General Education goals: (example: reflective thinking)
4. Individual course goals: (example: enhance student ability to put course content into a cognitive matrix that facilitates note-taking)
5. Co-curricular goals: (example: increased use of academic supports)

At the MICRO level strategies come into play that facilitate the MACRO alignment. It is at this point that institutional leadership must find ways to facilitate faculty work. One way of looking at an effective teaching/learning model at HBCUs/MSIs is to discuss "Teaching for Retention and Diversity." The Provost/VP for Academic Affairs must lead the discussion with Deans, Department Chairs and faculty on a discipline-based approach to this type of emphasis. Teaching for Retention and Diversity could utilize the following framework:

Teaching for student outcomes:

- Discipline-based course content
- Cognitive outcomes
- Course grades (example: C-wall courses)
- Competency testing
- Service learning

Teaching with support services:

- Tutoring
- Advising
- Mentoring
- Connection to centers (learning and writing)
- Connection to developmental programs

Faculty development and support (incentive-based efforts):

An example of combining elements from this framework could be a Freshman Seminar where instructors target a cognitive outcome such as "reflective thinking" in the course content. Students are also enrolled in a service-learning project that emphasizes reflective learning and, through the Writing Center, learn to write persuasively about one's reflective experiences. Another example of how the framework could be utilized would involve asking faculty to identify "bottlenecks" or conceptual difficulties that their students experience in gateway courses. We compare that to what students report as their difficulty in the same courses. Students are then enrolled in an academic support such as Supplemental Instruction that can supplement the course outcome of reflective thinking. The following are examples of such "bottlenecks in gateway courses." If students don't negotiate the early bottlenecks in a course, then they won't likely grasp conceptual relationships later in the course:

Accounting—debits
Biology—cell division
Chemistry—molarity
Physics—vectors
Geology—hydraulic flow gradients
Engineering—statics and dynamics
Languages—verb tenses
Philosophy—conceptual relationships among varied philosophical positions
Psychology—classical conditioning and operant conditioning
Statistics—concept of variance

Faculty members have the responsibility of monitoring which bottlenecks are most problematic across their courses, and then utilizing proven strategies to address student difficulty. To do any less is to doom a certain category of students to failure. Sometimes the change that is necessary is as simple as reordering the course sequence in the major. I have worked with several nursing programs at HBCUs that exhibited high failure or dropout rates in their programs. We targeted the anatomy and physiology course, taught in the first semester of the first year, as a primary culprit. I asked why did the less prepared students have to take this course in the first year. The answer was usually the same: "This is the way the course sequence has always been." I suggested that this course be moved to the third semester and replaced by a first-year seminar that allowed the less prepared students to work on skill development and competency building. Once implemented, the success of at-risk nursing students was almost immediate.

When I arrived at FSU in 2008, I committed $400,000 to faculty development. I indicated that faculty could submit competitive proposals to enhance teaching/learning outcomes in their courses or department. More important was my promise not to touch those funds even in the face of mandated state budget cuts. From 2008 to 2014, the UNC system experienced six consecutive years of budget cuts.

An example of how a program outcome gets translated into a learning outcome with an attendant set of metrics occurred at North Carolina State University, where I served as Vice Provost and Dean of Undergraduate Affairs (1992–2003). At that time, the data on the academic performance and first-to-second year persistence of the incoming classes did not jibe with the profile of those incoming students, which would have predicted more positive outcomes. The data were even more troubling for students of color. The decision was made to do two things: (1) establish a First Year College (FYC) where students could choose to enter without declaring a major and where all of the best practices on student success could be applied, and (2) bolster the quality of the existing Summer Bridge program (the Transition Program) for entering minority students. That program was moved to start in the fall semester. One of the major outcomes that faculty, staff, and administrators committed to for both programs was the following:

Program outcome: Students in the program will develop positive attitudes towards learning and increase their own commitment and responsibility for their own learning. As part of our commitment to fund this outcome, we wrote and received two consecutive grants from the William and Flora Hewlett Foundation. A key aspect of this grant was to buy out release time (one course per semester) for one year for faculty to develop their courses in line with the outcome. The faculty developed a teaching/learning community known as the Hewlett Fellows and their focus across disciplines was on Inquiry-Guided Learning (IGL). They shared their strategies across disciplines. Among the metrics for the initiative were:

(1) Examine pre/post gains when comparing the FYC cohort with a matched pair of non-FYC freshmen on dimensions such as academic skills, incoming admissions scores (ACT or SAT), critical thinking, values toward learning, academic self-confidence, etc.).
(2) Ask students to develop a comprehensive plan of study to cover four years.
(3) Train students to develop learning portfolios so they could track their own learning gains.

(4) Administer the Learning Environment Preferences Survey (based on the cognitive developmental scheme of William Perry) or the CLA (Collegiate Learning Assessment) which assesses critical thinking.

The First Year College at North Carolina State University became the seminal model of student success for many similar programs around the country, and the students in the Transition Program consistently outperformed a significant percentage of non-Transition freshmen (mainly White) who entered with stellar academic profiles. Both programs succeeded because they integrated multiple areas; were well funded; utilized best research, best models, and best practices; were developed and supported by committed leadership; and the faculty took ownership of their components.

ENSURING THAT HBCUs AND MSIs ARE ADDRESSING ALL COMPONENTS OF ACADEMIC QUALITY IN THE COMPETITIVE EDUCATIONAL MARKET

In the aforementioned SEF survey/interview of HBCU presidents, quality programs and academic reputation were listed as high priorities. Yet, the development and assessment of program outcomes and learning outcomes were of a lesser concern. While many HBCUs and MSIs market that their academic programs are of high quality and that they are committed to student success, it is often difficult to identify whether there is an institutional commitment to strengthening the connection between strategic planning, academic quality, program outcomes, student success outcomes, and learning outcomes. Such clearly was the case when I arrived at FSU in 2008. There was no strategic plan or business model that could fund quality programs in the future, and the Board of Trustees had not been included in the critical discussions about academic quality and the future of the University, and they only had a surface knowledge of who their students really were. Many minority-serving institutions find themselves in this dilemma. Yet, it would be so easy to start students off with a reading like that of Laura Rendon et al. (2004) that delves into the first-year experiences of students of color, or my book *Change and Transformative Leadership in the Academy* (Anderson, 2008). It would also be easy to scan the websites of successful peer institutions to get examples of successful models, and perhaps to arrange a visit for a closer examination. Currently, several foundations and higher education organizations are involved in transformative grants for HBCUs (e.g., Bill and Melinda Gates Foundation, Lilly Foundation, United Negro College Fund, Association of American Colleges and Universities, Lumina Foundation, and Thurgood Marshall Foundation).

The critical question becomes: If HBCU and MSI Board members and campus CEOs are not part of the critical discussion about student success and educational quality, then how do they know that the resource investments are the right ones? How do they know if they are supporting an institutional model that is long-term as opposed to isolated and unconnected strategies that may/may not work in the short term? If these leaders are really concerned with finding cost-effective ways to ensure student success and educational quality, then they should be an integral part of the development of a plan and business model that provides historical evidence of effectiveness and future success. Campus Boards, senior leadership, and faculty should currently be in discussions about the future high-quality academic programs that need to be developed to serve as new revenue streams and sources of institutional excellence, marketing, and branding. To do anything less is to vacate our responsibility as leaders to transform our institutions.

REFERENCES

Allen, D., & Bir, B. (2012). Academic confidence and summer bridge learning communities: Path analytic linages to student persistence. *Journal of College Student Retention* 13(4), 519–548.

Anderson, J. A. (2008). Driving change through diversity and globalization: Transformative leadership in the academy. Sterling, VA: Stylus Publishing, LLC.

Arnett, A. (2015a). HBCU Presidents Offer Advice to New Leaders. Diverse Issues in Higher Education. Retrieved from http://diverseeducation.com/article/77987/

Gasman, M. (2013). The changing face of historically Black colleges and universities. Center for Minority Serving Institutions, University of Pennsylvania, Philadelphia.

Rendon, L. I., Garcia, M., and Person, D. (Eds.), (2004). Transforming the first-year experience for students of color. Monograph No. 38. Columbia, University of South Carolina, National Resource Center for the First Year Experience and Students in Transition.

Report by the Association of Governing Boards of Universities and Colleges (2014). Top strategic issues facing HBCUs now and into the future. Retrieved from www.agb.org

CHAPTER FOURTEEN

Energizing Higher Education IN Tough Times

A Historically Black College President's Perspective

KEVIN D. ROME
President, Lincoln University (Missouri)

Most successful organizations typically have overarching guiding principles. These principles are the essence of their purpose; they guide actions and set institutional culture. We have all heard the trite phrases that comprise goals, objectives, values, mission, and the like. It is very important that organizations reflect about what these principles are because they form identity and engender external perceptions. Higher education has become a commodity that makes careful crafting of goals and values particularly relevant. There are certainly differences in institutional focus, quality, and reputation; but the public often looks at colleges and universities in a general sense. Therefore, higher education institutions must be able to distinguish themselves by cutting through the clutter and establishing an identity. Historically Black Colleges and Universities (HBCUs) pride themselves in their missions, values, and purpose. From the founding of Cheney University of Pennsylvania in 1837 to the present, HBCUs have focused on creating a family-oriented environment directed at providing educational opportunities for those who otherwise may not have an opportunity to pursue higher education. The topic beckons the question: what should be the core values and goals for these colleges?

At the outset, it must be specified that the author's perspective is that of someone who has worked at three different HBCUs and received an undergraduate degree from an HBCU. I will thus focus on the student experience at HBCUs and use "college," "university," and "institution" interchangeably.

HBCUs strive to help students improve their life by nurturing them as holistic contributors to society and by aiding them to find gainful employment in a vocation they love. People seek education for a myriad of different reasons: status, prestige, job prospects, career earnings, successfully raising a family, discovering self, etc. However, cultivating holistic contributors to society with substantial prospects in their chosen field is an underlying commonality for all institutions. Now, we shall treat some of the main topics of concern at HBCUs today.

ARTICULATING GOALS AND VALUES

HBCUs' goals must be aligned with a need for student growth as a continuous pattern among many other considerations. One goal of higher education is to graduate students. Most industries are judged on their end product, and higher education is no different. An end product cannot be judged on its merits until it has completed its goal, that is, student graduation. For both state-assisted and private institutions, there is a call for more accountability and increases in graduation rates. Performance funding has been introduced to address accountability at state-supported institutions. HBCUs understand the challenges that are faced by matriculating students who may not be as prepared for college, that is, many are from economically challenged backgrounds. Another equally important goal is for students to enjoy their experience. If they do not enjoy their experience, negative perceptions about the university will quickly spread and the stream of students seeking to enter it will slowly begin to dissipate.

Conversely, if students enjoy their experience, their word-of-mouth endorsement will become the college's strongest marketing tool. A great predictor of student satisfaction and the effect of university support structures is retention. Retention is measured by the percentage of students who begin a fall academic school year and return the following fall semester. Two of the most salient contributing factors in attrition are nonsatisfaction with their experience, and not faring well enough academically to meet the minimum qualifications to return. Retention percentage is weighed heavily by prospective students.

The final process goal has garnered much attention amid the growing scrutiny of higher education: timeliness of job placement upon graduation and the type of jobs students are hired for. Those factors are monitored by many people and agencies, especially regulatory bodies. Given the rising cost of tuition, students' return on investment is exceedingly important. Institutions must ensure that they are preparing students to be competitive in the job search process—with the goal of quickly finding a suitable job in their chosen fields.

Lincoln University in Missouri, like many other HBCUs, has dedicated significant time and resources to improving retention and graduation rates along with addressing student satisfaction. We have sent faculty and staff to conferences and workshops, surveyed students, created and modified programs, revised curriculum, participated in state and national initiatives, and attempted to promote a culture of student success. We realize that such efforts are necessary and that it is imperative that students do their part by embracing the notion of student success.

Values are more intrinsic and indicate what an institution believes. The definition of value, according to the *Meriam-Webster* dictionary, is as follows: "something (as a principle or quality) intrinsically valuable or desirable" (*Merriam-Webster*). Values are highly esteemed by an institution. Colloquially, they are what an institution is "all about." They should inspire people within and outside the institution; to an extent, they should be idyllic. College values should be incessantly expressed, and evidenced, in all actions the university takes. HBCUs take pride in espousing values that transcend the campus and permeate the world at large.

Some values are common to many institutions. Despite the perceptions of some, HBCUs should, and do, contain the following: rigorous pedagogy, civic engagement, universal interdisciplinary competence, and heuristic learning. Rigorous pedagogy describes an educational experience that pushes students to expand their knowledge and perspectives through exposure to intensive theoretical material. This type of education attempts to instill a solid ethic. Students at HBCUs should be actively involved in their communities and exercise their human agency. Holistic contributors to society has been cited as a crucial goal, and that notion entails maximizing students' benefit to society. It is vitally important that students be exposed to diverse, divergent information and experiences. Universal interdisciplinary competence attempts to achieve that exposure and is exhibited in students being comfortable and knowledgeable in various locations and disciplines. Globalization is making the world smaller and more interconnected. Students should show prowess in synthesizing information and being able to function at a high capacity irrespective of location. Discovery is quite valuable and is frequently arrived at after trial-and-error. Many of the greatest discoveries (e.g., Thomas Edison's lightbulb or Benjamin Franklin's bifocals) required resilience and inquisitiveness to achieve success. HBCUs have very high expectations for students to achieve greatness throughout the world.

IN THE CLASSROOM: CHANGING DYNAMICS AND METHODS

Colleges are ever changing and must be nimble enough to adjust with the changing dynamics of their environment. Constantly changing dynamics greatly impinge on curricula. Some of these dynamics include changes in generation, industry, economy, and politics. Higher education must be vigilant and sensitive to these changes since they must prepare students for the workforce in the world they will live in today and tomorrow. Curricula should be modified with the goals outlined above—graduating holistic, global citizens with strong prospects in their desired fields. Modifications should occur in a manner that adequately prepares students for the various careers they will be pursuing. Colleges should have regular dialogue with industry professionals to glean what industry wants and needs in professions and occupations, with the goal of infusing the curriculum with those wants and needs. Lincoln University, like other HBCUs, is grappling with such issues in our own unique way as those changes impact student learning and success.

The world is becoming increasingly technological, and curricula should adjust to incorporate more technology in classrooms. To clarify, each class should require students to interact with some form of an online resource or new form of technology befitting their discipline. One example of an online resource is the extensive use of the software Basecamp. It allows online collaboration and tracks created information by housing group work in a convenient location. The software is not only simple enough for students to grasp relatively easily, but also requires them to learn current software, further bolstering their ability to interact with technology. As technology advances, many HBCUs struggle with the resources to maintain current, or even moderately recent, technology. Additionally, curricula should further integrate classwork that is increasingly collaborative with longitudinal and interrelated content. Many professions and occupations require working with counterparts on simultaneous projects that span an extended duration of time. For example, most marketing schemes are not developed in the vacuum of a single person's mind. They usually require much thought and collaboration by a team designated for the task. Curricula should reflect this reality by including longitudinal, group projects that overlap with other simultaneous projects. Various HBCUs are at different points of development but embrace this notion.

ON- AND OFF-CAMPUS EXPERIENCES: IMPROVING STUDENTS' ACADEMIC AND SOCIAL LIVES

Colleges provide a unique environment in which a large cluster of individuals are educated in the exact same location of residence. A significant portion of college students' lives is experienced outside the classroom, presumably on the campus in interaction with their colleagues. Thus far, this essay has focused on the intentional and organized components of the college experience: classroom learning. However, the outside-the-classroom collegiate experience is equally as important. The academic and social components of college overlap frequently, but are rather distinct. Given this Venn diagram of coinhabitance, how should colleges improve both the academic and social life of students? HBCUs take pride in providing students with well-rounded social and academic experiences that prepare students for life.

The academic experience can be improved in several different ways. A common query amongst students is how course content will benefit them in their chosen career path. Faculty should sincerely vet their curricula to extirpate all "busy work." Classwork should be very intentional and closely connected to students' chosen fields.

I would be remiss if I did not take this opportunity to mention the two predominant philosophies in higher education that have an effect on coursework being readily tied to one's chosen field. Two classifications for institutions are research universities and liberal arts colleges. Liberal arts institutions focus on providing students with a "well-rounded" base of education before entering a major. Research institutions tend to focus primarily on a student's major or focus on ancillary content related to the student's major. It is often more difficult to tie all coursework to the student's chosen major at a liberal arts college as opposed to a research institution. Some fail to acknowledge that HBCUs are as diverse in their institutional types, classifications, and sizes as other types of higher educational institutions. I believe the connection should be done at all types of institutions.

Another way the academic experience could be improved is by reducing the reliance on lecture-based learning. This type of teaching has become increasingly ineffective because it does not reflect how individuals learn on the job or in "real" life. Additionally, the attention spans of students have become shorter due to our fast-paced technological world. Lecturing, as opposed to more dynamic learning, tends to lose students and does not accomplish the goal of reaching them with the expressed intention that they will learn and retain. There is still a place for lecture-based teaching, but it should be part of an arsenal of teaching styles, and not necessarily the dominant one. Class sessions should vary among lectures, group discussions, guest speakers, and hands-on learning. Group discussions should embrace the "flip" classroom concept which, according to Educause, is a pedagogical model in which the typical lecture and homework elements of a course are reversed (Educause). Essentially, students read literature and watch videos for homework in preparation for class discussion. When students arrive in the classroom, the discussion is engaging and encourages more participation. Guest speakers are intriguing to students because they provide a different dynamic and change from usual class time. Students tend to be more attentive during these sessions generally. Hands-on learning allows students the opportunity to implement the principles and concepts learned in the classroom. These sessions hold the attention of students in that they are required to use additional cognitive resources to concentrate on the task at hand. Some may have the perception that HBCUs are slow to change (which may or may not be true of higher education in general); changing instruction to fit the ever-changing student is a necessity for HBCUs.

Enhancing the social aspects of the student experience should be focused on more deeply. HBCUs attempt to create a family-type environment where students develop meaningful relationships that last for a lifetime. Returning for Homecoming and renewing such relationships is ingrained in the HBCU experience. I return to my undergraduate institution for Homecoming as often as possible. Colleges should focus on facilitating interaction among the different groups on campus. A tactic employed to engender this interaction is requiring students to attend educational events on campus. Often this requirement is levied by a required, general course, which all freshman students must take. I fondly remember my freshman assembly and understand the value in requiring the current generation of students at Lincoln University to participate in such a course. The course tends to provide freshman students with foundations for success at the institution and in life.

There is great value in allowing students to participate in the development of the life experiences being crafted for them. Colleges can begin to improve social life for students by conducting regular focus groups and using the information gathered to enhance social life. Similarly, periodic surveys could guide future decisions on how to better prepare social experiences for students.

Too often most of the focus on improving student social life is restricted to the campus. I believe more consideration should be given to arranging interaction between the college students are enrolled in and their peer institutions. Such circumstances exist to an extent with institutions providing buses to away-athletic events and their engaging in intellectual competitions (e.g., quiz bowls). However, there should be more intentional opportunities for students to attend educational and social events at other universities. Lincoln University and Harris-Stowe State University participate in athletic and academic programs that promote competition and unity between the two universities. Colleges should communicate regarding which activities are being offered at certain times of the year and work to provide opportunities for students to attend. I do caution about the over-use of this idea. If universities utilize the tactic too often, they risk cannibalizing attendance at their own events and weakening social life on their own campus.

WORKING WITH LIMITED RESOURCES

Higher education funding across the United States has been trending downward in recent years, especially for public institutions. Limited resources are leading to hard decisions about where to invest time, money, and personnel. Colleges and universities have become more introspective about where resources are not being utilized effectively and efficiently. Smaller and/or lower-resourced institutions, such as most HBCUs, find themselves more frequently making difficult decisions. As a president of an HBCU, I find myself in a position that requires me to make extremely tough decisions that are not popular but critical to the future existence of the institution. A strategy to counteract the angst of shrinking resources is to analyze each offering a university provides on a cost-benefit ratio basis. Academic programs need to undergo periodic review of their goals, value, and viability. If an academic program is not meeting expectations set forth for it, it needs to be either restructured, deactivated, or (in the most extreme cases) eliminated.

Universities need to imbue a culture highlighting "everyone's responsibility." For example, traditionally it has been the task of an admissions office to seek out and recruit students. With this approach, if their campuses do not enroll enough students, it is attributed to the recruiters not being able to entice or persuade them to attend. This logic fetters the institution by pigeonholing a major component of its existence to solely one office. Instead, it should be an expectation that faculty participate in student recruitment in their own way. If a culture of "everyone's responsibility" is successfully communicated, faculty members feel the same onus of ensuring they recruit students as well. I spend more time recruiting students than I ever imagined would be part of my duties. If everyone feels it is his/her duty to help recruit, a broader and stronger university effort is the likely result, and more students will likely come to the university.

Institutions need to be more receptive to opportunities for synergy when facing limited resources. Universities that are part of a state system should explore opportunities to use equipment, which may have been phased out on another campus, to help supply their own needs. If a university is phasing out expensive lab equipment and another college is looking to upgrade its legacy equipment, a discussion should be conducted with the goal of an arrangement for future upgrades. A different way to capitalize on synergy is to allow students to take classes at another institution when their home institution does not offer it.

Limited resources can be counteracted, in part, by aligning the university with those who find value in what the institution offers and are willing to pay for access. Revenue can be generated by developing and leveraging partnerships with industry. Naming rights opportunities, endowed professorships, and sponsored programs can all supplement limited budgets. Academic buildings on campus can be named in honor of benefactors if they give a large monetary or in-kind gift. Endowed professorships allow positions at the university to be named in their honor, while they receive recognition each time the positions are uttered. Sponsored programs are increasing in popularity. This concept involves a benefactor paying for his or her recognition to be associated with a program, usually an academically stellar program. The naming of the program usually is packaged with the perquisites of having first access to students during career fairs, a guarantee of a certain amount of student interns per year, and the ability to propel real-world projects to the sponsored academic program for worthwhile solutions.

MAKING THE MOST OF GOVERNMENTAL RESOURCES

State and federal governments are absolutely critical to the success of colleges and universities. A fruitful relationship with the state legislature is not a panacea due to the fraught nature of the appropriations process; however, an ambivalent, apathetic, or negative relationship with it can be crippling. Colleges should incessantly communicate their various needs—why they are important, and why they should receive primary attention. In short, a vigorous, effective strategy to interface with state and federal government is crucial. As I speak with other state HBCU presidents, I note that there is a common theme of legacy issues of underfunding and continued neglect of needs compared with sister institutions.

Inviting state and national legislators to campus is a great opportunity to begin the process of building relationships and highlighting the university's importance in solving the needs of the state and nation. In these instances, it behooves colleges to not only show the needs of the institution, but to also showcase their unique offerings. Optimally, this offering is in an area not many other institutions provide. Conversely, the university's outbound efforts to meet and greet legislators is equally as important. Some institutions coordinate a day to have faculty, staff, students, alumni, and community members descend upon the Capitol to showcase the vital strengths of the school. The expansiveness of the representation shows legislators the depth and breadth of people positively impacted by the campus community.

SOLVING ISSUES OF COLLEGE COSTS

As funding for institutions from state and federal governments has diminished, college costs have risen substantially since 2008 (Leachman, Mitchell & Palacios, 2014). As more attention has been diverted to the costs of obtaining a college education, universities grapple with how to reduce the burden of costs that dissuade students from attending. At HBCUs, we are very aware of the significant number of students who have scant personal resources or financially stretched families. A very large number of our students rely on the institution for financial support outside of any state or federal aid received.

College can be made more affordable for students if institutions garner more grants from the federal government. I serve as the chair of the Association of Public Land-Grant Universities' Council of 1890s Institutions and am quite aware of the important research being conducted and grants received. Many grants are earned due to the research of faculty and staff at any given institution. Although many universities focus on the attainment of grants as a faculty requirement, broadening that requirement is especially relevant in today's environment. Laying out a minimum number of grants to be obtained by faculty and staff departments would be advisable. Another sensible strategy is democratizing the responsibility to develop a plan to make college more affordable for students. Often, the administrative leadership, or a specific university department, feels it must bear the brunt of devising a solution. Creating a university standing committee focused on reducing college costs allows many more constituents to own a difficult and entrenched problem.

Reevaluating the cost of renting facilities on campus is another way to create additional resources to improve college affordability. Frequently, outside organizations and groups request the use of university facilities. Quite often, colleges charge for this type of usage. If not, it is otherwise due to a special relationship or a quid pro quo arrangement. Facility rental fees need to be examined, and perhaps raised, periodically. Even if the raise is negligible, the volume of events throughout the year should aggregate additional revenue.

Cost-benefit analysis has extreme relevance in this section. University offerings need to be scrutinized for their impact and juxtaposed to their cost. For example, if $500,000 is spent on a program that services a very small faction of students, a reduction should be considered, with the residual being earmarked for some activity that brings satisfaction to a larger swath of the student population. HBCUs can no longer expend significant resources to support small populations if they do not produce real success. Programs must justify their existence.

DIVERSITY IS "EVERYONE'S RESPONSIBILITY"

"Diversity" has become a commonplace term that usually symbolizes an organization making some sort of an attempt to increase the representation of differences. There is a wide spectrum of authenticity (and inauthenticity) in these efforts. However, Diversity is often seen as solely the observable and quantifiable presence of different races, ethnicities, nationalities, genders, religions, creeds, sexual orientations, and the like. Areas that are less discussed are equity and inclusion. Equity refers to the equal opportunity of individuals who constitute a diverse group. Inclusion comprises the two aforementioned concepts, but also extends to fostering an environment where all parties feel a sense of welcome and belonging.I heard a great analogy regarding the relationship between diversity and inclusion: "Diversity is being invited to the dance. Inclusion is being invited to dance."

HBCUs must work toward sustaining all these concepts simultaneously in their campus spaces and beyond. We do not receive a pass when it comes to promoting and embracing diversity. The social and business environment is becoming increasingly diverse. Issues of egalitarianism are becoming a larger component of campus associations—and why individuals and groups associate with an institution. Colleges should address this issue by instilling the value of diversity, equity, and inclusion as tantamount to the value of education per se. It is recommended that universities make the pursuance of these concepts "everyone's responsibility." Paradigms on campus must embrace that notion: it is not the responsibility of a single department to ensure the plateau of diversity, equity, and inclusion is reached.

The concept of everyone's responsibility begins with creating an inclusive educational orientation at the beginning of every academic year for faculty, staff, and students. Each person hired by the institution should be required to master its educational content and be evaluated on it. HBCU leaders need to lead the charge of valuing the existence of diversity and equity. Whenever these leaders speak to audiences, they should include references to diversity and equity. A university committee should be appointed to address the interplay and enhancement of diversity, equity, and inclusion on campus. The hiring of a Chief Diversity Officer signals a clear commitment to not only addressing the topic but changing the campus atmosphere. As president of Lincoln University, I created a chief diversity officer position in 2016. Since the concepts of equity and inclusion are rarely formally discussed at many campuses, university-sponsored programs should analyze the concepts with a pragmatic lens toward enhancing those values.

FACILITATING STUDENT SUCCESS

Institutions attempt to identify which attributes have the highest likelihood in assuring students will be successful at their campuses. The process relies on a few metrics: heavily weighted GPA, unweighted GPA, SAT/ACT score, class rank, school rank, grading scale, etc. Those admissions criteria do not always predict how students will fare in their new environment. Often students become overwhelmed with the massive amount of sensory input once they arrive on campus. Furthermore, students can become discouraged in the face of more intensive or unfamiliar challenges. HBCUs must ask themselves if they have the resources and infrastructure to assist the students they attract.

Colleges have attempted to address these variables by looking for ancillary components of students' high school experience. Community service, athletics, or leadership involvement are looked at to show a student's ability to multitask. Universities should take this a step further and standardize the process. I believe that a more serious tone should be placed on college admissions. Students should be made aware of the high expectations and importance of academic success. Colleges also need to weigh extracurricular experience more heavily. If students are involved in several commitments outside of school, they are likely to be much more adept at handling competing demands and being resilient. These components are woefully underrated when predicting student success. Furthermore, admissions criteria should consider what is required to succeed once students arrive on campus and not solely on what it requires for entrance. Aptitude is very important and research should be devoted to which qualities lead to the highest likelihood of success. But personality assessments need to be used more frequently. The Myers-Briggs Type Indicator, or a similar instrument, could inform decisions on how to situate students on campus. This process could help students succeed, because placement in a living-learning community based on their personality attributes may have a positive impact on their retention. Being surrounded by individuals with similar personalities could assist young (and older) adults in weathering the psychological storm that accompanies venturing into a new environment.

ASSESSING FACULTY SUCCESS

Faculty are often judged by their research, irrespective of their university's classification as a research or teaching institution. In recent years, more attention has been devoted to the success and satisfaction of students in the various courses taught by faculty. Many institutions have adopted a post-course survey that must be completed by students. These surveys include questions pertinent to students' satisfaction with their overall experience. HBCUs must look at their faculty and make sure that adequate faculty development is available and provided. Lincoln University, like many other HBCUs, struggles with the issue of aging faculty, attracting and retaining younger faculty, and creative ways to energize faculty to be more innovative (without adequate resources). An area not currently being given adequate attention is how engaged students are in their classes. More focus on this area might allow for fairer assessment of faculty teaching—and more communication about how effective pedagogies could be shared across campus. If classes and coursework are to simulate, and carry over to, the working environment, they should require faculty to emphasize student engagement. However, the institution has a responsibility to make sure that faculty have the needed tools and resources to accomplish that goal.

BALANCING ACADEMICS AND ATHLETICS

I must first state that I believe that HBCUs utilize athletics to garner community, alumni, and national visibility. Winning makes a tremendous difference, especially in terms of local support. The recent success of the Lincoln University men's basketball team marked a phenomenal increase in community and alumni support. However, balancing academics and athletics can be a delicate activity on many college campuses, particularly at lower resourced institutions and HBCUs. A focus on academics is the primary reason institutions exist, while athletics provide social experiences and outlets for students and can serve as a potent recruiting tool. Determining the divide on each campus is usually unique, but the overall goal for students should be the guiding principle: to improve student-athletes' lives by developing them as holistic contributors to society and by helping them attain gainful employment in a vocation they love. A myopic focus on either academics or athletics misses the holistic part of the goal. Unfortunately, many schools create a schism in how the balance is proportioned. It is quite obvious that academics should be weighed higher than athletics, but their respective values can ideally coexist in relative harmony. Academics provide students the learning power and intellectual rigor for a robust understanding of their future life pathways. Athletics afford students an environment to express camaraderie, spirit, and solidarity with fellow student-athletes and fans.

Athletics should be in the strategic plan and supported by senior university leadership because it affects many areas of the institution. I measure the spillover effect of intercollegiate athletics on the quantity and quality of college applicants on the notion popularly known as the "Flutie effect" (Chung, 2013). That kind of influence triggers a virtuous cycle. When teams win in major sports, they garner acclaim for the entire campus. When they attain such accolades, more students tend to apply to the university. When more students apply, more revenue is generated by the institution. The surge in the pool of applicants allows the college to be more selective. When an institution is more selective, it is able to acquire a better crop of college-ready students. College-ready students are able to be retained in greater numbers and tend to graduate at higher rates. College-ready students who graduate at higher rates lead to a higher overall grade point average for the institution. Furthermore, they lead to more money for the university, that is, less revenues are lost via attrition.

Colleges that have students with higher grade point averages, students who are retained, and who have improved graduation rates tend to ascend in college quality rankings. Colleges who win are able to recruit better coaches and better student-athletes and tend to perpetuate winning attitudes and results. When teams win, students tend to enjoy their collegiate experience more, and thus are more satisfied upon graduation. Students who are more satisfied upon graduation tend to give more money back to their university. Local communities galvanized by the winning of their "home" team tend to be more involved and magnanimous to the institution.

The aforementioned argument explains how athletics can affect recruitment, retention, residential life, alumni affairs, development, college average grade point average, and the like. Of course, there are perils to a disproportionate focus on athletics. It should not lead to an errant decline of attention to other areas of the institution. Quality of faculty, library resources for students, and residential and academic building facilities—all these should definitely be valued higher than athletics. Weighing the valuation of all components of the university constitutes a delicate balance. Student success and satisfaction is of the utmost importance, and decisions regarding where to dedicate resources should be weighed with a view toward which options maximize the two.

TAKING ADVANTAGE OF TECHNOLOGICAL RESOURCES

Technology permeates all areas of life and knowledge of it frequently offers a competitive advantage in the workforce. Leveraging technology properly can prepare students for their chosen fields. Having the resources to provide the technology infrastructure needed at HBCUs is a challenge for most. It is not reasonable to think that a technology fee charged to students can cover the associated costs at many HBCUs due to size and limited elasticity in cost of attendance. Nevertheless, in reality, most professions and occupations rely heavily on technology. Each course a student is enrolled in should have some interaction with technology. The use of technology should be infused in all majors and minors offered by an institution. Having familiarity with a certain technology could be the difference between obtaining the job of choice or settling for a lesser alternative. If someone majoring in sales management, or a similar area, has not interacted with the software Salesforce, that lack severely impacts her marketability in that field. (Salesforce is currently one of the most widely known and used customer-relationship management database systems.) It would be a tragedy for a student to have accrued debt and dedicated years to obtaining a degree in sales management to not be competitive in the workforce due to a deficit in software skills.

Each professor at an HBCU should be required to use a learning management system in making assignments and interacting with students. Each course lesson plan should include a blend of in-person and online assignments to condition students to regular use of technology. Students should be informed about the latest technology and software in their fields. Each year, each course lesson plan should include a new software, or new form of technology, to ensure continual exposure in every class. This does not suggest new software or technology be purchased each year; it recommends that students be cognizant of its function and capability. Students need to be conditioned to be flexible and fluid when approaching new software or other technological products.

Faculty should also consult internal and external parties about how to incorporate software and other technologies. The information technology staff are a valuable resource and collectively have vast areas of knowledge and interests. Soliciting their opinion on how to incorporate technology, and which technology should be used, is important. Conversely, industry partners should also be consulted about assisting students in building technological proficiency. This can be accomplished by universities locating organizations in which their students seek employment in large numbers and asking them what technological prowess is needed.

Finally, as president of an HBCU, I know one fact personally from interacting, observing, and conversing with dedicated faculty, staff, and students in those institutions: Increased resources may not be the panacea for HBCUs, but they certainly would resolve many of the issues that HBCUs are facing. I am one of the first to acknowledge that an overhaul is needed in higher education, and HBCUs are not exempt from the greatly needed changes. Yet HBCUs have provided an invaluable contribution to this country since the 1800s and continue to play a significant role in American higher education. We could do even more with more adequate resources and public commitment.

REFERENCES

Chung, D. J. (2013). The dynamic advertising effect of collegiate athletics. *Marketing Science* 32(5), 679–698.

Educare. (2012, February). Things you should know about … flipped classrooms. Retrieved from http://net.educare.edu/ir/library/pdf/eli7081.pdf

Leachman, M., Mitchell, M., and Palacios, V. (2014). *States are still funding higher education at below pre-recession levels*. Washington, D.C.: Center on Budget and Policy Priorities, pp. 1–27.

Merriam-Webster.com. (2016). Retrieved from https://www.merriam-webster.com (November 8, 2016).

CHAPTER FIFTEEN

Making Community Colleges Better

EDWARD E. RASPILLER
President, John Tyler Community College

> [T]he hard truth is that some of the jobs that have been lost in the auto industry and elsewhere won't be coming back. They are casualties of a changing economy. And that only underscores the importance of generating new businesses and industries to replace the ones we've lost, and of preparing our workers to fill the jobs they create. For even before this recession hit, we were faced with an economy that was simply not creating or sustaining enough new, well-paying jobs.
>
> That is why, at the start of my administration I set a goal for America: by 2020, this nation will once again have the highest proportion of college graduates in the world ... Today, I am announcing the most significant down payment yet on reaching this goal in the next ten years. It's called the American Graduation Initiative. It will reform and strengthen community colleges from coast to coast so that they get the resources students and schools need—and the results workers and businesses demand. Through this plan, we seek to help an additional five million Americans earn degrees and certificates in the next decade.
>
> —Barack Obama (2009)

In his speech that day on July 14, 2009, U.S. President Barack Obama thrust community colleges across the country into the national spotlight. While many of us have worked in this industry for twenty or thirty years, this is the first time community colleges have been seriously considered to lead the United States not only out of the confines of a recession we still grapple with in many parts of the country, but also to play a central role in maintaining a qualified workforce. Thus, we have been challenged to serve as an economic development engine in the post-great recession economy. Nimble by nature, this call has challenged community colleges to redefine their mission and definition of student success.

In 2011, the American Association of Community Colleges launched a major initiative called "The 21st Century Initiative," which began with a multi-state listening tour led by AACC President and CEO Dr. Walter G. Bumphus and senior AACC staff (21st Century listening tour brief). They held fourteen meetings in twelve states and what quickly emerged was a comprehensive list of objectives that centered on student completion (American Association of Community Colleges, 2012). Since then, several colleges have developed their own student success agendas, which focus on student recruitment, retention, and completion. This chapter will illustrate strategies colleges are using to move students from college to work in viable career fields, or successfully transferring students into baccalaureate programs, at a time when resources are more volatile than ever before.

Historically, community colleges have focused on credit programs designed for transfer to four-year colleges and universities, or credit programs in various vocational fields, often referred to as career and technology programs, that are designed to move students directly from the community college to work. Secondary to this has been their focus on noncredit workshops and courses typically known as workforce education or workforce development. As we are finding out in this new century, requirements for entry-level jobs, mid-career jobs, and beyond require training beyond high school, but less than baccalaureate degrees. In response, community colleges are reassessing the role of noncredit programming in their colleges, and the nature of their relationship with local economic development initiatives in the communities they serve.

In addition to maintaining adequate funding for programs and services in the classroom and beyond, community colleges are working to enhance current internal collaborative efforts and sharpen data collection and analysis techniques as well as developing effective partnerships with external public and private sector partners to identify high-demand occupations, and the consequent training required. This has caused the need for leadership across the institution, not simply at the top, and professional development programs to begin to develop and refine leadership skills. As Eddy et al. (2015) postulate, leadership development programs, particularly those at the graduate level, are often geared toward developing leaders with the same skills required by community colleges as they were developing a half century ago. While not completely outdated, the skills required by effective leaders today have many more dimensions.

CORE VALUES AND GOALS

The typical community college mission statement speaks towards providing coursework designed for transfer, career entry, and noncredit workforce training and development. It likely includes the tenets of open-admission, diversity, and building stronger communities. While bold in intent, are these aspects of our work still doable in an age of declining resources? Do we need to prioritize these to meet the expectations of business and industry, state and local elected officials, and communities at large or can we continue with the often-cited mantra *everything to everybody*?

One thing we know for sure is if all we focus on is access into credit programs, which has been the case for decades, we have only taken the first step toward student success. However, many if not all, state reimbursement formulas have been designed around reimbursement for headcount, that is, enrollment. This is in direct contrast to the need for students to enroll, remain enrolled in programs semester to semester, and then completing a credential that allows them to successfully transfer their coursework to four-year schools, or enter the workforce with gainful employment in the area of their study.

To cause a shift in focus, over the past ten years many states have developed performance-funding formulas for postsecondary education based on student retention and completion. The Virginia Community College System spent over eighteen months developing their formula, which stair-steps into 20% of college funding based on performance by the year 2020. Their indicators of success are focused on FTFT (first-time, full-time) students and include measures of retention from semester to semester, year to year as well as completion of developmental education and consequent college-level coursework. It also rewards colleges for students that successfully complete certificates and degrees designed for transfer or moving directly into the workplace. As our data capture and processing systems integrate new technology and strengthen their accuracy and timeliness, colleges are beginning to see trends and develop alternatives to help insure student success (Virginia Community College System, 2015).

As colleges have designed academic programs and services to insure access, retention, and completion, it has caused a need to refocus the institution's resources specifically around teaching and learning. While academic and student support have long been the hallmarks of community colleges, this initiative has taken it to the next level. This typically includes expanding advising and tutoring services, as well as building comprehensive electronic data capture and analysis systems. The financial burden, at a time of diminishing state resources and maintaining conscientious tuition increases, is causing institutions to rethink how nonacademic and student support functions are delivered.

SHARED SERVICES

In 2016, community colleges across the country find themselves at the apex of working to fill expectations: they will graduate more students with credentials in high-demand occupations, in a time of dwindling financial revenues. The surging enrollments we experienced during the height of the great recession are beginning to level off, and at many colleges actually decline. As discussed earlier, the focus for community colleges must remain centered around student enrollment, retention, and completion; however, the only way to effectively do this is to constantly find and strengthen alternative means to maintain adequate financial resources.

We take for granted that public tax dollars will remain constant, at best. Several schools have employed differential tuition costs as a means to raise revenue to offer more general education courses or expand offerings in high demand/high cost programs. As a recent study by Friedel and Thomas (2013) points out, differential tuition can be a double-edged sword. While it can indeed help colleges expand courses and start new programs, it can also put tuition costs at a prohibitive level for some potential students. Regardless of the innovative ways colleges develop to drive alternative revenue, administrators must continuously look for ways to bring the costs of those functions outside the realm of direct services to students.

Over two years ago, the Virginia Community College System Governing Board made up of fifteen members appointed by the governor, many of whom are from the private sector, directed the chancellor and staff to closely examine the transactional processes related to business services, including procurement, collections, accounts receivable, and accounts payable as well as human resource and information technology functions in the System office and across the twenty-three colleges in Virginia. This directive had the dual purpose of identifying the preferred process for all to follow, and then to utilize a collaborative approach to create a Shared Services Center to relieve the individual institutions of this work so their resources can be repurposed to support student success initiatives. Separate work teams, made up of Subject Matter Experts (SMEs) from the System office and individual colleges, were formed around business services, human resources, and information technology. An analysis of transactional functions was examined to identify similarities, differences, and best practices.

While in many public sectors this concept of shared services is new, it has been going on in the private sector for many years. There are states, such as Ohio and Alaska, that have launched shared service initiatives in public, statewide government, but it certainly is not typical in community colleges. The states and public agencies that have developed shared service initiatives have learned two things: (1) the process is not an easy one and (2) as the private sector has found, there is significant cost reduction, but perhaps more valuable is the consistency and efficiency of the transaction processing itself (examples include: travel reimbursement processing for employees, shared CIO or ISO positions, and web design and maintenance services). The real value in shared services is performing these functions in aggregate, as opposed to each individual institution doing its own, that allows for shared value by all.

Many public, postsecondary institutions have become bloated with bureaucracy. This is particularly evident in those that are actual state agencies. As accountability in higher education begins to mirror that in K–12 education, brought on by the "No Child Left Behind Act of 2001," assessment of all practices and processes take a central role. While there are rather sophisticated assessment practices at the course level, assessment at the program and department level is beginning to proliferate across instructional and non-instructional areas of the college. Needless to say, these new practices can cause a lot of angst for personnel at all levels if they are imposed with little input and design by the stakeholders. The key to success is ownership by the individuals involved. Developing this process includes identifying and involving those who will be affected up front, and seeking their input relative to the design and functions involved.

The work of the Virginia community colleges SME work teams morphed into a shared services management structure that includes: a governance board, made up of five presidents and two vice-chancellors, and a management committee, made up of representatives from each of the twenty-four institutions. A shared services center manager was hired and the first of several employees are in place. It is unclear at this time the exact number of employees the Center will ultimately have as the transactional process design centers on the utilization of software and information systems to process the work, thus limiting the need for transaction-based jobs and personnel. It should also be noted that the Center itself has been placed in a rural part of the state to help support local and statewide economic development initiatives and to do our part in helping maintain vibrant local economies at a time when rural communities are hurting for new employers and jobs.

As a consequence of this initiative, community colleges across the state are reexamining their organizational structure to identify positions that are either no longer necessary, or that can be combined with other work. Any savings from the elimination of positions or partial positions will be reallocated to support the student success initiatives that include focus both on the classroom and on support for students outside the classroom. Effective and clear communication at the institution and individual level is critical to successfully shifting to a shared services environment with minimal disruption to end-user satisfaction and minimal employee confusion or fear for their job. Successful organizations that have done this have started with a focus on the "human" side of our work, and the need for people to understand and see their place in the newly designed operations. It would be naïve to think there will be no employee displacement, as the purpose is in part to reduce personnel costs. But by carefully examining relative practices across the institution, and the individuals that perform the daily tasks, employees can likely be given alternatives to their next steps, and certainly be treated with the dignity and respect they deserve.

WORKFORCE DEVELOPMENT

Today's public community college can be thought of as having three major aspects to its mission: (1) credit programs and support services leading to certificates and degrees designed for transfer to four-year schools or preparation to go directly into the workforce, (2) support services outside the academic components of the organization, and (3) noncredit classes and programs that often lead to an industry-recognized credential, often referred to as workforce development or workforce education. As stated earlier, the noncredit classes and programs are typically not central to the mission, and often do not even operate in a cost-recovery fashion, let alone an actual profit-center for the college. Given the changing nature of work in our modern society, the reliance upon non-credit workforce development continues to increase. The demand for ongoing skill-enhancement opportunities for employees that results in credential attainment continues to grow across all sectors of the workforce, particularly in the healthcare, information technology, and advanced manufacturing fields. This trend seems to follow the reliance on technology in the workplace of which there is no end in sight.

As community colleges work to provide state-of-the-art training in a just-in-time environment, noncredit programming has quickly emerged as the most viable, flexible option. Historically, funding for noncredit programs has been left to the college, and costs have often been recovered solely by fee-based classes, or direct funding from the organizations that participate in the training itself. As such, colleges struggle to offer classes in the same state-of-the-art labs credit classes are offered in, or in classrooms that are outfitted with current learning technology and modalities.

In 2016, the Virginia general assembly enacted legislation that allowed Virginia to join the nineteen other states that provide funding for training programs that lead to industry-recognized credentials. This process began the prior year when the General Assembly, based on feedback and input from business and industries across multiple sectors of the economy, requested a proposal from the VCCS chancellor that will help community colleges meet the training needs for jobs requiring more than a high school diploma, but less than a postsecondary degree. Comprehending this misalignment requires an understanding of the staffing ratio consistent throughout today's workplace. In general, for every one job that requires an advanced degree, there are two jobs that require a bachelor's degree, and seven jobs that require postsecondary training that leads to an associate's degree or industry-recognized credential.

In the months leading up to the 2016 Legislative Session, VCCS Chancellor Dr. Glenn DuBois held over twenty town hall meetings across the state to gather input from business and industry leaders as well as other stakeholders, representing small, medium, and large companies in rural, suburban, and urban environments.

While the audience make-up differed based upon location, several themes developed that transcended these differences. According to the *VCCS Workforce Credentials: The Pathway to Virginia's New Middle Class* publication (2005, p. 5), these included the identification of several gaps:

- The Skills Gap—Businesses cannot find qualified candidates.
- The Affordability Gap—Traditional financial aid options for students did not cover noncredit programs.
- The Interest Gap—People do not pursue these workforce prep programs because they are often not aware or not encouraged to pursue them.
- The Competitiveness Gap—To compete in a global economy, businesses need a workforce that can grow, learn, and change to meet demand, and there are limited resources in Virginia to entice employers to locate or expand their operations.

Guided by ongoing input from these stakeholder groups, the VCCS developed a funding proposal that was based on completion, not simply enrollment. Perhaps the first of its kind in the world, this funding formula relies upon the participant (or organization, if company-sponsored) to pay 1/3 of the instructional costs. Upon completion of the course the institution gets its second 1/3 of funding from the state, and upon being awarded the actual credential, the institution gets its third 1/3 of funding from the state. Like any other innovation in a bureaucracy, there are myriad details that have been or are being worked out. Ultimately, this formula will likely prove to be not only reasonable, but appropriate in the eyes of taxpayers, participants, employers, and the colleges themselves.

Regardless of the funding, it is clear from multiple sources that today's workplace requires job-specific skills beyond a high school diploma, but less than a bachelor's degree. A recent study by Georgetown University's Center for Education and Work (2013) finds that 65% of jobs will require some form of education or training beyond high school. The highest demand will be in those jobs related to STEM, then e.g., science, technology, engineering, and math careers. As individuals understand and embrace this concept, community colleges will be relied upon to provide the necessary learning for a majority of workers. This expectation is quickly changing the community college mission to include a stronger focus on workforce education and insures its place as economic development engines for local and statewide efforts.

LEADERSHIP

Since their inception, community colleges have required strong leadership at the top. Initially, presidents led the establishment of college campuses, curriculum, and articulation agreements between four-year colleges, and more recently dual enrollment programs in high schools. It took many years for community colleges to establish their identity and place in America's educational system. They had to get past the notion of high schools with ashtrays or junior colleges for those not academically or financially prepared for four-year college study. As community colleges continue to evolve, they are quickly becoming the go-to place as a next step for those completing high school, as well as for employees and will-be employees that want to enhance their skills in preparation for high-demand occupations and high tech workplaces. This is causing us to rethink both traditional graduate programs that prepare community college leaders as well as programs offered by various organizations through professional development conferences and workshops.

Several years ago, community colleges began to develop internal leadership development programs. These are designed with varying degrees of competency around the institution's specific programs and operational procedures, up through the community college mission itself. The program at John Tyler Community College, called TylerLEADS, is designed with both in mind. The third cohort of students is entering this academic-year-long program in fall 2016. Cohorts are up to ten employees that are selected through a competitive admission process from all levels and departments across the college. Through formal, monthly meetings and special topics work, participants gain a comprehensive understanding of how the institution and community colleges in general operate, and then they identify a special project to complete individually or in small teams. The goal of their project is to develop an approach or procedure that will positively impact an aspect of the College, typically in the participant's area of work and in support of the six-year strategic plan.

While still in its infancy, TylerLEADS has already proven itself to be a program that brings people from across the institution together in a forum otherwise not possible to learn from and with each other. In addition to positive impact the individual projects have had upon how we do our work, we are already seeing leadership traits develop and grow in participants. While it is not designed to be a succession-planning tool, it has helped nurture the lead-in-place characteristics that are critical in today's evolving community college environment.

TYLER 2021

The Virginia Community College System has developed comprehensive strategic plans that span six years. Its most recent plan (2015–2021) has one bold goal: to triple the number of credentials awarded across the twenty-three-college system. Credentials are defined as degree, certificates, or industry certifications. Each of the twenty-three colleges develops its own six-year plan that dovetails with the overarching VCCS plan. John Tyler Community College's plan, referred to as Tyler

2021, includes specific goals and strategies around student recruitment, retention, and completion, as well as goals and strategies to create a culture of excellence with regard to the student experience and the employee experience. This includes creating student pathways and restructuring around the shared services initiative. It has also caused resources to be directed to support non-credit programs and services. Last year we also created a council for diversity and inclusion, and it has developed a comprehensive plan that will allow us to understand and be able to work across differences in the classroom as well as across the entire college.

Last year, we began a monthly practice of reviewing our progress towards meeting the goals of our strategic plan. This brief monthly meeting, referred to as "Tyler21," includes all managers and is open to all College employees. Initially, we developed a data dashboard, inclusive of our strategic plan goals, that reflects our progress as well as opportunities to do more or seek alternative strategies to complete. After several months, participants got comfortable providing positive feedback as well as brainstorming as a group, alternative ways to accomplish the goals that remain elusive. In short, Tyler21 has become the safe forum for critical review of our goals and accomplishments, and perhaps more importantly, the forum that has kept our strategic plan alive, and helped insure engagement across the organization.

CONCLUSION

In this chapter, we have discussed several strategies being used now to make community colleges better. Perhaps they are best summoned up in the following five best practices below:

- Pathways—Community colleges should design and develop their programs and course sequences by identifying the clearest "pathway" students can follow to accomplish the credential they are pursuing. This requires focus on majors and meta-majors, and then designing all published materials, including the college catalog, to best express these pathways. Likely, this will include a mix of credit and noncredit instruction resulting in stackable credentials for the student. Perhaps the key is the work done with students upfront to identify the appropriate field of study and consequent pathway.
- Data systems and utilization—As the data systems in community colleges continue to become more sophisticated, college stakeholders need to continue to utilize data to guide the decisions made by administrators, faculty, staff, and students themselves. By developing sophisticated data dashboards around strategic plans and goals, the stakeholders can monitor what works and what does not work in an ever more real-time environment. This may

be the only way cogent decisions can be made in a timely fashion. Sophisticated data can also inform decisions and processes that allow community colleges to thrive in performance-based funding environments.

- Shared services—Since the great recession, public resources have continued to diminish with regard to funding public higher education in many states. This is likely not a point-in-time occurrence, but rather our new reality. As such, in order to keep costs down in what often is a very competitive environment, community colleges will need to look for ways to cut the cost of operations, particularly those outside of the academic areas of instruction and direct student support services. Likely areas to identify that can be shared with other public agencies include transactional services in the business office, human resources, and information technology.
- Workforce development—For years now, noncredit workforce development courses and programs have taken a back seat to those on the credit side of the house. This made sense in the last century. What we know now is access to a well-trained workforce is a critical factor in the decisions businesses make relative to where they should locate or expand operations. This phenomenon, coupled with ever-changing technical needs and requirements in the workplace, has moved non-credit instruction to the forefront of the community college mission. Likewise, individuals looking to have rewarding middle-class and above lifestyles, will need a series of stackable credentials, likely through a mix of credit and noncredit instruction, that enables them to assimilate new knowledge in their profession as well as in technological advancements.
- Leadership—Given what we know about the dynamic, ever-changing environments that our community colleges are today, the need for effective leadership is critical. What used to be thought of as "at the top" has quickly changed to the need for leadership across the organization. While graduate education programs specifically targeting community college leaders continue to developed at universities nationwide, this is simply not enough. Community colleges need to continue to develop and support internal leadership programs that prepare people to move up in the organization or simply have fulfilling careers by understanding the mission and scope of their school.

The community college story in this nation continues to unfold as we learn more and more about the need for learning in today's workplace, and the need for lifelong learning compels us to seek opportunities to learn. A hallmark of a community college is its ability to be agile, when compared to other higher education institutions, and to reflect the local and regional needs of the communities they serve. In order to continue to do this, community colleges must develop strategic plans that allow them to provide services in the most efficient way possible, to serve the most students. By doing this, colleges will be seen as a community's lifelong-learning provider that insures vibrant economies as well as productive and engaged citizens.

REFERENCES

American Association of Community Colleges (2012). *Final Report on the 21st-Century Initiative Listening Tour.* AACC: Washington, DC.

Eddy, P., Sydow, D., Alfred, R., & Garza, M. R. (2015). *Developing Tomorrow's Leaders: Content, Challenges, and Capabilities.* Lanham, MD: Rowman & Littlefield.

Friedel, J., & Thomas, G. (2013). Differential tuition: A community college budgetary strategy. *Community College Journal of Research and Practice* 37 (3): 147–152.

Georgetown University Center for Education and Work (2013, July 26). New study finds there will be 55 million job openings by 2020. Retrieved from https://cew.georgetown.edu/wp-content/uploads/2014/11/Recovery2020.Press-Release.pdf

Obama, B. H. (2009, July 14). Excerpts of the president's remarks in Warren, Michigan, and fact sheet on the American Graduation Initiative. Retrieved from https://www.whitehouse.gov/the-press-office/excerpts-presidents-remarks-warren-michigan-and-fact-sheet-american-graduation-initiative

Virginia Community College System (2015). *Workforce credentials: The pathways to Virginia's new middle class.* Retrieved from https://leg2/state.va.us/dis/h&sdocs.nsf/By+Year/RD2262015/$file/RD226.pdf

Contributors

James A. Anderson has been chancellor of Fayetteville State University in North Carolina since 2008. Prior to that he held various leadership positions in academic and student affairs at the University of Albany (New York), North Carolina State University, and Texas A & M University. He has been a member of the Board of Trustees of the Southern Association of Colleges and Schools and the American Council on Education's Commission on Inclusion. His books include *Driving Change through Diversity and Globalization: Transformative Leadership in the Academy* (2007) and *The Unfinished Agenda: Brown v. Board of Education* (2004).

Steven C. Bahls has served as the eighth president of Augustana College in Rock Island, Illinois, since 2003. He has also been dean of the Capital University Law School and a professor at the University of Montana School of Law. His book, *Shared Governance in Times of Change* (2004), is one of the best-selling books published by the Association of Governing Boards Press. President Bahls has served on the boards of the Council of Independent Colleges and the National Association of Independent Colleges and Universities.

Jonathan M. Brand has been president of Cornell College in Mount Vernon, Iowa, since 2011, after serving six years as president of Doane College and seven years as a senior staff and faculty member at Grinnell College. Holder of a J. D. from Cornell University, he has taught courses in political science and constitutional law at Cornell, Doane, Grinnell, and Nanjing University in

China. President Brand has written numerous articles and columns for higher education publications, including *The Chronicle of Higher Education* and *The Huffington Post.*

Joseph L. DeVitis is a retired professor of social foundations of education and higher education. Two of his seventeen books have earned *Choice* awards from the American Library Association (ALA) and four others have won Critics Choice awards from the American Educational Studies Association (AESA), including his latest book, *Popular Educational Classics* (Peter Lang, 2016). DeVitis is a past president of the AESA, the Society of Professors of Education, and the Council of Learned Societies in Education. Recipient of the Distinguished Alumni Award from the University of Illinois at Urbana-Champaign, he lives with his wife Linda in Palm Springs, California.

Carine M. Feyten is serving as the eleventh president and second chancellor of Texas Woman's University in Denton, with additional campuses in Dallas and Houston; it is the largest university in the country primarily for women. Feyten was formerly dean of the College of Education, Health and Society at Miami University of Ohio for eight years and associate dean and faculty member in the College of Education at the University of South Florida for over twenty years. Her research interests lie in the areas of listening, second language acquisition, cross-cultural communications, digital learning, and the integration of technology in education. She has authored or coauthored over 100 journal articles, conference papers, addresses, book chapters, and books.

Timothy L. Hall has been the president of Mercy College in Dobbs Ferry, New York since 2014. Prior to that, he was president of Austin Peay State University in Clarksville, Tennessee. Before he became a college and university president, he was for many years a professor at the University of Mississippi School of Law and associate vice chancellor for academic affairs at the University of Mississippi. President Hall is a regular keynote speaker on the topic of student success. An active scholar, he is the author of *Religion in America* (2007), *American Religious Leaders* (2003), *Supreme Court Justices: A Biographical Dictionary* (2001), and *Roger Williams in America* (1998).

Sandra J. Jordan is the fourth chancellor of the University of South Carolina Aiken, where she is the chief executive and principal spokesperson for the University. She has served in a number of leadership positions at other universities, including department chair, dean, vice provost, and provost. Chancellor Jordan has focused on increasing student access, enhancing graduation and student success rates, expanding community partnerships, and aligning academic programs to regional workforce needs. She serves on numerous local, state, and national boards of directors.

Patricia McGuire has been president of Trinity University Washington (District of Columbia) since 1989. Previously, she was assistant dean for development and external affairs at Georgetown University Law Center. She is the recipient of the Hesburgh Award for Leadership Excellence from the Teachers Insurance and Annuity Association (TIAA) in 2016; the Carnegie Award for Academic Leadership from the Carnegie Foundation in 2015; and the Henry Paley Award from the National Association of Independent Colleges and Universities in 2012. President McGuire also holds honorary degrees from Georgetown, Howard, Hope, Liverpool, and the College of New Rochelle. In 2007, she was named "Leader of the Year" by the Greater Washington (D.C.) Board of Trade.

Elsa M. Núñez is in her eleventh year as president of Eastern Connecticut State University (Willimantic, Connecticut). For more than 20 years, she was a senior administrator at City University of New York (CUNY) and the University of Maine System. She has been the leader of a campus with the highest percentage of minority faculty in the nation and the largest gain in the six-year graduation rate of Latino students from 2004 to 2010 (The Education Trust). The *Hartford Courant* has listed Eastern as one of the "Top Ten Workplaces" in Connecticut. Author of *Hanging Out and Hanging On: From the Projects to the Campus* (2014) and *Pursuing Diversity* (1992), President Núñez has published numerous articles on language acquisition, diversity, and other education issues.

J. Randall O'Brien is the twenty-second president of Carson-Newman University (Jefferson City, Tennessee). Previously, he was the executive vice president, provost, professor of religion, and visiting professor of law at Baylor University. He has held appointments as a research scholar at Yale University and as a fellow at Oxford University. He is a past president of the American Academy of Religion, the Society of Biblical Literature, and the National Association of Baptist Professors of Religion, Southwest Region. President O'Brien serves on the boards of the Tennessee Independent Colleges and Universities Association, the Consortium for Global Education, and the Center for Justice and Peace. He is a noted author with over 115 scholarly and popular articles and numerous books on religious themes.

Paul C. Pribbenow is the tenth president of Augsburg University, a comprehensive university affiliated with the Evangelical Lutheran Church in America (ELCA) and located in Minneapolis, Minnesota. A social ethicist, Pribbenow earned the bachelor's degree from Luther College (Decorah, Iowa) and the master's and Ph.D. from the University of Chicago. Under his leadership, Augsburg University has gained national and international recognition for its civic engagement and interfaith initiatives.

Edward E. Raspiller has been president of John Tyler Community College (Chester and Midlothian, Virginia) since 2013. He has served in community college administrative roles over the past twenty years. A community college graduate (College of DuPage in Illinois), he began community college work in 1989, teaching adult and workplace literacy. He earned his doctorate in adult and continuing education at Northern Illinois University. From 1996 to 2010, he directed the Community College Leadership Program at Old Dominion University. Raspiller has written numerous book chapters and articles, both national and international (China).

Kevin D. Rome is now the president of Fisk University in Nashville, Tennessee, after serving as the nineteenth president of Lincoln University in Jefferson City, Missouri. From 2008 to 2013, he was the vice chancellor for student affairs and enrollment at North Carolina Central University in Durham. President Rome has also been vice president for student services at Morehouse College (Atlanta), his alma mater; vice president for campus life at Clayton State University (Morrow, Georgia); and assistant vice chancellor for student life and diversity at Indiana University-Purdue University (Indianapolis).

Brian Rosenberg became the sixteenth president of Macalester College (Saint Paul, Minnesota) in 2003. He was educated as a scholar of Victorian literature and is the author of three books and many essays and opinion pieces. He is a past chair of the board of the Associated Colleges of the Midwest, the American Council on Education's Commission on International Initiatives, and the Presidents' Council of Project Pericles. Rosenberg is also a member of the Board of Directors of the Teagle Foundation.

Elizabeth (Beth) J. Stroble is the eleventh president of Webster University, a worldwide independent non-profit institution serving students in eight countries on four continents. She has held academic and administrative appointments at the University of Akron, the University of Louisville, and Northern Arizona University. In the eight years of her presidency at Webster, it has expanded into Africa and Greece, established its first four endowed faculty positions, improved its bond ratings, and increased its assets by $100 million. The University has more than doubled enrollment and increased previous scholarship dollars by 500%. Investments in infrastructure will result in an Interdisciplinary Science Building on the Webster Groves (Missouri) campus in 2017.

Beverly Warren is the twelfth president of Kent State University (Kent, Ohio), one of the nation's largest university systems, with a distinctive blend of teaching, research, and creative excellence. She is leading the University's bold vision to emerge as an exemplar among the country's best public research universities. Warren previously served as provost and senior vice president at Virginia Commonwealth University (VCU), where she also served as dean of the School of Education and professor and head of the Division of Health, Physical Education, and Recreation. She held faculty positions at Smith College, Auburn University, Appalachian State University, and Lander University.

AC | SS Adolescent Cultures, School & Society

Joseph L. DeVitis & Linda Irwin-DeVitis
GENERAL EDITORS

As schools struggle to redefine and restructure themselves, they need to be aware of the new realities of adolescents. This series is committed to depicting the wide variety of adolescent cultures that exist in today's troubled world. It is primarily a qualitative research, practice, and policy series devoted to contextual interpretation and analysis that encompasses a broad range of interdisciplinary critique. The series addresses such issues as curriculum theory and practice; multicultural education; adolescent literacy; aggression, bullying, and violence; media and the arts; school dropouts; homeless and runaway youth; gangs and other alienated youth; at-risk populations; peers, family structures, and parental involvement; identity formation; race, ethnicity, class, and gender/LGBTQ studies; and overall social, biological, psychological, and spiritual development.

Send proposals and manuscripts to the general editors at:

Joseph L. DeVitis & Linda Irwin-DeVitis
Darden College of Education
Old Dominion University
Norfolk, VA 23503

To order other books in this series, please contact our Customer Service Department at:

(800) 770-LANG (within the U.S.)
(212) 647-7706 (outside the U.S.)
(212) 647-7707 FAX

or browse online by series at:

WWW.PETERLANG.COM